Truth, Community, and the Prophetic Voice

Truth, Community, and the Prophetic Voice

Michael Walzer, Stanley Hauerwas, and Cornel West on Justice and Peace

Christopher J. Libby

LEXINGTON BOOKS
Lanham • Boulder • New York • London

Published by Lexington Books
An imprint of The Rowman & Littlefield Publishing Group, Inc.
4501 Forbes Boulevard, Suite 200, Lanham, Maryland 20706
www.rowman.com

Unit A, Whitacre Mews, 26-34 Stannary Street, London SE11 4AB

British Library Cataloguing in Publication Information Available

Library of Congress Cataloging-in-Publication Data

Names: Libby, Christopher J., author. | Walzer, Michael. | Hauerwas, Stanley, 1940- | West, Cornel.
Title: Truth, community, and the prophetic voice : Michael Walzer, Stanley Hauerwas, and Cornel West on justice and peace / Christopher J. Libby.
Description: Lanham : Lexington Books, 2018. | Includes bibliographical references and index.
Identifiers: LCCN 2018014980 (print) | LCCN 2018017552 (ebook) | ISBN 9781498551465 (Electronic) | ISBN 9781498551458 (cloth : alk. paper)
Subjects: LCSH: Prophecy—Christianity.
Classification: LCC BR115.P8 (ebook) | LCC BR115.P8 L53 2018 (print) | DDC 230.092/2—dc23
LC record available at https://lccn.loc.gov/2018014980

∞™ The paper used in this publication meets the minimum requirements of American National Standard for Information Sciences—Permanence of Paper for Printed Library Materials, ANSI/NISO Z39.48-1992.

Printed in the United States of America

Contents

Acknowledgments

This book is a revision of my Emory University Graduate Division of Religion Ph.D. dissertation, but its deepest roots lie in my master's degree in philosophy at the University of Colorado-Boulder. At both institutions, I was fortunate to have professors who were not only brilliant scholars and teachers but also friends and mentors. Among many, Claudia Mills, who directed my thesis at Colorado, and Timothy Jackson, who directed my dissertation at Emory, stand out most prominently.

Claudia is not just a philosopher, but also a children's book author. Befitting both roles, she combines, in equal parts, rigor and intellectual heft with kindness and a keen sensitivity to persons. As a young graduate student looking for direction, she not only provided me with the intellectual encouragement and space to trust and pursue my own interests, but also affirmation and enthusiasm at just the right time. I likely would have travelled a radically different intellectual and professional path had it not been for Claudia. I certainly never would have written this book.

Tim is easily one of the finest Christian ethicists of his generation, and this book bears the indelible mark of his influence, as a cursory glance at its argument quickly reveals. He is a model of generosity and charity to others in his thinking. He seeks to draw constructive insight wherever he might find it, and he is concerned, above all, to get his arguments right. I hope there are at least intimations of these intellectual virtues in what follows.

Colleagues and friends at Missouri Valley College provided much necessary support and distraction as I completed the book. Pam Sebastian, Claire Schmidt, Debbie Olson, Jamie Gold, and Matt and Anmarie Rahner make my work easier and my laughs louder. Librarians Pam Reeder and Mary Slater have been helpful in ordering books and tracking down references, often with short notice.

At Lexington Books, editor Joseph Parry and his assistants, Madhumitha Koduvalli and Emily Roderick, have made publishing this book easier than I had any right to expect it to be.

My deepest and most profound thanks go to my family. My parents, Edward and Evelyn Libby, wife, Elizabeth Webb, and daughter, Emma, have been unfailing sources of love and support. That I know anything about the values that I seek to give voice to in this book is in large measure a result of the good luck of having been their son, husband, and father. My daily life is immeasurably enriched by all of them.

Some of the material contained herein originally appeared as "Rorty or Kierkegaard: Social Amelioration, Truth, and the Ground of Cornel West's Normative Commitments," *International Journal of Public Theology* 5, no. 2 (January 2011): 165–86. I am grateful for permission to reproduce this material. I also extend my thanks to the Denver Art Museum for permission to reproduce the image of Edward Hicks' *The Peaceable Kingdom* in chapter 5, and to Emma Libby for permission to reproduce *Cityscape*, the photograph that appears on the cover.

Introduction

Setting the Stage—The Prophetic Voice in Contemporary Context

We live in an era in which the top one percent of Americans control forty percent of the nation's wealth; in which violence rooted in racial, ethnic, and religious animus continues nearly unabated; and in which looming environmental disaster is too often met with denial and indifference, to name just a few of our challenges. Such a context seems to call out for prophetic voices, for those voices that condemn injustice and seek peace. Yet, what might it mean for Christians to speak or act in a "prophetic mode" today? How can the voices of the biblical prophets be brought to bear on the realities of our contemporary world? When one speaks or seeks to speak prophetically, it is generally understood that, even if one does not literally speak the words of God, one does mean to speak on behalf of God or in defense of values expressive of or resonant with the covenant or Kingdom values expressed in the Christian Scriptures.[1] One, in short, means to uphold or defend God's truth. But how can one witness to the truth in this manner if, as is broadly agreed to be the case today, there can be no unmediated access to truth, when all of our claims reflect particular social contexts, locations, and historical influences? In a world without foundations, can we continue prophetically to uphold or defend God's truth? If so, how?

The central concern of this book, then, is to ask how it might be possible today to uphold an understanding of the prophetic voice that comports in essential ways with its expression in the biblical vision, while attending especially to contemporary judgments regarding the epistemological significance of community and concerns about the nature and function of claims to truth. Ultimately and more specifically, I hope to gain some purchase on what an adequate contemporary Christian theological rendering of the prophetic looks like. Can, in short, there be a prophetic voice without foundations? I will argue that it is not only possible to provide a non-foundationalist account of the prophetic voice, but that that voice is able to come truly into its own when cast in a non-foundationalist frame.

This is conceived as an offering in political or public theology, broadly construed, in that it is especially concerned with how a faithful retrieval of concepts and terms central to Christian biblical and theological tradition may constructively inform contemporary social and political institutions and practices. So conceived, this project has three argumentative movements. The first movement is largely descriptive, and is concerned, above all, to give an account of the prophetic voice as it finds biblical expression. The second (and longest) movement is primarily critical in nature, and is concerned, in light of the biblical witness, to evaluate the thought of three contemporary figures—Michael Walzer, Stanley Hauerwas, and Cornel West—who find in the prophets a model for ethical and political engagement and/or who conceive of their own work in prophetic terms. The third movement is constructive in nature, and is concerned, in light of the first two movements, to offer suggestions about the shape and content of an adequate contemporary theological expression of the prophetic voice. In short, then, this book is concerned with *retrieving* and *reviving*, while also *rethinking*, the biblical witness of the prophets in light of contemporary concerns and conceptual categories.

THE BIBLICAL WITNESS

Chapter 1 offers an account of the central conceptual elements of the prophetic voice through engagement with the biblical text. Despite diversity internal to the biblical text, it is possible to identify in it a set of assumptions and commitments that, taken together, can be summarily identified as constitutive of the prophetic voice. Though there are prophetic *voices*, there is also, I argue, a discernible prophetic *voice*. Biblically understood, this voice is, above all, concerned to defend and uphold the vision of reality that constituted the normative communal understandings and practices of ancient Israel and that finds expression in and through Jesus Christ's proclamation of the Kingdom of God. It is embodied in distinctive forms of community that are animated by an understanding of justice shaped by God's own attention to those who are most vulnerable or live at society's margins and that envision the fundamental transformation of the social order toward peace and reconciliation. Though there are identifiable differences between Old and New Testament expressions of the prophetic voice, the continuity that exists is of greater significance, with the New Testament constituting not a break with the Old, but, rather, a dynamic intensification and extension of its central theological and normative logic. Across the whole of Scripture, then, the prophetic voice is united by its determination to give communal expression to an understanding of divinely grounded reality defined above all by commitments to justice and peaceableness. This discussion grounds this project as a whole and themes that emerge as central from it—community, truth, justice, and violence/nonviolence—establish the framework for discussion in subsequent chapters of the book.

CONTEMPORARY CHALLENGES

In chapters 2, 3, and 4, I am concerned with determining how successfully the ethical and political vision one glimpses in Israel's prophets and in Jesus Christ finds contemporary expression. This second movement engages with and evaluates the work of three influential contemporary American exponents of the prophetic voice: Michael Walzer, Professor Emeritus of Social Science at the Institute for Advanced Study in Princeton; Stanley Hauerwas, Gilbert T. Rowe Professor Emeritus of Theological Ethics at Duke University Divinity School; and Cornel West, Professor of the Practice of Public Philosophy at Harvard University.

These figures all share central assumptions and emphases. Each finds in the prophets exemplary expressions of moral and political insight that provide important resources for normative engagement today and/or they conceive of their own work as in some way resonant with the prophetic voice or a prophetic standpoint. All three share a non-foundationalist epistemological orientation, and each finds in particular communities and those communities' shared practices the raw materials necessary for articulating their respective moral visions and for standing in critical relation to the surrounding culture.

Despite these shared assumptions and emphases, however, there are significant differences between each of these figures. Walzer is a secular Jew, committed liberal democrat, and one of the foremost contemporary defenders of just war theory. By contrast, Hauerwas is a United Methodist deeply influenced by Catholic and Anabaptist theologies, unswerving critic of liberal democracy, and one of the chief contemporary theological advocates of pacifism. West is a black Baptist and radical democrat whose liberationist political ethic is aimed at fostering contemporary expressions of King's "beloved community." Examined together, the similarities and the differences that exist between these figures can aid in the articulation of the challenges of, and prospects for, a satisfactory contemporary articulation of the prophetic voice.

Both the task of evaluating resonances between these figures and the prophetic voice and the constructive task that follows it face considerable challenges, however. Perhaps above all, in both its critical and constructive movements, this account must be wary of anachronism. This pitfall cuts two ways, both in the attempt to move from the biblical text to the contemporary world, as well as in the attempt to move from the contemporary world to the biblical text. In addition to asking what the biblical witness has to say descriptively or exegetically, it is also necessary to determine how we might appropriate what it has to say to us today. In attempting to discern the contemporary shape of the prophetic voice and of prophetic discipleship, we encounter the challenges of what Richard Hays has called the hermeneutical and pragmatic tasks of biblical ethics. First, we must determine how we might "take our moral bearings from a world so different from our own."[2] Second, we must discern how to embody the imperatives of scripture within the life of the believing community. These are closely related tasks which Hays suggests might profitably be grouped together under the heading of "application": "The hermeneutical task is the cognitive or conceptual application of the [Bible's] message to our situation, and the pragmatic task is the enacted application of the [Bible's] message in our situation."[3]

Interpretive adequacy finds expression in what Wayne Meeks calls a "hermeneutics of social embodiment," in which present-day interpreters or performers, in seeking to interpret and apply those texts to their own social setting, are "tuned to the way in which the text worked in time past." The goal of such interpretation is formation in terms that "correspond to the symbolic universe rendered or signaled by the text."[4] For Meeks, the interpretation and application of biblical texts in relation to our present context is to be guided—though never wholly determined—by its use or function in its original context. What good performers "do" is capture, in the present context, the material essentials of the original context. In other words, interpretive adequacy is measured in terms of performative adequacy, which is best understood *analogically*. The point of such an approach, as William Spohn has made clear, is not to give expression to an imitation of, for example, Jesus Christ that is finally little more than a parroting; rather, it is to capture that to which Meeks points us: how the witness of the biblical text, understood in light of its social setting, might inform our witness, understood in light of our social setting. Jesus did not command his disciples to "Go and do exactly the same." He commanded them to "Go and do *likewise*" (Luke 10:37). Implicit in this final word of the command is recognition of the creativity implicit in any adequate expression of faithfulness. Summarizing the foregoing, we thus say that today's Christian communities should be to their worlds as the New Testament communities were to their worlds.[5]

THEMATIC BRIDGES BETWEEN THE BIBLICAL AND CONTEMPORARY WORLDS

What, then, can serve to guide us in attempting to discern how the prophetic voice as expressed in the biblical text might be brought to bear on the contemporary world? What themes or concepts might be highlighted that would allow a faithful reading of the biblical text to be brought to bear on a charitable reading of the figures examined here? My critical discussions of Walzer, Hauerwas, and West are guided by four themes: community, truth, justice, and violence/nonviolence. Though these are not the only themes that a discussion of the contemporary nature and shape of the prophetic voice might highlight, these four themes are central both to biblical expressions of the prophetic and to the thought of the three figures examined here. These themes can serve as useful heuristic guides in assessing how well the contemporary figures examined here depict and/or exemplify the prophetic voice and in the broader task of articulating an adequate contemporary expression of that voice. Bearing in mind especially the determination to avoid anachronism, it will be helpful at this point to discuss briefly the nature and significance of these themes, and how they will shape the discussion that follows. For reasons that will become clear, how contemporary understandings of community and truth are rendered is of particular importance.

Community: Affirming a Non-Foundationalist Epistemology

In *The Origins of Christian Morality*, Wayne Meeks highlights the centrality of community for the early Christians. "The early Christians, for practical as well as principled reasons, had to have a past. Without scripture and tradition they would have had no identity."[6] Much the same may be said about the ethical insights of Hebrew moral tradition. As I will argue in chapter 1, the prophets are centrally part of, and speak to, a community. What was unique about the prophets had less to do with their charisma or other particular individual characteristics and almost everything to do with the community out of which they arose and the convictions that animated that community. Though they might bear messages from God individually, those messages are *mediated* through religious tradition. The authority of the prophets is inseparable from their place in the community. Without the background assumptions of an animating religious tradition, prophetic authority would be unintelligible.

At least two features of prophetic community are significant here. First, the prophets were concerned to articulate and defend a *particular* conception of community, a particular tradition and way of being. Within the Ancient Near East, Israel's covenant community was conceptually distinctive, standing as an alternative to competing forms of community, and in many ways inverting the animating assumptions of other surrounding communities. Much the same can be said for the "upside-down Kingdom"[7] of Jesus within its Roman context. Second, this distinctiveness was rooted in and is constituted by a particular concern to respond to God's concern for those at society's margins. It is the *content* of prophetic community that gives it its distinctive shape.

Communal distinctiveness is thus not something sought for its own sake, but, rather, is the result of the embodiment of a particular view of reality. The degree to which prophetic community contrasts with surrounding communities and traditions will depend, in part, on the character of those communities and traditions and the degree to which they comport with, or depart from, prophetic understandings of reality.

Like the prophets, a focus on community occupies a central place in contemporary thought. For contemporary philosophers and theologians, however, this emphasis on community derives from broadly epistemological considerations regarding how we hold or come to hold beliefs. Generally speaking, modern thought is dominated by "foundationalist" conceptions of knowledge. Modern thinkers, stretching back at least to Descartes, tended to argue that in order to avoid an infinite regress in the justification of claims about knowledge, there must be some foundation of beliefs upon which we can know that all other claims rest. These grounds were generally sought either in sense experience (Locke, Hume) or in given, a priori principles or categories of mind (Descartes, Kant). Though a thorough review of the debates surrounding foundationalism would take us rather far afield, suffice it to say for present purposes that, over the course of the twentieth century, dissatisfaction with these approaches grew, and a consensus among philosophers gradually emerged that our knowledge of truth—of reality—is never had raw, never apprehended directly. With regard to the empiricists, most now recognize that all observations are theory-laden, perspectival, and contextually interpreted. With regard to the rationalists seeking self-evident truths or principles, most now contend that there is no way to identify one right conception, as the rationalist quest for an interpretation-free account of first principles fares no better than the empiricist's quest for interpretation-free sense experience.[8]

Taking seriously the lessons of the American pragmatists, Ludwig Wittgenstein, Wilfrid Sellars, Willard Van Orman Quine, Richard Rorty, and others who have revealed the deficiencies of foundationalism has fundamental implications for the nature and tasks of theology. William Placher writes, "If theologians try to defend their claims by starting with basic, foundational truths that any rational person would have to believe or observations independent of theory and assumption, they are trying to do something that our best philosophers tell us is impossible—not merely for religious beliefs but for any beliefs whatsoever."[9] Theology, just as much as philosophy, must now realize that claims to truth are mediated in and through a variety of interconnected contexts: histories, social and political practices, traditions, and communities. We all stand, so to speak, in the cave; our ideas, beliefs, claims, and so on are inevitably shaped by a panoply of contextual and contextualizing factors. Any adequate contemporary understanding of the prophetic voice will have to contend with this fact.

The bulk of this book will be concerned with what happens when such non-foundationalist assumptions influence or are brought to bear on contemporary understandings of the prophetic voice. Walzer, Hauerwas, and West are all non-foundationalist thinkers who find in some conception of community the content for moral and political claims. In this shared concern for the distinctiveness of community, they give contemporary expression to, and resonate in important respects with, the prophetic voice's reliance on an animating tradition and its emphasis on the distinctiveness of such a community from surrounding communities. As with biblical expressions of the prophetic, community both grounds the ability to speak and act ethically in an intelligible manner and it provides leverage for social criticism.

What may be less clear, however, is how these respective affirmations of community are compatible with the second notable feature of prophetic community I have identified: communal expression of, or responsiveness to, God's concern for the margins. Many critics of the contemporary turn to community worry that a focus on communal distinctiveness and identity makes difficult the very sort of attention to the margins that characterizes the prophetic voice. The key question about community, then, as conceived by Walzer, Hauerwas, and West is whether it can accommodate the prophetic concern to uphold both a distinctive vision of formative community *and* attention to those on society's margins. This is a question that, in turn, leads naturally to consideration of how the prophetic understands, and how each of the figures dealt with here understands, truth, justice, and violence/nonviolence.

Truth: Upholding Alethiological Realism

Though community and tradition are fundamental to the prophetic voice, undergirding the role and function of community are convictions about the nature and shape of *reality*. For the Hebrew prophets, for example, the most fundamental reality is God, for it is God who animates, gives shape to, and regulates the beliefs and practices of the covenant community, and it is to God that the covenant community is finally accountable. The biblical prophets' claims about meaning and value, though expressed and embodied communally, were not *reducible* to Israel's communal belief nor were they mere self-descriptions of what Israel happened to affirm collectively; rather, the claims that undergirded and were expressed through the covenant community's beliefs and practices were claims about, and gave expression to, reality.

Expressed in contemporary conceptual categories, the biblical prophets assumed what philosophers and theologians would today call a realist conception of truth and value. Though we do need to keep in mind the need to refrain from imposing contemporary categories on the biblical text, as well as the fact that such terminology is foreign to the biblical world—it has its home in contemporary philosophy and theology—clearly realist commitments are nonetheless discernible in the biblical text. In characterizing the prophets as assuming realist commitments, I have in mind alethiological realism, in which the meaning of truth claims is understood to be dependent upon, and measured in terms of, some form of correspondence or adequation between words spoken or ideas expressed and the metaphysical or transhistorical reality or object to which the words or ideas refer. The key insight here—an insight clearly discernible in the prophets and the biblical text more generally, even if not expressed in these terms—is that moral truths are not merely human constructions or social conventions, even if they are necessarily expressed through human categories and language.[10] An adequate contemporary expression of the prophetic voice will likewise uphold such a realist conception of moral value.

There may appear, however, to be a tension between a commitment to an alethiological realism and the affirmation of non-foundationalist epistemological commitments. Concerns about the tenability of foundationalist epistemologies often travel closely with concerns about the tenability of claims to represent reality, to uphold the truth, and this may seem to present problems for the contemporary expression of the prophetic voice. These latter concerns have both a conceptual and a moral dimension.

For some, the implications of the non-foundationalist turn in epistemology are quite radical for how we understand the nature and meaning of truth. A number of philosophers, and a significant number of theologians in their wake, have claimed that, with the demise of foundationalism, we must not only affirm that our ideas emerge from, and are expressed through, history, but that they are reducible to it. What William Dean has called the "new historicism" in philosophy and theology holds that there are no deeper truths "behind or beneath the events of social history." Whatever truths there are "are entirely historical creatures, conceived within history, directed at history, and grown in a historical chain, as interpretation refers to interpretation refers to interpretation throughout history."[11] For the new historicism, imagination is central, though this is not an understanding of imagination that seeks the articulation of transhistorical meanings, but, rather, one that is concerned "to interpret the past, sometimes rather freely, and always with the contribution of the interpreter and its community. . . . [I]ts purpose is really to communicate with the past—not merely to reproduce but to interact, to initiate, to create, as one does in a conversation."[12]

Part of the appeal of Dean's position is precisely that it aims to keep conversations going, that it resists premature closure and certitude, characteristics often attributed to realist construals of truth. The worry, of course, that attends those who position themselves as the bearers of certainty and truth is that such assertions may lead to manipulation, compulsion, or coercion. In a generally affirmative discussion of moral realism, Robin Lovin captures nicely the hermeneutics of suspicion that underlies many instances of its rejection: "Moral realism is doubly suspect, because it not only claims that there is one and only one correct view of moral reality, but also—because it is *moral* reality that is under consideration—claims moral authority to impose the imperatives that the one correct view dictates on those who hold to other interests and opinions."[13]

Though an adequate contemporary articulation of the prophetic voice will affirm the fallibility entailed by a non-foundationalist epistemology, it will be loath to give up a realist construal of moral value. It will affirm both a non-foundationalist epistemological orientation and an alethiological realism with regard to the nature of moral claims. Though the message does not find expression apart from social mediation, it must not be reduced to, or conflated with, the medium through which it is expressed. A contemporary articulation of the prophetic voice will rightly affirm the non-foundationalist insight that our ideas about and ways of understanding reality are shaped by a variety of social and historical forces, and, perhaps above all, by language. It will, accordingly, be marked by a heightened awareness of the difficulty of speaking of truth in a straightforward manner. All of our claims, insofar as they are historically and linguistically mediated and shaped, at best disclose reality only partially. It will reject, however, what Dean and others seem to affirm in upholding non-foundationalist commitments, namely, that our claims reduce to their historical or communal expression, that there is no reality transcending our claims by which they may be measured or to which they are held accountable.

The contemporary task, then, seems to be to determine how it might be possible both to uphold the distinctiveness and formative influence of communal tradition, understood in terms of its particular animating understandings—its "grammar"—*and* a commitment to an understanding of truth as finally transcending, regulating, and judging that, or any, tradition. If such a conception can be articulated, it will mark a significant contemporary theological rethinking of the prophetic voice, as it will denote a way of speaking and acting prophetically that is both self-consciously fallibilist in character, and affirmative of what is theologically assumed by the biblical prophets, namely, that it is God's truth that is being expressed and defended.

Justice: Attending to the Margins

One way this may be accomplished, or at least one aspect of it, may lie in the fact that, in the biblical text, reality is not primarily understood in cognitive or propositional terms, but as something that is embodied and that is to be experienced. In the biblical witness, one knows truth/reality by experiencing or doing it.[14] As I discuss in the next chapter, in the biblical witness, this is seen especially in the intimate connection between knowledge of God and the doing of justice. There was no division in Israel's life between faith and justice, between theory and practice, for the doing of justice, in imitation of God's own compassionate care for Israel, was understood to be the substance of faith; without it one could not claim to know God. As a response to God's steadfast love, acts of justice are those focused on extending compassionate care, especially to those at society's margins, in an effort to redress social grievances and inequalities in a manner that approximates the genuine equality of all before God.

Within contemporary political theory, liberal democracy is frequently offered as the form of political expression that best embodies a commitment to the equal well-being of all within society, particularly those whose voices are least likely to be heard. The intention of many expressions of liberal democratic theories of politics and justice is to give expression to a fundamental commitment to the dignity and equality of all human beings. Within such expressions, rights are expressly conceived as checks on expressions of power that could lead to the domination of the few, the weak, or the otherwise marginal by those who hold power. As will become clear in the pages that follow, prophetic and liberal democratic commitments and practices often give expression to similar core normative claims.

Though a contemporary expression of the prophetic voice will affirm core liberal democratic commitments, this is secondary to the more fundamental commitment to form and sustain communities devoted to embodying God's truth. We must be concerned not only with whether the prophetic voice ought to affirm such commitments, but why it ought to do so. For some influential contemporary liberal theorists, commitments to liberal democracy are grounded not in substantive ontological claims about the shared humanity or sanctity of persons—that is, the sorts of claims a realist construal of value will be likely to prioritize—but, rather, in broadly pragmatic or strategic considerations about the how to achieve social consensus in a pluralistic society and/or in claims about the historic commitments that shape and form a political culture. However, because it marginalizes substantive ethical claims, such prioritization of communal understandings and practice is problematic.

There are at least two problems here. First, where the prophetic voice will seek to uphold the integrity of the neighbor out of love and respect for the neighbor *qua* neighbor, on this sort of construal of liberal democratic commitments, respect for others is extended by virtue of its historical or cultural importance within a particular society. But this constitutes less attention to and respect for the integrity of the neighbor herself—her inviolability, for example, as a bearer of the *Imago Dei*—than it does attention to the conventions and commitments of tradition. Second, and often related to this, insofar as a liberal democratic conception of justice and its commitments are derived from the shared practices or commitments of a political culture, it will inevitably exclude voices on society's margins who have not figured, or figured sufficiently, in the articulation and formation of that conception and its commitments. Shared understandings cannot provide the substance of an account of justice, even if it is through such understandings that we speak or argue about justice.

In short, though the prophetic affirmation of the value and integrity of human beings will find various forms of expression *in and through* the languages or "grammars" of various historical and political communities, it is not something *derived from* the various practices and beliefs of those communities. In fact, it is inadequately realist construals of the normative commitments of the prophetic voice that, however unintentionally, tend to harbor marginalizing exclusions and/or lack adequate resources for self-criticism of distorted practices. A contemporary construal of prophetic justice must be realist in character to prevent its communal domestication and distortion.

Violence/Nonviolence: Just War, Pacifism, and Peace

The justice that the prophetic seeks is finally animated by the hope for the establishment of true peace. The vision of *shalom* one finds expressed in the prophets is one in which society is no longer hierarchically organized, but is instead based upon true equality and liberty, the equitable sharing of power, participation of all—particularly the formerly marginalized—in political and economic institutions, and forms of distributive justice that attend not to individual desire but to communal well-being and care of the most needy. The vision is one of the cessation of violence and the conditions that lead to violence and of the healing of broken relationships.

How or when this is all to be achieved may seem to be a matter of some debate within the biblical text itself, however. While such a vision is central to the Hebrew prophets, it is also clear that it is an eschatological vision that awaits the establishment of true justice for its full expression. In the interim, while there are important gestures toward forgiveness and peacemaking as crucial elements of Israel's religious vocation, violence, it seems, is not renounced wholesale, as it may be a proper expression of just divine judgment upon sin. In the New Testament, the peaceable thrust of Israel's prophets is intensified and radicalized, as Jesus proclaims God's Peaceable Kingdom as fully present in his life and work. Nonviolent practices of forgiveness, reconciliation, and peacemaking are the central elements of Jesus' witness and are to shape the witness of his disciples. Even measured recourse to violence in response to injustice is finally incompatible with the *full expression* of the Kingdom that Jesus embodies and proclaims.

In the centuries hence, debate about the moral licitness of violence in response to injustice has tended to revolve around two approaches. Traditionally inspired by biblical considerations, but also finding various nontheological justifications expressions, the just war tradition and pacifism have long been the two primary normative responses to unjust violence. Both take a presumptive stance against political violence. Because the world is not the Kingdom, the just war tradition contends that, in exceptional circumstances and under highly circumscribed conditions, properly motivated violence (e.g., by a concern to protect innocent others) may be a morally permissible response to injustice. By contrast, pacifists characteristically contend that, while we are not necessarily to refrain from resisting injustice, a morally credible response to injustice excludes the use of violence.

While strictly political or pragmatic approaches to the problem of political violence will not suffice, considerations about such matters as the nature and function of the state, and the nature and demands of political responsibility within the state, *do* rightly figure in determining how the biblical text best finds expression. From a prophetic standpoint, however, judgments about such matters can never be divorced from fundamental moral judgments and so will, again, be tied up with prior considerations about the nature of community, truth, and justice. Furthermore, when theologically rendered, the prophetic voice will be concerned to ask especially about the demands of discipleship, the responsibilities of love for one's neighbor, the nature of eschatology and its relation to the possibilities and/or limits of moral action, the nature and significance of sin, and other associated matters in determining the normatively proper response to injustice. Finally, beyond interrogating critically these two approaches to political violence, a contemporary articulation of the prophetic voice will want to ask if these ways of understanding and embodying the prophetic vocation to seek peace is adequate.

THREE CONTEMPORARY PROPHETS?

With these thematic and conceptual issues in mind, I move in chapters 2–4 to a critical examination of how well Walzer, Hauerwas, and West give expression to the prophetic voice. Chapter 2 analyzes prophetic resonances within Michael Walzer's political philosophy. Here, I am above all concerned to examine the implications of his attempt to construe the prophetic in non-realist terms. Though Walzer finds resonances between his community-based political philosophy, which is concerned to foster resistance to a particular understanding of domination and to enable a grounded form of social criticism, and the biblical prophets, his position is unsatisfactory. The fundamental difficulty with his project is that its non-realist social conventionalism cannot adequately render the normative commitments of the prophetic voice. This is seen, above all, in the constriction of moral vision that results from his emphasis on the "shared understandings" of a political community as the content of justice and social criticism. Such an emphasis makes difficult attention to those who figure only marginally in the articulation of those understandings and it threatens to make the political community an end to itself.

As I discuss in chapter 3, though Stanley Hauerwas, no less than Walzer, emphasizes the centrality of community, he means for his position to be grounded in realist assumptions. In Hauerwas' forthrightly theological project, the church possesses a distinctive grammar or language through which truth is performatively displayed and that enables it to stand as a distinctive witness in the world. He is especially concerned to oppose those distortions he argues characterize the animating assumptions and practices of liberal modernity, particularly insofar as they are judged to underwrite violence. In his opposition of the church to liberal modernity, Hauerwas' work shares much rhetorically with biblical depictions of prophetic confrontation, but substantively his work falls short of the prophetic. The sharp contrast he draws between the church and all other stories or grammars blinds him to voices from the margins, voices that would not only reconfigure his rather insubstantial account of Christian justice but also his pacifist leanings. More sustained attention to the margins is necessary to correct his tendency to conflate the church (the medium of truth) with truth itself, his characterization of rights and liberation as thoroughgoing Enlightenment concerns, and his tendency to portray almost any justification of political violence as a Constantinian subsumption of theological integrity to the concerns of the nation-state.

Though community occupies a central place in Cornel West's thought, he is less interested, as I explain in chapter 4, with their constitutive self-understandings than he is with how communities may foster liberation and the alleviation of suffering. In seeking to articulate such a vision, his project, which he terms "prophetic pragmatism," draws upon a variety of sources, most notably American pragmatism and prophetic Christian moral vision. West's intellectual eclecticism and overriding focus on social amelioration cuts both ways, however: while, on one hand, his work does not succumb to the closure one finds in Walzer and Hauerwas and seeks self-consciously to attend to the margins, on the other hand, his thought gives rise to tensions regarding the nature of truth and to the adoption of an overly general conception of democracy as the normative shape and substance of his thought. While an adequate contemporary rendering of the prophetic voice is not opposed to democratic norms and practices, there are reasons to worry that West's own normative position is too thin and thereby unable to give sufficient expression to prophetic understandings of justice and peaceableness that his own convictions demand. His conception of community does not fall victim to the same pitfalls that beset Walzer and Hauerwas, but it too is his Achilles heel. Despite his self-professed Christian convictions, he does not judge the character of community in terms of theological considerations, but in terms of its ability to foster a rather general understanding of democratic practices.

TOWARD A CONSTRUCTIVE UNDERSTANDING OF THE PROPHETIC VOICE

In chapter 5, I seek to outline a constructive Christian understanding of the prophetic voice that is both faithful to the biblical witness and self-conscious of the challenges posed by contemporary concerns and conceptual categories, particularly the non-foundationalist turn. Though I argue in chapters 2–4 that Walzer, Hauerwas, and West all fail to offer sufficient accounts of that voice, their failures are instructive and help to point us toward an adequate Christian theological account of the prophetic. In seeking to show how it is possible to hold together a realist account of truth with an account of how truth is communally mediated and an articulation of prophetic commitments to justice and peaceableness, I suggest, first, that it is with truth, rather than community, that we must first of all be concerned. Building upon the distinction between alethiology (which concerns the nature or meaning of truth) and epistemology (which concerns the justification of truth claims), I argue that a non-foundationalist affirmation of theological realism will highlight the aspirational and unfolding, yet fallible, character of truth claims. As the primary communal embodiment of such an understanding of truth, the church will possess a "wayfaring" character as it seeks to become an ever more faithful expression of what it means to be Christ's body. Central to this understanding of Christian community will be recognition of the significance of "others" for shaping and reshaping the identity and mission of the church, a recognition that marks the congruence between the foregoing affirmation of truth and its communal embodiment and the normative commitments of the prophetic voice. With regard to justice, the church's being, which is also always a becoming, is marked by a commitment to solidarity, as both its identity and that of society, at large, is constructed from the outside, in. With regard to violence/nonviolence, though recognition of the eschatological futurity of the Kingdom underwrites a just war ethic, the more fundamental drive of the prophetic voice and of the vision of the church outlined here is toward active forms of just peace*making*.

A NECESSARILY RELIGIOUS VISION?

Before moving to the main argument of the book, it may be helpful to anticipate what might appear to be a couple of difficulties lurking in this project. First, given my inclusion of Walzer here and his nontheological/nonreligious reading and appropriation of the biblical prophets, one might wonder if there may be nonreligious construals of the prophetic voice, or if it must be construed in religious terms. If it *must* be construed in a self-consciously religious or theological manner, then my inclusion of Walzer is suspect, as his is manifestly not a theological project and so will necessarily fail to inform in any substantive way. Though it is to the biblical text that one will naturally look when inquiring into the ethical and political nature of the prophetic (hence, chapter 1), and though a *Christian* account of the prophetic voice (such as I am ultimately interested in defending) will read that text and construe that voice theologically and its adequacy will be measured theologically, it is possible to imagine characterizing as prophetic a normative position or project that coheres in central respects with the vision of the biblical text, but that does not self-consciously affirm or uphold its theological assumptions. Such an account would bear a close family resemblance to a theological reading of the biblical text, and it may look to that text in some sense (as Walzer does) as exemplary. In terms of its ethical substance, in particular, it would resonate with it analogically in key respects. Were a nonreligious account to do this, I would be more than happy to concede its congruity with a contemporary theological expression of the prophetic.

What I do doubt, however, is whether such an account could also be non-realist. Realist assumptions, in short, lie at the center of an account of the prophetic, whether religiously or nonreligiously construed. The fundamental defect in Walzer's account is not that it is not theological, but that it is animated by a non-realist social conventionalism. Without attention to and recognition of the independent integrity of the other—attention and recognition, in short, finally *not* dependent upon (though mediated through) the shared understandings or linguistic practices of a community—attempts to act prophetically will be stillborn. But this demand to understand such action in a realist manner need not be construed so narrowly as to exclude those whose moral vision is not self-consciously religious in character.

THEORY AND PRACTICE

But does this *really* matter? In fact, one might argue, Walzer is on the side of the saints. He *wants* us to attend to the margins, to construct inclusive communities, to seek more egalitarian social policies and practices. Much the same could be said for Cornel West and Stanley Hauerwas. Each of these three figures, in their own distinct ways, *enacts* what could reasonably identified as prophetic commitments; they each, in varying ways and to varying degrees, *embody* the prophetic voice. In this, none of them is arguably considerably different from prominent figures, like Martin Luther King, Jr., who might uncontroversially be identified as paradigmatic contemporary prophets. Why worry, then, about the theoretical articulation of the prophetic voice or the analytical categories I highlight here?

This is centrally an issue of the relationship between theory and practice and the respective importance of each. By and large, the practices of Walzer, Hauerwas, and West, we might say, outpace their theoretical accounts of the prophetic. They are each largely successful in enacting the prophetic *in spite of* their respective theoretical accounts or articulations of it. This is all to the good, but it is insufficient. Though the prophetic voice does not find expression apart from practice, such practices are not self-sustaining or self-justifying. Without an adequate theoretical articulation of the prophetic, in addition to and apart from its expression in particular communal practices, we lack sufficient resources to resist or correct distortions of those practices when they do occur (as will inevitably happen) or to guide us upon encountering new or unexpected challenges to our practices. The realist account of moral value that the prophetic voice assumes, for example, provides leverage for resisting the tendency of practices to take on a reactionary character upon encountering challenges, the tendency of practices to underwrite the erection of boundaries around considerations of what constitutes "us" as opposed to "them." Especially when rendered in a non-foundationalist idiom, such an understanding of moral value is naturally open to the other and suspicious of the sorts of closure to which I will argue a conventionalist account, however successful its practices tend to be, is susceptible. This broader argument is, as I have already indicated, rooted in considerations about the prophetic voice as it finds expression in the biblical witness. It is to providing an account of that voice that I now turn.

NOTES

1. Here, "Christian Scriptures" is meant to refer inclusively. In this book, I will be concerned with the prophetic voice as it finds expression beginning with Hebrew Scripture and extending through the New Testament.

2. Richard Hays, *The Moral Vision of the New Testament: A Contemporary Introduction to New Testament Ethics* (San Francisco: HarperSanFrancisco, 1996), 6.

3. Ibid., 7.

4. Wayne Meeks, "A Hermeneutics of Social Embodiment," *Harvard Theological Review* 19, nos. 1–3 (1986): 184–185.

5. William C. Spohn, *Go and Do Likewise: Jesus and Ethics* (New York: Continuum, 2000), 4, 54–55.

6. Wayne A. Meeks, *The Origins of Christian Morality: The First Two Centuries* (New Haven: Yale University Press, 1993), 214.

7. I draw the image from Donald B. Kraybill, *The Upside-Down Kingdom*, updated edition (Scottdale, PA: Herald Press, 2011).

8. For brief, but instructive overviews, see John E. Thiel, *Nonfoundationalism* (Minneapolis: Fortress Press, 1994), 1–37; and William C. Placher, *Unapologetic Theology: A Christian Voice in a Pluralistic Conversation* (Louisville: Westminster/John Knox Press, 1989), 24–35.

9. Placher, *Unapologetic Theology*, 34.

10. As Christopher J. Insole puts it, with regard to religious realism, "Religious realism is the claim that truth is independent of our beliefs about truth, and that we can in principle hope to have true beliefs about God." "Why Anti-Realism Breaks Up Relationships," *Heythrop Journal* 43, no. 1 (January 2002): 20. For a good survey of the debates surrounding realism, see David Fergusson, *Community, Liberalism, and Christian Ethics* (Cambridge: Cambridge University Press, 1998), Chapter 4.

11. William Dean, "The Challenge of the New Historicism," *Journal of Religion* 66, no. 3 (July 1986): 261.

12. Ibid., 263–264.

13. Robin W. Lovin, *Reinhold Niebuhr and Christian Realism* (Cambridge: Cambridge University Press, 1995), 21.

14. For a very brief treatment, see Mary Joan Winn Leith, "Know," in *The Oxford Companion to the Bible*, ed. Bruce M. Metzger and Michael D. Coogan (New York: Oxford University Press, 1993), 416–417.

Chapter 1

Doing Justice at the Margins

The Prophetic Voice in Biblical Perspective

BIBLICAL FAITH, ETHICS, AND THE PROPHETIC VOICE

Israel's prophets—with Jesus, the prime biblical exemplars for this study—have been imaged or studied in a wide array of ways: as visionaries or mystics bearing reports of messages from God, as seers who predict the future, as poets noted for powerful and creative literary productions, as bearers of charisma proclaiming religious doctrine or God's commandments, and so on.[1] Here, I am interested in focusing primarily on the import of the prophets for Christian ethics and Christian political theology. In this regard, my approach resembles that of Michael Walzer, about whom I will have much to say in the next chapter. Walzer claims that it is only when prophetic pronouncements are set "within a moral frame, when they are an occasion for indignation, when prophecies are also provocations, verbal assaults on the institutions and activities of everyday life, that they become interesting."[2] This focus is, indeed, quite natural for a study interested in the contemporary implications of biblical faith. Ethical concerns are central to the religious revolution begun in ancient Israel, rendering it "a radical redefinition of what we now term religion."[3] What Walzer misses, as I will clarify later in the book, is the way in which the prophets' moral frame is essentially theological in character.

As "verbal assaults," "provocations," "occasions for indignation," and prophetic claims tend to be articulated in a critical, oppositional mode. Prophets stand against something—social evil, injustice, apathy, moral laxity. Judgment of sin is an ineliminable element of prophetic activity. Of course, the standpoint is not wholly oppositional; in standing *against*, prophets also stand *for*. Positively, what is essential to the normative message of the prophetic voice? To understand how the prophetic voice may inform the understanding and practices of contemporary Christians, it will be necessary to specify the particular grounds for such moral claims and criticism. Through an articulation of the biblical and theological vision of the prophetic, this chapter will lay the foundation for the remainder of the book. What, then, is the core message of the prophets of ancient Israel? How does Jesus embody and extend this prophetic message?

The central claim forwarded here is that, from a Christian ethical perspective, the prophetic voice finds its fullest embodiment as the church articulates its identity in terms of, and seeks to provide witness to, the character of God as disclosed through the radical theological vision of Israel's prophets and Jesus Christ. Some readers, particularly those who are textually minded and sensitive to the complexities and discontinuities of scripture, may recoil at the suggestion here that there is any singular vision to be found in the prophets and Jesus Christ. Does it make sense to speak about *the* prophetic mode or voice? While it would be foolish to deny the complexity and diversity of concern, emphasis, and social context of the various prophets, it is possible to identify a discernible family resemblance that enables the more general characterization of *the* prophetic voice that will guide the argument of the book. There are prophetic *voices*, but it is also possible to speak meaningfully of the prophetic *voice*. And this should hardly be surprising, for it is the one God to whom the prophets witness and for whom they serve as spokespersons. Ultimately, "the prophetic" is not about the prophets, but about God and God's character. Specifically, the prophetic voice, biblically understood, is concerned to *defend and uphold the vision of reality that characterized Israel as a covenant community and Jesus Christ's proclamation of the Kingdom of God and the normative values that follow from this vision of reality: an understanding of divinely grounded justice that attends particularly to the claims of those who are most vulnerable in society and that envisions the fundamental transformation of the social order toward peace and reconciliation.*

The task of this chapter is to explicate the nature of the prophetic voice as it finds expression in Israel's prophets and in Jesus Christ. In discussing Israel's prophets, particular attention will be devoted to prophetic indictments of distortions of Israel's covenantal identity and material commitments by its kings, especially insofar as these reflect special concern for how economic and sociopolitical injustices harm those most marginal in the community. Jesus' pronouncement of the Kingdom of God is rooted in this prophetic vision, as it is likewise focused centrally on "denouncing and unmasking real injustice and oppression,"[4] though it extends it in significant ways. Thus, Jesus proclaims, reading the words of the prophet Isaiah, "good news to the poor," "release to the captives," and freedom for the oppressed (Luke 4:18–19). In attending to the margins in this manner, prophetic justice is aimed, ultimately, at the establishment of true peace.

CENTRAL VESUS CRITICAL PROPHECY

Following Robert Wilson,[5] Paul Hanson divides ancient Near Eastern prophecy into two types, one of which is most characteristic of Israel's prophets. The first, central—or court—prophecy, functions to support the interests, institutions, and authority of a given society. Ancient Near Eastern texts, including the Bible, abound with examples of such prophets. By contrast, what Wilson calls peripheral prophecy exists outside the mainstream and exerts a critical function over against it. Although, as Hanson notes, the term "peripheral" is misleading ("critical" would perhaps be more accurate), it is this critically oriented type of prophecy that is normatively central in Israel's history. The prophets whose messages are preserved by biblical faith as normative were opponents of the established order. They were reformers and critics of kings and priests, and were "less interested in supporting official policy than in exposing it to a very distinct and unflinching critique."[6]

Such criticism was exerted from a distinct perspective and sphere of power, for and in defense of a particular, recognizable theological tradition and worldview. The prophets do not represent some *sui generis* religious understanding; rather, they constantly appealed to and reiterated the ancient religious traditions of Israel.[7] What is true of prophetic authority is true of any form of authority, in general: It does not "stand apart from established ways of doing things," rather, "it stands to them in a very special relation. Apart from the tradition to which it stands in such relation, it is quite unintelligible and inconceivable."[8] Thus, Israel's traditions, which grounded and gave rise to distinct understandings of religion, ethics, and politics, provided the substance of prophetic criticism. If anything is unique here, it is not the prophets themselves, but the community out of which they arose and the theological vision in which that community was rooted. Such traditioned reiteration, however, is not reducible to the exegesis of settled or static tradition. Tradition is living, ongoing, and dynamic. Reiteration in this sense is perhaps best understood as a verb—a faithful enactment of divine reality in ever-new contexts and in the face of ever-new realities. Ultimately, faith is not to the tradition itself, but to the God about whom the tradition testifies.

ISRAEL IN ITS ANCIENT NEAR EASTERN CONTEXT

The distinctiveness of Israel's theological (and, by extension, ethical and political) vision is seen in its contrast with other ancient Near Eastern conceptions of divinity and society. In the ancient Near East, society was centrally and dominantly characterized by monarchy,[9] with kingship understood in highly cosmogonical terms. Governance in the earthly realm was understood to be tied to, and reflective of, governance of the cosmos. This understanding of earthly kingship underwrote authoritarian and repressive conceptions of society that found an explicit counter in Israel's covenantal and egalitarian model of society.

Throughout the ancient Near East, earthly kingship was bound to governance of the cosmos. The primary task of the gods was understood to be the establishment and maintenance of order in the universe. In the creation out of chaos myths of the ancient Near East—such as in the epic narratives of the Babylonian Marduk defeating Tiamat, the mother and personification of chaos, or of the Canaanite Baal defeating Yam, god of the chaotic sea—a hero-god was depicted as battling and defeating a personified monster of chaos.[10] Earthly kingship was thought to be established with, and to reflect in mirror image, the creation of the earth. In Canaan and Mesopotamia, for example, because the king is the god's representative on earth, the king's palace along with the main temple is thought to be the center of the earth, the place from which the primary god establishes peace and prosperity. In like manner, the Egyptian hieroglyph for the divine order of nature and society is "represented by a stylized form of the pedestal of the royal throne, which symbolizes the primeval mount. When the creator-god stands upon the primeval hill to put order in the place of chaos, it is the Pharaoh as his earthly representative that does it in his place."[11] Just as a hero-god's authority in heaven was predicated on maintaining order and overcoming chaos, an earthly king's authority in the mundane realm depended on establishing and maintaining order.

This led directly to distinctive conceptions of society and politics, a fact to which Israel, on the basis of its memory of oppression in Egypt, could attest. The structure of ancient Egyptian society may, appropriately enough, be conceptualized as a pyramid. The deity stood atop the pyramid, with the pharaoh just below, followed by the social classes in progressive descent, each less well off than its predecessor, followed by the slaves, the largest and poorest group, at the bottom. The luxury of the upper classes was enabled through the exploitation of those living close to the subsistence level at the bottom of society.[12] Because the earthly ruler was God's representative on earth, no questioning of authority was tolerated, for to rebel against the king was to rebel against the order of creation. Above all, subjects were to be obedient and faithful in fulfilling their assigned duties in the universe.[13] Thus, as in other surrounding societies, a "religion of static triumphalism" underwrote a politics of oppression and exploitation in Egypt. As with other ancient Near Eastern gods, the gods of Egypt were "the immovable lords of order," who called for, sanctioned, and legitimated "a society of order" that allowed for "no breaks for freedom."[14]

In contrast to such conceptions of divinity and social order, Israel's confession and imaging of God's activity in the world is significantly different, with profound social and political ramifications. Israel believed in "*creation continua*, the continuation of God's work as Creator throughout the history of creation,"[15] and Yahweh is understood to be a dynamic character, whose covenanting and liberative activities stand in continuity with his creative activity. The God who creates is also the God who liberates and covenants. Israel's conception of God's kingship images God predominantly in organismic terms, as standing in intimate relationship to the world.[16] Yahweh's deliverance of Israel from Egyptian oppression and subsequent covenanting at Sinai paradigmatically exemplify the *character* of this new understanding of God, for it is in liberating and initiating covenant with Israel that Yahweh's relational character is made most clear.[17]

LOVING JUSTICE: THE CHARACTER OF GOD, THE CHARACTER OF THE COVENANT COMMUNITY

Unlike the gods of the surrounding cultures, who could not relate faithfully to or in solidarity with humanity, except perhaps for self-serving alliances, the "primal disclosure of the Bible" is that the God of Israel "*makes a move toward* earth to identify a faithful covenant partner, responding to the groans of oppressed people."[18] The God Israel confesses is a God who *loves* and suffers *with* and *for* Israel. In the biblical witness, God's love is marked by *pathos*; it is a suffering love.[19] Through—indeed, *because* of—its experiences of and with this suffering God who liberates and covenants, Israel confesses Yahweh to be Holy, steadfastly loving, righteous, and just, all attributes with deep ethical significance.

Divine activity within the covenant relationship is characterized by Israel perhaps most centrally in terms of God's steadfast love (*hesed*). Paradigmatic expression of this is found in Exodus 34:6–7, where God confesses Godself to be

> The Lord, the Lord, a God merciful and gracious, slow to anger, and abounding in steadfast love and faithfulness, keeping steadfast love for the thousandth generation, forgiving iniquity and transgression and sin, yet by no means clearing the guilty, but visiting the iniquity of the parents upon the children and the children's children, to the third and the fourth generation.[20]

The meaning of *hesed* is difficult to specify precisely in English, and has been understood to capture, variously, God's mercy, grace, loyalty, goodness, loving-kindness, and compassion.[21] However, some of the basic conceptual elements of the term include the following: First, "God's steadfast love is always demonstrated in the context of relationship, and most often in relation to the need of the other in relationship." Second, *hesed* is an expression of fidelity in such relationship. It is a concrete expression of loyalty, manifest in concrete action. Finally, in the context of covenant relationship it is used to characterize the relationship of God to Israel. As Bruce Birch notes, "God's *hesed* points to God's actions of loving fidelity to the covenant relationship."[22]

From the perspective of the ethical dimensions of the prophetic, two of the most important expressions of God's steadfast love are God's righteousness (*sedaqah*) and God's justice (*mispat*). Proclamations of God's righteousness and justice are oft repeated and clear in the Hebrew Bible: "the Lord is a God of justice" (Isa. 30:18), whose reign is established and upheld "with justice and with righteousness" (Isa. 9:7). "Righteousness and justice are the foundation" of God's throne, before whom goes "steadfast love and faithfulness" (Ps. 89:14; see also Ps. 97:2). God declares, "I am the Lord; I act with steadfast love, justice, and righteousness in the earth, for in these things I delight" (Jer. 9:24).

As the foregoing illustrates, righteousness and justice are closely allied in meaning, and are frequently used in parallel manner as variants of one another.[23] While the terms are not strictly identical, the differences between them are difficult to establish sharply, and seem to be largely a matter of emphasis. *Mispat* is a mode of action. In judging on behalf of those who have been denied their right, God upholds justice. *Sedaqah*, righteousness, is a quality of the actor known through her actions. It connotes someone or something shown to be true, particularly in a legal context. While justice and righteousness are not strictly identical, then, in the biblical witness they coincide, with righteousness reflected in the law or just action. Thus, to claim that God is righteous is to claim "that he is a just and reliable judge (Ps. 9:4) who keeps his side of the covenant and who thus delivers Israel from her enemies, so that they experience that righteousness as punishment, while Israel experiences it as salvation and vindication."[24] Because of the close proximity with which the terms lie relative to one another, and judging that a focus on justice is often veiled from the English reader of the Hebrew Bible by virtue of the ambiguity of the term "righteousness," Stephen Mott suggests that, when found in a context of social responsibility or oppression, "righteousness" is better translated as "justice."[25] Given that what follows is concerned almost exclusively with such contexts, I will follow Mott in reading justice and righteousness as coterminous and mutually implicating terms that may profitably be read in shorthand simply as "justice."

God's concern for justice is focused especially on those in the community who are most marginal or vulnerable. Yahweh "executes justice for the orphan and the widow, and . . . loves the strangers, providing them with food and clothing" (Deut. 10:18). Nicholas Wolterstorff characterizes "the undoing of injustice and the bringing about of justice" as "Yahweh's own abiding cause."

Such concern is a function of God's love for humanity and desire for the flourishing of God's creatures and is focused in particular on what he calls the "quartet of the vulnerable": widows, orphans, resident aliens, and the poor.[26]

We determine whether justice is done, then, not by looking at whether the economically or politically powerful have enough to eat or speak with a voice that is heard, but, rather, whether the economically or politically power*less* are fed and heard.[27] The *victim* of *in*justice occupies center stage. Central to biblical justice is what Mott calls "the principle of redress," whereby those inequalities which undermine well-being are to be corrected in a manner that approximates equality.[28] This principle underlies the provisions of the Year of Jubilees (Lev. 25), which, in decreeing that all land be returned to the original owning family every fifty years, had the effect of institutionalizing "the relative equality of all persons in the landed means of production."[29] It finds explicit expression, for example, in Psalm 107:39–41, which speaks of God's action, rooted in his steadfast love, on behalf of victims of injustice:

> When they are diminished and brought low through oppression, trouble, and sorrow, he pours contempt on princes and makes them wander in trackless wastes; but he raises up the needy out of distress, and makes their families like flocks. The upright see it and are glad; and all the wickedness stops its mouth. Let those who are wise give heed to these things, and consider the steadfast love of the Lord.

Guided by this principle, the first priority of justice is to meet the needs of the members of the community: "give me neither poverty nor riches; feed me with the food that I need." (Prov. 30:8).[30] One of the dominant themes of God's liberation of Israel from bondage, pervading not only the law, but also much of Israel's liturgical, wisdom, and prophetic literature, is that Israel is obligated to those in need.

Israel's obligation to attend to the needs of the neighbor is a response to God's own action on Israel's behalf: "You shall not deprive a resident alien or an orphan of justice; you shall not take a widow's garment in pledge. Remember that you were a slave in Egypt and the Lord your God redeemed you from there; therefore I command you to do this" (Deut. 24:17). Thus, while the just individual is one who "preserves the peace and wholeness of the community," particularly as it relates to those who are most marginal or vulnerable in the community, this concern for the defenseless is not simply a concern for social harmony, "but is rooted in the nature of Yahweh himself who is defender of the oppressed."[31] This point may be generalized to characterize the shape of Israel as a whole. Indeed, Israel's communal character is *incoherent* if it is not understood as a response to God's character and activity in the world. In Israel's effort to live as a distinctive community, there was an organic connection between the exodus event and the communal structures that were true to Israel's origins in God's gracious act of deliverance. That connection could not be preserved solely by abstract formulations of belief, but *demanded a quality of life relating inextricably to systems of justice, land distribution, use of capital, treatment of vulnerable classes within the society, and the like*. These institutions are not formal accidents, but essential structures already implicit in the nature of the God revealed in the exodus.[32]

This concern for justice is thus not abstract or episodic, but is to be embodied in Israel's communal life through its most central social structures—political, legal, and economic.

In embodying God's justice, Israel is not only acting faithfully; such response is central to knowledge of God. This divine concern for justice sets the pattern not only for human understandings of justice, but also for human understanding of God. If God is the pattern of reality, God's concern for justice establishes for human action concrete priorities and patterns for right action toward and relationship with others. To fail to act justly toward others is to fail to know God, for there can be no true religion absent the doing of justice. In the biblical witness "there is no division between *theoria* and *praxis*, between faith and the doing of justice . . . . The doing of justice is not the application of religious faith, but its substance; without it, God remains unknown."[33] This connection between justice and the presence of true faith is made clear in Jeremiah's contrast of the just reign of Josiah with the unjust reign of his son Jehoiakim:

> Woe to him who builds his house by unrighteousness, And his upper rooms by injustice; . . . . Are you a king because you compete in cedar? Did not your father eat and drink and do justice and righteousness? Then it was well with him. He judged the cause of the poor and needy; then it was well. Is this not to know me? says the Lord. (Jer. 22:13, 15–16)

It is thus responsiveness to this radically different understanding of God as an active character in history, with purposes to be fulfilled with, for, and on behalf of humanity, that gives rise to Israel as an alternative community with a radically different social system.

COUNTERING ROYAL IDEOLOGY IN ISRAEL: PROPHETIC ATTENTION TO THE MARGINS

Against this background of Israel as a covenant community of justice, the generally negative view of kingship conveyed by the biblical text is comprehensible, for kingship threatened this understanding of biblical justice in several ways. While the royal and the prophetic stand alongside one another as two distinct and competing political trajectories in the Hebrew Bible, the latter is normatively and canonically granted pride of place. As Gunther Wittenberg has pointed out, "the Old Testament historians have a very critical, one could even say a biased view of the monarchy. The real actors of history are the prophets. History is written from the perspective of the prophets."[34] Early calls for or experiments with kingship (see, e.g., the stories of Gideon and his son, Abimelech, in Judges 8 and 9) were rejected as incompatible with God's kingship and contrary to the character of Israel's community.

The central dangers of earthly kingship lay in its threat to God's rule over Israel and to the religious, economic, and political practices reflective of that rule. In short, kingship harbored the "potential for introducing a social system . . . antithetical to the very notion of community to which they were called by God's deliverance."[35] It threatened to undermine Israel's essential, identity-constitutive character as an alternative, covenantal community of justice. Indeed, the institution of prophecy seems to have arisen simultaneously with kingship in ancient Israel.[36] If there were to be kings, there would be prophets, for the dangers posed by kingship must be kept in check. As Michael Walzer notes, "God's interests are represented by his prophets, while the full and often contradictory set of human interests—personal, dynastic, and national—is represented by the king. Prophecy is born together with monarchy lest divine law have no voice in the world."[37]

If earthly kingship would be legitimate and successful, Yahweh's kingship would provide the model. God's reign provided the blueprint for the earthly exercise of power. Under David, a developing royal theology coupled positively the reign of God with the reign of an earthly king. In this coupling, "the king is considered to be Yahweh's regent," and "the qualities of God's rule are to be reflected in the rule of the earthly king."[38] While the promise of this royal ideal may have been glimpsed, however ambiguously, under David, it largely fell from view under those who reigned subsequently.

Solomon and his successors ushered in "a radical shift in the foundations of Israel's life and faith," which threatened to undermine the radical, alternative character of Israel as a covenant community. The whole of Solomon's program "appears to have been a self-serving achievement" aimed solely at "the self-securing of king and dynasty." The politics of Solomon's "state-sponsored syncretism" led to the abandonment or erosion of much that characterized Israel as an alternative community.[39] This movement by Israel, from a distinct and distinctly religious community to a bureaucratic, political state with its own ends has been characterized by George Mendenhall as a systematic reversion to Bronze Age paganism. He argues that "by the end of Solomon's regime the Jerusalem state was a thoroughly paganized Syro-Hittite regime and was condemned as intolerable by the prophets, who represented the continuity of the Yahwist tradition."[40] This characterization is applicable not only to Solomon's kingship, but to most all who followed in his wake. Indeed, the bulk of Israel's story of kingship "from Solomon to the exile can be understood as the struggle between the calling to be the alternative community of covenant and the pattern of royal ideology which sought to make Israel 'like all the other nations.'"[41]

Prophetic condemnation of Israel's monarchs for this rejection of the community's constitutive commitments and practices in favor of a paganized state focused centrally on three broad, but conceptually interrelated, areas: economics, politics, and religion. The biblical picture here, one must be clear, is holistic; there is no compartmentalizing the political, the economic, and the religious into separate spheres, each with its own autonomy. Failures in economic or political practice frequently reflect and reinforce one another, and are themselves understood to be rooted in failures of religious practice. The failures of kingship in these areas are centrally—in most cases, essentially—a failure to embody the moral values which characterize covenant obedience: justice and righteousness, particularly in relation to the most vulnerable and marginal members of the community. For the remainder of this discussion of prophetic confrontation with Israel's kings, I will discuss each of these areas of prophetic condemnation in turn.

The distortions of Israel's character ushered in by royal ideology are particularly noticeable in terms of its upholding of an "economics of privilege" or an "economics of well-being and affluence." The egalitarian impulses that characterized Israel as a covenantal community and focused on need were shunned in favor of economic policies favoring the king and others in privileged positions. This was clear, for example, in the following description of Solomon's provisions:

> Solomon's provision for one day was thirty cors of choice flour, and sixty cors of meal, ten fat oxen, and twenty pasture-fed cattle, one hundred sheep, besides deer, gazelles, roebucks, and fatted fowl . . . . Solomon also had forty thousand stalls of horses for his chariots, and twelve thousand horsemen. Those officials supplied provisions for King Solomon and for all who came to [his] table . . . ; they let nothing be lacking. (1 Kings 4:22–23, 26–27)

These provisions were not those of the average Israelite, but, rather, reflected the grossly inequitable forms of distribution common under Solomon. Indeed, mirroring "the pattern of Phoenician and Egyptian royal courts Solomon created a new hierarchy of elite classes." In addition to the growth of an administrative class, the ostentatious and avaricious policies and building campaigns undertaken by Solomon, which led to hefty tax burdens, gave rise to "a growing class of the poor, some of whom were forced into indentured servitude by their indebtedness."[42] These policies of Solomon, as well as similar policies under other Israelite kings, were anathema for the prophets.

The economic crisis brought about by Israel's emergence as an efficient political state was particularly focused on the issue of the land and its ownership. In the traditional economy of Israel's covenant community, "security and freedom" were dependent upon "a relatively inclusive distribution" of small farms owned by kinship groups as well as common public territory for grazing and water. Israel's understanding of the significance of the land was rooted in more than its simple economic importance, however; it was central to identity. The land was owned by God, and each family was to receive a portion, an "inheritance" (*nahalah*), to manage in stewardship. "It was their inheritance from God. To lose their inheritance was tantamount to losing their identity as a member of the people and the privileges that went with that identity." Land was "the instrument of participation in the society as an equal," it "was a corollary to membership in the society."[43] The land as a whole was Israel's "possession," God's gift and sign of salvation. Within this rich theological context, then, not only was the land the basic economic good in society, essential to the well-being of the population, it was also central to Israel's identity.

The egalitarian community of justice to which Israel as a covenant community was called was threatened by exploitative policies focused on the accumulation of land and wealth. Such practices were the object of unswerving condemnation by Israel's prophets:

> Ah, Those who add house to house And join field to field, Till there is room for none but you To dwell in the land! (Isa. 5:8 [*Tanakh*])
>
> Alas for those who devise wickedness and evil deeds on their beds! When the morning dawns, they perform it, because it is in their power. They covet fields, and seize them; houses, and take them away; they oppress householder and house, people and their inheritance. (Mic. 2:1–2)

For the land, a fundamental element of Israel's egalitarian counter community, to become the basis of the oppression of the many by the few was a fundamental perversion of its purpose.[44]

Such economic exploitation was closely related to, and frequently enabled, political injustices in Israel. Indeed, indictments of economic and political injustices frequently stand side by side in prophetic texts. Of particular concern for the prophets was corruption in the administration of justice. Both local justice "in the gates," as well as the larger judicial system of the monarchy had become corrupted—by the greed of judicial officials, by bias toward the powerful, by bribery. Such corruption, not surprisingly, was most intensely felt by those who were most marginal in society: the poor, the widow, the orphan. The convergence of these concerns is clear in the following passages from Isaiah and Amos:

> Your princes are rebels and companions of thieves. Everyone loves a bribe and runs after gifts. They do not defend the orphan, and the widow's cause does not come before them. (Isa. 1:23)

> For I know how many are your transgressions, and how great are your sins—you who afflict the righteous, who take a bribe, and push aside the needy in the gate. (Amos 5:12)

Bribery in the gate—in the courts—was not a victimless crime, but had oppressive effects on those who were most vulnerable in society, most in need of the equitable administration of justice.

Political corruption extends, however, well beyond the courts, and infects every level of leadership in Israel. Kings and their advisors are indicted for their "trust in diplomacy and military might in their quest for extended power rather than trust in God."[45] Hosea is particularly forceful in his wholesale condemnation of the institution of kingship on this score:

> You have plowed wickedness, you have reaped injustice, you have eaten the fruit of lies. Because you have trusted in your power and in the multitude of your warriors, therefore the tumult of war shall rise against your people, and all your fortresses shall be destroyed, ... At dawn the king of Israel shall be utterly cut off. (Hosea 10:13–14, 15)

This movement away from covenant commitments in economic and political practices was accompanied and enabled by a similar movement away from such commitments in religious practice. Two areas were of particular focus: the persistence of idolatry and the perversion of religious life due to a failure to embody covenantal righteousness and justice. Idolatry was a persistent threat to Israel's loyalty to Yahweh:

> My people consult a piece of wood, and their divining rod gives them oracles. For a spirit of whoredom has led them astray, and they have played the whore, forsaking their God. (Hosea 4:12)

Likewise, religious observance had become perverted in Israel's failure to embody standards of justice and righteousness. Recall the earlier discussion of the intimate connection between knowledge of God and acting justly. In the absence of justice, religious observances are hollow and empty. Religious observance was not an end in itself:

> When you stretch out your hands, I will hide my eyes from you; even though you make many prayers, I will not listen; your hands are full of blood. Wash

> yourselves; make yourselves clean; remove the evils of your doings from before my eyes; cease to do evil, learn to do good; seek justice, rescue the oppressed, defend the orphan, plead for the widow. (Isa. 1:15–17)
>
> I hate, I despise your festivals, and I take no delight in your solemn assemblies. Even though you offer me your burnt offerings and grain offerings I will not accept them; . . . . But let justice roll down like waters, and righteousness like an ever-flowing stream. (Amos 5:21–22, 24)

Finally, the domesticated religion of the monarchy was problematic not only because of such perversions in practice, but also because it was harnessed to royal power, and served as a source of its legitimation. The endurance of political and economic corruption in Israel was rooted in theological forms of justification. Theological warrant was provided for this royal ideology via what Walter Brueggemann has called "the establishment of a controlled, static religion in which the God and his temple become part of the royal landscape, in which the sovereignty of God is fully subordinated to the purpose of the king." With the establishment and institutionalization of such religion, "God is now 'on call,' and access to him is controlled by the royal court." This arrangement serves to sanction "every notion of the king because there can be no transcendent resistance or protest," and it "gives the king a monopoly so that no marginal person may approach this God except on the kings terms."[46] Indeed, as was the case with other ancient Near Eastern political cultures, this domesticated "religion of immanence" was a crucial support for the monarchical corruption of politics and economics, and it resulted in a "captive God" wholly at ease with royal ideology.[47]

JUSTICE AS SHALOM

Though often a harshly judgmental, critical voice, the prophetic call to justice is dynamic, future-oriented, and centrally animated by a hope for repentance, the restoration of the community, and the establishment of the true justice and true peace. The covenantal justice the prophets called for in opposing the distortions of royal ideology aimed at what E. Clinton Gardner has termed a "reconciling justice." This stands in stark contrast to the classic, Aristotelian,[48] manner of conceiving justice in terms of the preservation or restoration of the existing social order. In this conception, order is measured according to "conventional criteria of personal, ability, merit, rank, or wealth." Such a position leaves existing disparities and injustices in place. The marginal remain marginal, even after justice is done.[49] In contrast to such preserving justice, reconciling justice aims at the transformation of the social and political order.

> From a biblical perspective, all historical systems of justice are corrupted and perverted by sin; therefore, they fall ultimately under judgment by the righteousness and justice of God. Covenantal justice demands the transformation of hierarchical forms of society upon the basis of the fundamental equality and liberty which all share through their creation in the "image of God." Reconciling justice means equal justice. It means sharing of power with those who are oppressed. It means participation of marginalized groups in institutionalized forms of economic and political power. Reconciling justice demands the resignation of proportionate (retributive and distributive) justice out of compassion for the needy and for the sake of the well-being of the community as a whole. Creative justice forgives in order that broken relationships may be restored.[50]

While classical justice assumes the presence of ongoing social disparity, biblical justice, as the prophetic witness makes abundantly clear, will have none of this.

The biblical witness, instead, envisions a profound, robust understanding of peace (*shalom*). Ultimately, it is to this that calls for justice are directed. This peace is not merely an absence or lack of conflict, but, rather, is an ontologically fundamental harmony and wholeness, originally present at and grounding divine creation. God's ordering of the "cosmos created harmony and peace. Justice, righteousness, and peace are all present in this 'original state.'"[51] Although humanity's sinfulness has distorted this harmonic peace, it is the goal to which creation is to be restored, the eschatological end of God's good work. Justice and righteousness are essential in this restoration.

Indeed, peace—wholeness in human relationship and throughout the whole of creation—and justice are frequently depicted in prophetic literature as standing in intimate and essential connection. This vision is vividly presented, for example, in Isaiah 11 and Micah 4. In Isaiah, the ideal Davidic king is depicted (v. 4) as judging the poor with righteousness and deciding "with equity for the meek of the earth." The effects of the justice of such rule will be peacefully manifested throughout the whole of creation, as the wolf lies with the lamb, the leopard with the kid, and a child plays near the hole of the asp (vv. 6, 8). In Micah, an eschatological vision of justice among the nations is the foundation of a universal peace in which military armaments are beaten into agricultural tools, nations cease to go to war or to learn its ways, and all will possess a share of the land ("sit under their own vines and under their own fig trees") (vv. 3–4). Positively stated, then, the prophetic vision is one of a "future transformed society in which human beings live together in peace with themselves and in harmony with the whole of creation (*shalom*), and in which the glory of Yahweh would be revealed."[52]

JESUS THE PROPHET

The prophetic voice is most closely associated with the witness of the Hebrew prophets, but it is also clearly embodied, and importantly extended, in the person and work of Jesus Christ. While numerous titles have been ascribed to Jesus Christ in the biblical text—Son of Man, Messiah, Teacher, and so on—he is also centrally confessed to be a prophet, in the same line as Elijah, Jeremiah, and John the Baptist. The various titles ascribed to Jesus are rightly understood as mutually implicating—he who is prophet is also Messiah, for example. Indeed, it may reasonably be argued that Jesus' distinctive character as Messiah is more decisively significant than his role as a prophet in that he does not just call the community to its roots, but enables it to realize its salvation. Without denying this, my focus here, however, will be largely on how, in terms of his social vision and practice, it may be that the latter title is rightly ascribed to Jesus. The central contention here is that, in a manner analogous to and in continuity with, but ultimately going beyond, Israel's prophets, Jesus' message and mission was centrally and essentially concerned with exposing and critiquing the injustices of his day, and bringing about social renewal and transformation through an inclusive, peaceable vision of God's reign in the world. In the words of Jon Sobrino, Jesus' "prophetic praxis" consists of his "direct denunciation of the anti-Kingdom"; it is concerned "with denouncing and unmasking real injustice and oppression."[53]

The identification of Jesus with the prophetic tradition is variously represented in the gospels, perhaps most significantly as issuing from Jesus' own mouth. Luke, for example, depicts Jesus' own understanding of his ministry and mission, from its public inception, in prophetic terms. The Spirit of the Lord, in Luke's witness, has been conferred upon Jesus to, in the prophet Isaiah's terms, "bring good news to the poor[,] . . . to proclaim release to the captives and recovery of sight to the blind, to let the oppressed go free, to proclaim the year of the Lord's favor" (Luke 4:18–19; cf. Isa. 61:1–2, 58:6). In Jesus' reading these words, "this scripture has been fulfilled" (Luke 4:21). Although there may be good reason to doubt the veracity of Luke's description of Jesus' reading of these words in the synagogue, it is clear that Luke conceived Jesus' identity in prophetic terms and the nature of his ministry in justice terms. There can be no spiritualist or pietistic reading of these words without fundamentally distorting them. "We do violence to the realism of Judaism if we choose to hear the terms which connote poverty, bondage, deprivation and oppression as metaphors referring to the 'spiritual' life. If they do not mean what they say, if Luke's Jesus is suggesting that the political and economic order and the world of social systems are to be circumvented in order for his hearers to be religious, then he has certainly chosen a peculiar text for saying so."[54]

Elsewhere, those who hear Jesus' words and witness his actions are presented as identifying him prophetically. In Matthew 16:14, as well as in the parallel passage of Mark 8:27–30, Jesus is confessed to be a prophet: "'Who do people say that the Son of Man is?' And they [the disciples] said, 'Some say John the Baptist, but others Elijah, and still others Jeremiah or one of the prophets'" (Matt. 16:14). In the Fourth Gospel, Jesus is on several occasions named a prophet by those who witness or experience miracles (for example, by the crowd after the feeding of the five thousand—"This is indeed the prophet who is to come into the world." [6:14]—and by a blind man healed on the Sabbath—"'What do you say about him? It was your eyes he opened.' He said, 'He is a prophet.'" [9:17]). It is the case that some of these attributions of prophetic identity are clearly regarded in the text as failing by themselves to render Jesus' identity fully (in addition to the previously cited texts from Matthew and Mark, see, e.g., Matt. 11:9), but the identification is not denied or negated, and "it is clear that if the crowds place Jesus in the line of the prophets, then he must have led a prophet's life . . . . Jesus transcends his propheticism, yes, but he does so from a point of departure in, and an ongoing exercise of propheticism itself . . . . It is via the prophetical dimension that the crowds, and his disciples as well, come to grasp what Jesus is in his ultimate reality."[55]

Jesus transcends his propheticism, but he does not deny or destroy it. One might worry that to highlight Jesus' prophetic identity runs the risk of reducing his life to that of a political figure and his message to that of a political program or ideology, such that they might be appropriated to underwrite a Christology more concerned with political effectiveness than with Christian faithfulness. As important as the prophets might have been in giving voice to God's intentions for humanity, they were not themselves divine. To speak of Jesus primarily in terms of prophetic identity, then, may seem to render his divinity a matter of secondary importance. On the basis of such worries, one might suggest, in the interest of such faithfulness and of attending to that which makes Jesus truly unique, that one highlight other titles, such as "Messiah/Christ" or "Son of God" or "Son of Man" or even "God." These titles are properly ascribed to Jesus, and each helps to illumine important dimensions his uniqueness, but they do not render marginal his prophetic identity. If anything, they intensify the significance of that identity. If Jesus is God incarnate, then in his prophetic identity he is not simply a messenger of God's intentions for humanity, he is the very embodiment of those intentions. Jesus does not simply proclaim the Kingdom of God, he performs that kingdom in and through his very self, thereby rendering the prophetic voice central for an adequate understanding of Christian discipleship.

JESUS' PROPHETIC PRAXIS: CHALLENGING THE DOMINATION SYSTEM

While Jesus' prophetic activities were not directed at distortions of Israel's communal character by its ostensible keepers, his critique of the Greco-Roman culture of his time was focused on social, political, and religious practices that were similar in key respects to those condemned by Israel's prophets. He denounced what Walter Wink has called the "Domination System," a system in which domination was multifaceted and pervasive throughout the whole structure of social relationship:

> The rich dominated the poor; men, women; Romans, their subjects. Power was patriarchal, hierarchical, autocratic, and androcratic, and was exerted through conquest, deception, competition, and force. Violence and war were regarded as inevitable and redemptive. Ethnic barriers separated Jew from Gentile. Status distinctions were jealously preserved; a man's place at a banquet was a delicate matter of relative ranking. The more powerful surrounded themselves with clients; patrons exercised control through honor and shaming, gifts and obligations. Slavery was ubiquitous. Women's reproductive capacities and sexual expression were subject to male control, and their freedom in relationships and movement were sharply circumscribed. Divine beings were scarcely distinguishable from human tyrants, demanding propitiation by means of bloody sacrifices. A coterie of priests held a monopoly on temple wealth and power. Nature itself existed to be exploited by a single one of its species.[56]

Not only were oppressive social configurations multifaceted and pervasive, but within these configurations of social relationship in ancient Mediterranean society, modes or spheres of being that are now often thought to be highly differentiated and relatively independent—for example, religious, economic, political, educational, and familial spheres—were neither. One's status in one sphere generally correlated with one's status in another. Furthermore, in contrast to modern assumptions of abundance, in this system, the range of material and social/political goods available was presumed to be limited and was tightly channeled—it was a zero-sum society.[57]

It is within and against society structured in this manner that the prophetic dimensions of Jesus' message and mission are most apparent. Jesus represented and embodied an alternative structure of reality that stood over and against reality structured in terms of the domination system or what Jon Sobrino calls the anti-Kingdom.[58] In fact, Jesus' "positive proclamation of the Kingdom has to be made in the presence of the anti-Kingdom. Its purpose is to overcome and destroy the anti-Kingdom by upholding the true God. This is carried out in the midst of conflict, and therefore implies struggle."[59] Upholding justice, truth, and the moral worth of the oppressed, the Kingdom introduces "truth into a world of lies . . . compassion into a world of insensibility and cruelty," and "life into a world of death."[60] Struggle against and destruction of the anti-Kingdom/domination system ought not to be understood in violently agonistic terms, however, for, as I will discuss shortly, one of the chief and unique attributes of the prophetic dimensions of Jesus' message is its unswerving commitment to peaceableness.

In many respects, Jesus' prophetic message stands in an explicit and direct line of continuity with the focus on reconciling justice found in Israel's prophets. Like them, he resisted religious corruptions of his day, especially insofar as they depicted one's relationship to God in a manner that legitimated inattention to real human needs: for example, distortions of the purity system, legalistic interpretations of the law, corruptions of the sacrificial and temple system, and so on. Much of this prophetic critique of the religious abuses of his day was reflective of an unwavering concern for all manner of practices of economic and social exclusion. What Jesus maintained and defended in his prophetic critique of the domination system, like Israel's prophets before him, was a particular vision of the reality of God, a vision in which religious and social rules and practices were judged in terms of their effects upon, and attention to, those most marginal in the community.[61]

This, then, helps to explain the central concern in Jesus' message and ministry for "the poor." Poverty and wealth were understood by Jesus to stand in an inverse and oppositional relationship to one another. The riches of the few were the cause of poverty, and the Kingdom proclaimed by Jesus was primarily addressed to, and stood unequivocally on the side of, those poor who were the victims of others' abundance. "The gospel of Jesus is founded on economic equality, because economic inequalities are the basis of domination. Ranking, domination hierarchies, classism and the caste system are all built on accumulated power provided by excess wealth."[62] In resisting domination so constituted, God's bias was clearly expressed in favor of those who were poor and oppressed.

This contrast is explicit throughout the New Testament, but perhaps most especially in the Gospel of Luke. In Luke's Sermon on the Plain (Luke 6:17–46), the oppositional relationship between wealth and poverty is explicit. Luke's is "a radical judgment . . . that brings poverty and its praise, and wealth and its reprehension, into relative confrontation."[63] In the order proclaimed by Jesus, the poor will have a place in the Kingdom of God, and those who are hungry will be filled. By contrast, however, the rich already have their consolation in wealth and will not possess the Kingdom of God, and the presently satiated will be the ones who will be hungry. A similar contrast between wealth and poverty, accompanied by a parallel depiction of reversal of fortunes, is found in the parable of the rich man and Lazarus

(Luke 16:19–31). While poor Lazarus was, while alive, dependent upon the scraps that fell from the abundant table of the rich man, it was the rich man who, having died and descended into Hades, sought out Lazarus, who had been "carried away by the angels to be with Abraham," so that he might feel on his tongue the coolness of water from Lazarus' finger.

If the implications of Jesus' prophetic critique of the domination system are not to be understood in an overly narrow manner, it is important that "the poor" not be understood here too restrictively. While poverty is frequently depicted in terms of one's economic status, or lack thereof, "the poor" is a more encompassing term than this economic meaning alone conveys. There are the economic poor, but there are also those Sobrino calls the sociologically poor: "those despised by the ruling society, those considered sinners, the publicans, the prostitutes." These groups of people are poor "in the sense that being a *socium* (the symbol of basic interhuman relationships) is denied them, and with this, the minimum of dignity." As an encompassing category, the poor are those who are not recognized as possessing moral worth. They are those at the bottom of history, those oppressed in society and cast out of it. "Both economic poverty and lack of moral dignity can express this being at the bottom."[64] Thus, for example, in the parable of the great dinner (Luke 14:15–24), clearly a metaphor for the Kingdom of God, those invited to the banquet include not only the poor but also the blind, the crippled, and the lame. Similarly, Jesus' miracles, through their satisfaction of concrete material needs, were not apolitical acts which merely authenticated the gospel or Jesus' religious authority, but, rather, were understood as robustly social and political signs of the presence of the Kingdom.[65]

Enacting this alternative, domination-free order proclaimed by Jesus—acting as Jesus' disciples—is predicated on a radically altered set of values and assumptions aimed at upsetting regnant ideas about social power, prestige, and the like.[66] This is perhaps best illustrated in the dispute, recorded by Luke, between the disciples regarding who among them was the greatest. Jesus responds, "The kings of the Gentiles lord it over them; and those in authority over them are called benefactors. But not so with you; rather the greatest among you must become like the youngest, and the leader like one who serves. For who is greater, the one who sits at the table or the one who serves? Is it not the one at the table? But I am among you as one who serves" (Luke 22:25–27; cf. Matt. 20:24–28; Mark 10:41–45). Neither ambition nor aspiration nor power nor greatness are values repudiated by Jesus, but they are to be focused not on one's own status, but on service to the needs of those others who are most vulnerable or marginalized. The true greatness to which one ought to aspire is marked by Christ-like service to others.

This understanding of discipleship as service to vulnerable others finds expression in the story of Zacchaeus (Luke 19:1–10). As a tax collector,

Zacchaeus is an oppressor of the economically poor, a person one might well expect, as in the case of the rich man/ruler (Luke 18:18–30; Matt. 19:16–30; Mark 10:17–31), to receive word of the necessity of service to vulnerable others with sadness and grief. Instead, Zacchaeus pledges to give half of his possessions to the poor, and, in keeping with the strictest provisions of the law, to repay four times anyone he has defrauded. In this only recorded conversion of a rich man, Jesus rejoices and declares that salvation has come to Zacchaeus' house not because he is hospitable, although hospitality is certainly a central biblical virtue, but because he has promised to refrain from oppressing. "Zacchaeus ceases to be a sinner because he has stopped being a rich oppressor."[67]

INTENSIFYING AND RADICALIZING THE PROPHETIC TRADITION

To this point, it may seem that there is little in this account of Jesus' prophetic praxis that is new. This focus on resisting unjust, hierarchically configured domination through attention to marginalized others is clearly continuous with the calls for justice proclaimed by Israel's prophets. However, although standing in clear continuity with the prophetic tradition in essential ways, Jesus' prophetic praxis was also comprised of dimensions that led that tradition in largely new and innovative directions, without abandoning its core insights or commitments. I will focus here on two of the most important ways in which Jesus intensified and radicalized the prophetic tradition: a more expansive understanding of solidarity, and an unwavering upholding of peaceableness, discernible particularly in his identification of nonviolence and forgiveness as defining characteristics of the Kingdom of God. Both of these emphases are essential aspects of Jesus' prophetic praxis in that they mark those commitments and methods of resistance to domination that are most central to, and characteristic of, his ministry and message.

Before discussing these elements of Jesus' teaching, I want to be clear that what follows is not a brief against Judaism or another hackneyed version of the claim that the Old Testament portrays a God of wrath or violence, while the New Testament portrays a God of love. The Old Testament imaging of God as characterized by steadfast love clearly resists such simple readings. Furthermore, it is important to remember here that Jesus was a Jew, and keeping this in mind helps to make clear that what is radicalized and intensified is his own tradition of religious thought and practice. It is more helpful to think of Jesus' teachings as giving expression to God's own dynamic creativity, by selectively taking up and extending in more radical directions already present themes from the diverse religious tradition of which he was part. It should hardly be surprising that there is a real diversity of moral thought and reflection in the Old Testament, from which some themes would find greater emphasis in Jesus' teachings than others, for Hebrew moral thought developed over the course of several centuries, in different historical, social and political contexts, and in response to a wide range of moral, political, and religious concerns. Nevertheless, while Jesus' teachings are not discontinuous with his inherited Judaism, it would be naive to deny that in the particular emphases of his message he offered nothing new.

Hebrew Scripture, with all of its moral diversity, does in places point to universal understandings of other-directed concern, as in the idea of a common human share in the image of God (Gen. 1), but alongside the universalistic thrust of Genesis stands the arguably more pervasive particularistic emphases of Exodus and of the law. Within Hebrew/Jewish moral teaching, such particularism roots moral obligation in judgments regarding moral respectability, relationships of dependence, proximity and intimacy in social relations, and the dynamics of social solidarity.[68] Thus, for example, Leviticus 19:34 ("You shall love the alien [NRSV]/stranger [Tanakh] as yourself"), often taken to entail a universal, indiscriminate commitment on the part of Israel to vulnerable others, is properly understood in more particularist terms. The word here for alien/stranger (*ger*) is best understood as referring not to anyone in need, regardless of their relation to oneself, but to the "sojourner," "one who lives with you." "From the beginning . . . the "stranger" did not refer to the word's intuitive meaning in English—to foreigners in general—but to a very particular type of foreigner who had actively affiliated herself with the Jewish community."[69] This particularist conception of moral obligation helps to explain other passages that more straightforwardly make distinctions between Jews and non-Jews regarding what is or is not permissible (e.g., Deut. 23:19–20 on lending with interest), as well as subsequent particularist emphases and distinctions in rabbinic thought.

While Jesus' message did not mark a wholesale departure from traditional Hebrew religious teaching—after all, he came to fulfill the law, not abolish it (Matt. 5:17)—his understanding of the proper breadth of one's range of moral concern does at least mark a broadened and more radical understanding of traditional Hebrew moral teaching. Thus, for example, one finds in his teachings concerning neighbor love, particularly those enjoining love of enemies, an understanding of solidarity perhaps intimated in Hebrew Scriptures, and so not utterly novel, but not yet fully developed.[70] In such teachings, he is "appealing for *an experience of solidarity with* [hu]*mankind*, an experience that is non-exclusive, an experience that is not dependent upon reciprocity because it includes even those who hate you, persecute you or treat you badly."[71] It is arguably a commitment to solidarity of this sort that underlies some of Jesus' hard sayings, such as, "Whoever comes to me and does not hate father and mother, wife and children, brothers and sisters, yes, and even life itself, cannot be my disciple" (Luke 14:26). Jesus is certainly engaged in hyperbole here,[72] but this is crucial for discerning his essential point: solidarity based in particularistic attachments to oneself and those one most loves is to be replaced by a "more basic solidarity with all [hu]mankind."[73]

This radicalization and intensification of Hebrew moral tradition is seen further in the central emphasis Jesus gives to peaceableness, which is centrally characterized by commitments to forgiveness and nonviolence. Images of peace do abound in and are central to Hebrew moral thought. Thus, I drew attention earlier to the concept of *shalom* as the central religious and ethical ideal of the prophetic tradition, and it is notable in passages, such as Proverbs 17:9, which enjoin forgiveness: "One who forgives an affront fosters friendship, but one who dwells on disputes will alienate a friend." Indeed, this demand to forgive is intimately bound to what it means for Israel to model its life individually and communally after God, for God's steadfast love finds characteristic expression in compassion and forgiveness. This is seen repeatedly in prophetic texts, as Israel violates the terms of its covenant with God, and is punished but ultimately forgiven for its misconduct. In Isaiah 54:8, for example, although God hides God's face from the people in a moment of wrath, this does not last, as "with everlasting love [God has] compassion" on Israel.[74]

Jesus' teachings affirm such commitments to peaceableness, but intensify them, thereby overriding elements of inherited Hebrew moral teaching, such as the *lex talionis* (eye for eye, tooth for tooth, etc. [Exod. 21:23–24; Lev. 24:17, 19–20; Deut. 19:21]),[75] which legitimated violence. For example, despite the abundance of references in the Old Testament to peace and forgiveness, "there is nothing in Moses or the prophets quite like Jesus' Sermon on the Mount in Matthew or Sermon on the Plain in Luke."[76] The injunction to love one's enemies is not simply a broadening of the range of moral concern, but an irreducibly peaceable practice, in which one refuses violence and seeks reconciliation with others. Similarly, Jesus' intensifications of traditional Hebrew teaching—"You have heard . . . but I say . . . "—all subvert any legitimate recourse to retaliatory violence, even of the most measured and proportional type.

It is common for these intensifications, and other aspects of Jesus' teaching, to be interpreted as positing impossibly high moral ideals or perfectionistic prohibitions, a misinterpretation that has dire consequences for a proper understanding of those teachings. Traditionally, Jesus' teachings are understood to have a twofold, dyadic, pattern consisting of a statement about traditional righteousness ("You have heard . . . ") followed by a more demanding teaching that is to replace the traditional injunction ("But I say to you . . . "). The new teaching is then commonly understood to be followed by illustrations (so in fulfilling what is taken to be the new command not to be angry with a brother or sister, one is to seek reconciliation with him or her [see Matt. 5:22–26]). On this common interpretation, then, one is not only not to kill, for example, one is not even to become angry. Taken in this manner, these injunctions seem highly unrealistic, even incapable of fulfillment. As David Gushee and Glen Stassen observe, this has led interpreters to "compartmentalize Jesus' teachings as meant for attitudes but not actions, or for repentance but not obedience, or for another future dispensation but not the present time, or merely as illustrations of general principles like love but not meant to be followed in particular."[77] It is this sort of interpretation that underlies worries, which I will discuss more fully later, that much of the history of Christianity can be written as the history of the "Constantinian" accommodation of the church to secular political authority.

In place of this twofold interpretation of many of Jesus' central teachings, Gushee and Stassen argue that such teachings actually have a threefold structure, offering what they call "transforming initiatives." The proper structure of such teachings does not follow a traditional righteousness/new teaching structure; rather, we find, first, a statement of traditional teaching, followed not by a command, but a diagnosis of a vicious cycle in which people often get stuck. This characteristically takes the form not of an imperative, but of an ongoing action. Following this, in what is often taken to be the illustrative section of the teaching, we come to the longest and climactic portion of the teaching, and it is here where the imperatives come, which Gushee and Stassen characterize as transforming initiatives that promise a way out of the vicious cycles in which we become stuck. Jesus' teachings recognize that we are liable to anger, to seek to retaliate revengefully, to practice righteousness for mere show, to look upon the other lustfully. The transforming initiatives that comprise the third portion of his teachings are meant to provide concrete practices through which we can extricate ourselves from such vicious cycles. They "are not mere inner attitudes, vague intentions, or moral convictions only, but regular practices to be engaged in. As we engage in them, we learn better and better ways to practice resolving conflict."[78]

This is seen, for example, in Matthew 5:38–42. Traditional righteousness ("You have heard it said . . .") counseled, "'An eye for an eye and a tooth for a tooth.'" The response generally attributed to Jesus, "Do not resist an evildoer," is better translated, Gushee and Stassen argue, along the lines of something like, "Do not retaliate revengefully by evil means." This translation better recognizes Jesus' own resistance of evil and gives better expression to the vicious cycle that seems to be the real object of his concern here: the cycle of revengeful retaliation. This also helps to show how the imperatives that follow (to turn the other cheek, give up one's undergarment, and carry a soldier's pack a second mile) counsel not forms of passive nonresistance, but creative practices through which one might actively and peaceably respond to evil. At the heart of such peaceable practices, Walter Wink argues, "is the 'unnatural' . . . refusal to mirror evil," a refusal "to let one's responses be determined by what one deplores." Such practices "do not at all mean acquiescing passively to evil, but are a studied and deliberate way of seizing the initiative and overthrowing evil by the force of its own momentum."[79] Thus, for example, the injunction to turn the other cheek is not a demand to acquiesce passively to evil. Instead, it is a method of active, nonviolent resistance that would have forced an attacker to strike a person in a manner that, by virtue of regnant social conventions, entailed the recognition of that person as an equal.[80] It was largely through such expansive, peaceable practices that Jesus sought to enact an alternative vision of society characterized by true peace, equality, and care for the oppressed, a vision all the more radical for its refusal of violence, even "'redemptive' violence."[81]

It may be unclear, however, in just what sense this peaceable vision may be said to be a political vision, a vision that may offer insights into how Christians might engage the public/political realm today. It is clear how Israel's prophets might be considered political figures; after all, most of their prophetic confrontations were focused on denouncing Israel's kings for distortions of the community's identity. It is generally not the case that Jesus may be said to be a political figure in the sense that he struggled with governmental politics, yet he is very clearly a political figure in his struggle with what might be called social politics. Although one does not find the same kind of direct confrontation with governmental policy that tends to be found in Old Testament accounts of prophetic activity, Jesus did come into conflict with the authorities of his day. Jesus' "exercise of a prophetic calling," in both its religious and social aspects, "interferes with the public and collective structure and by that very fact with the system of powers that shape society. From this viewpoint alone one can discern in Jesus' mission not only a public character, but perforce a political one."[82] This was not lost on Jesus, of course, who came proclaiming the *Kingdom* of God, nor was it lost on the authorities who opposed him and put him to death.

LOOKING BACK, LOOKING AHEAD

Though the prophetic voice finds varied expressions throughout the biblical text, there are broadly unifying themes discernible in the foregoing that characterize *the* prophetic voice and that can therefore serve to guide inquiry into its contemporary shape. Of particular importance are the themes of community, truth, justice, and violence/nonviolence. Furthermore, other prominent themes that might suggest themselves as central can be reasonably subsumed under at least one of these four themes. For example, it might be suggested that the naming and denunciation of sin is a central prophetic preoccupation. Certainly this is true, but this is not a concern distinct from these categories; rather, it is implicit in these categories, perhaps most especially the prophetic concern for justice.

As the prior discussion makes clear, the biblical prophets were concerned to uphold and defend the divinely grounded normative vision that characterized Israel as a covenant community. Though Israel's prophets and Jesus Christ often stood apart from other members of their communities, calling them to task for their deviations from the constitutive commitments of their communities, they did so precisely as defenders of and spokespersons for those communities. Though Israel's prophets and Jesus Christ bore messages from God individually, their authority was inseparable from the background assumptions of an animating religious tradition. Without community, their authority would be unintelligible.

However, as this broad canvassing of the biblical witness makes clear, in upholding community and tradition, Israel's prophets and Jesus were engaged, above all, in the articulation and defense of a particular and distinctive understanding of reality. For the biblical prophets, the most fundamental reality is God, for it is God who animates and gives shape to the community and its constitutive commitments, and it is therefore in terms of God's character and demands that the adequacy of a community's beliefs and practices were measured. Thus, the biblical prophets' claims about meaning and value, though expressed and embodied communally, were not *reducible* to Israel's communal beliefs nor were they mere self-descriptions of what Israel happened to affirm collectively; rather, they believed that the claims that undergirded and were expressed through the covenant community's beliefs and practices were claims about, and gave expression to, reality. For the biblical prophets, the adequacy of beliefs or practices—what we would now call the truth of beliefs or practices—is determined by how well they give expression to the reality that animates them.

Central to this vision of reality is a distinctive set of normative commitments. For the prophets and for Jesus Christ, one knows God's reality most especially by embodying God's character. For Israel, this was defined centrally by a concern for justice. In response to God's steadfast love for the covenant community, Israel's character was defined above all by acts of justice focused on extending compassionate care, especially to those at the community's margins. This understanding of justice was taken up by Jesus, and intensified and radicalized. The justice sought by the prophets and Jesus is aimed at establishing true peace, a form of peace in which unjust hierarchies are replaced by forms of social organization characterized true liberty and true equality, the full participation of all, and the equitable sharing of power. Ultimately, the normative vision of the biblical prophets hopes for true reconciliation and an end to violence.

The challenge to be addressed in subsequent chapters is how the normative theological vision canvassed here might find adequate contemporary expression. As the dynamism of this vision within the biblical text itself implies, this is not a static vision that can be simply parroted or copied as one seeks to embody it within contemporary contexts. Rather, while seeking to be faithful to the essentials of its biblical expression, what is sought is an articulation of this voice rendered intelligible through conversation with contemporary concerns and contemporary philosophical and theological conceptual categories. In the chapters that follow, I pursue this via engagement with the work of Michael Walzer, Stanley Hauerwas, and Cornel West. The analysis of these figures will be well-served by the foregoing exegetical discussion, as the categories that have emerged as central in this discussion also figure prominently in the work of these figures. In the final chapter, building upon the successes and failures identified in the work of these figures, I will begin to articulate an adequate contemporary theological expression of the prophetic voice.

NOTES

1. On the first three appellations (among others), see Gene M. Tucker, "The Role of the Prophets and the Role of the Church," in *Prophecy in Israel: Search for an Identity*, ed. David L. Petersen (Philadelphia: Fortress Press, 1987), 159–175; on the last, see Max Weber, *The Sociology of Religion*, Introduction by Talcott Parsons with a New Forward by Ann Swidler (Boston: Beacon Press, 1993), Chapter 4. See also, generally, Abraham J. Heschel, *The Prophets* (New York: Perenniel Classics, 2001), esp. part II.

2. Michael Walzer, *Interpretation and Social Criticism* (Cambridge: Harvard University Press, 1985), 70.

3. George E. Mendenhall, *The Tenth Generation: The Origins of the Biblical Tradition* (Baltimore: The Johns Hopkins University Press, 1973), 24.

4. Jon Sobrino, *Jesus the Liberator: A Historical-Theological Reading of Jesus of Nazareth*, trans. Paul Burns and Francis McDonagh (Maryknoll, NY: Orbis Books, 1993), 161.

5. See Robert R. Wilson, *Prophecy and Society in Ancient Israel* (Philadelphia: Fortress Press, 1980).

6. Paul D. Hanson, "The Origin and Nature of Prophetic Political Engagement in Ancient Israel," in *Let Justice Roll: Prophetic Challenges in Religion, Politics, and Society*, ed. Neal Riemer (Lanham, MD: Rowman and Littlefield Publishers, 1996), 2–3.

7. Tucker, "The Role of the Prophets and the Role of the Church," 167.

8. Peter Winch, "Authority," in *Political Philosophy*, ed. Anthony Quinton (Oxford: Oxford University Press, 1967), 107. Thus, for example, Weber's divorce of the charismatic authority of the prophet from tradition is mistaken (see Weber, *The Sociology of Religion*, 46).

9. Gunther Wittenberg, "Authoritarian and Participatory Decision-Making in the Old Testament," in *A Democratic Vision for South Africa: Political Realism and Christian Responsibility*, ed. Klaus Nürnberger (Pietermaritzburg, South Africa: Encounter Publications, 1991), 86.

10. For instructive discussion, see Henry Jackson Flanders, Jr., Robert Wilson Crapps, and David Anthony Smith, *People of the Covenant: An Introduction to the Hebrew Bible*, fourth edition (New York: Oxford University Press, 1996), 107ff.

11. Wittenberg, "Authoritarian and Participatory Decision-Making in the Old Testament," 86.

12. See Hanson, "The Origin and Nature of Prophetic Political Engagement in Ancient Israel," 7; and Paul D. Hanson, *The People Called: The Growth of Community in the Bible*, with a New Introduction (San Francisco: Harper and Row, 2001), 13–14.

13. Hanson, "The Origin and Nature of Prophetic Political Engagement in Ancient Israel," 6, 12; and Wittenberg, "Authoritarian and Participatory Decision-Making in the Old Testament," 86–87.

14. Walter Brueggemann, *The Prophetic Imagination*, second edition (Philadelphia: Fortress Press, 2001), 7.

15. Bruce C. Birch, *Let Justice Roll Down. The Old Testament, Ethics, and Christian Life* (Louisville: Westminster John Knox Press, 1991), 75–76. See also Bernhard W. Anderson, "Introduction: Mythopocic and Theological Dimensions of Biblical Creation Faith," in *Creation in the Old Testament*, ed. Bernard W. Anderson (Philadelphia: Fortress Press, 1984), esp. 18–21. As those familiar with the literature on the ethics of the Hebrew Bible and prophets may recognize, my discussion of the character of Israel as a covenant community and of the nature and function of the Hebrew prophets owes more to Birch's text than any other single work.

16. Birch, *Let Justice Roll Down*, 35. Relationality is a central focus in Carol Dempsey's treatment of the ethical vision of the prophets. See her *Hope Amid the Ruins: The Ethics of Israel's Prophets* (St. Louis: Chalice Press, 2000), esp. Chapter 2.

17. On the centrality of the nature of the *kind* of God one confesses, see Terrence E. Fretheim, *The Suffering of God: An Old Testament Perspective* (Philadelphia: Fortress Press, 1984), esp. Chapters 1 and 2.

18. Walter Brueggemann, "Covenant as a Subversive Paradigm," in his *A Social Reading of the Old Testament: Prophetic Approaches to Israel's Communal Life*, ed. Patrick D. Miller (Minneapolis: Fortress Press, 1994), 44.

19. For discussion of biblical treatments of God's pathos, see Brueggemann, *The Prophetic Imagination*; Fretheim, *The Suffering of God*; and Heschel, *The Prophets*. For theological and philosophical treatments, see Paul S. Fiddes, *The Creative Suffering of God* (Oxford: Clarendon Press of Oxford University Press, 1989); Warren McWilliams, "Divine Suffering in Contemporary Theology," *Scottish Journal of Theology* 33, no. 1 (1980): 35–53; Kenneth Surin, "The Impassibility of God and the Problem of Evil," *Scottish Journal of Theology* 35, no. 1 (1982): 97–115; and Nicholas Wolterstorff, "Suffering Love," in *Philosophy and the Christian Faith*, ed. Thomas V. Morris (Notre Dame: University of Notre Dame Press, 1988).

20. While the notion of intergenerational punishment for injustice contained in v. 7 is troubling, the central claim here, it seems clear, is that God's steadfast love,

radically outstrips God's judgment. Though the passage asserts that God's judgment is visited unto the third and fourth generation, its more fundamental claim is that God keeps steadfast love unto the *thousandth* generation.

21. Birch, *Let Justice Roll Down*, 152.

22. Ibid., 152–153.

23. Heschel, *The Prophets*, 256.

24. John Siesler, "Righteousness," in *The Oxford Companion to the Bible*, ed. Bruce M. Metzger and Michael D. Coogan (New York: Oxford University Press, 1993), 655. See also Birch, *Let Justice Roll Down*, 153–256; and Heschel, *The Prophets*, 256–257.

25. Stephen Mott, *Biblical Ethics and Social Change*, second edition (New York: Oxford University Press, 2011), 49–50. James Childress also closely associates justice with righteousness: "The most general meaning is uprightness, rectitude, or justice, and the word may be applied to God or humans. In the OT God's righteousness (*sedeq/sedaqah*) is seen in his covenant relations with his people; it involves both justice and compassion as expressed in God's concern for the weak and vulnerable." James Childress, "Righteousness," in *The Westminster Dictionary of Christian Ethics*, ed. James F. Childress and John Macquarrie (Philadelphia: The Westminster Press, 1986), 556.

26. Nicholas Wolterstorff, *Justice: Rights and Wrongs* (Princeton: Princeton University Press, 2008), 81–82, 75.

27. Nicholas Wolterstorff, "Why Care About Justice?," *The Reformed Journal* 36, no. 8 (August 1986): 10.

28. Mott, *Biblical Ethics and Social Change*, 54–59.

29. Ibid., 57.

30. Ibid., 58.

31. John R. Donahue, S.J., "Biblical Perspectives on Justice," in *The Faith That Does Justice: Examining the Christian Sources for Social Change*, ed. John C. Haughey, S.J. (New York: Paulist Press, 1977), 70, 73. Wolterstorff argues that Israel's obligation to aid those who are most vulnerable is, in part, "*a public remembrance, . . . a memorial*, of Yahweh's deliverance of Israel from Egypt." Wolterstorff, *Justice*, 80.

32. Hanson, *The People Called*, 23. Emphasis added. Likewise, commenting on the relational character of covenantal justice, E. Clinton Gardner notes that "justice was not only a rights claim arising out of the needs of the disadvantaged; from a covenantal perspective, it was a communal obligation grounded in Israel's vocation to be God's people. Justice was a demand for faithfulness in the life of the community as a whole, a demand which rested ultimately not upon human rights but upon Israel's covenantal relationship to God." Gardner, *Justice and Christian Ethics* (Cambridge: Cambridge University Press, 1995), 49.

33. Donahue, "Biblical Perspectives on Justice," 76.

34. Wittenberg, "Authoritarian and Participatory Decision-Making in the Old Testament," 85.

35. Birch, *Let Justice Roll Down*, 208.

36. Frank Moore Cross, *Canannite Myth and Hebrew Epic: Essays in the History of the Religion of Israel* (Cambridge: Harvard University Press, 1973), 223.

37. Michael Walzer, *In God's Shadow: Politics in the Hebrew Bible* (New Haven: Yale University Press, 2012), 67.

38. Birch, *Let Justice Roll Down*, 204–5.

39. Brueggemann, *The Prophetic Imagination*, 23–24.

40. George E. Mendenhall, "The Monarchy," *Interpretation* 29, no. 2 (April 1975): 160.

41. Birch, *Let Justice Roll Down*, 228.

42. Ibid., 222.

43. James Luther Mays, "Justice: Perspectives from the Prophetic Tradition," *Interpretation* 37, no. 1 (January 1983): 10–11.

44. Mays, "Justice," 11.

45. Birch, *Let Justice Roll Down*, 266.

46. Brueggemann, *The Prophetic Imagination*, 28–29.

47. Ibid., 30.

48. Aristotle, *Nicomachean Ethics*, 1131a.

49. Gardner, *Justice and Christian Ethics*, 52. See also the parallel discussion in Mott, *Biblical Ethics and Social Change*, 54.

50. Gardner, *Justice and Christian Ethics*, 52–53.

51. Joseph P. Healey, "Peace, Old Testament," in *The Anchor Bible Dictionary, vol. 5*, ed. David Noel Freedman (New York: Doubleday, 1992), 206–207.

52. John M. De Gruchy, *Christianity and Democracy: A Theology for a Just World Order* (Cambridge: Cambridge University Press, 1995), 44.

53. Jon Sobrino, *Jesus the Liberator*, 161. Seán Freyne also identifies Jesus as a prophetic figure and finds in his praxis—his life and ministry—his significance for ethics. Seán Freyne, "The Ethic of Jesus: The Sermon on the Mount Then and Now," in *Ethics and the Christian*, ed. Seán Freyne (Dublin: The Columba Press, 1991), 44. Walter Wink writes that it is out of the heart of the prophetic tradition that "Jesus engaged the Domination System in both its outer and spiritual manifestations." Walter Wink, *Collected Readings*, ed. Henry French (Minneapolis: Fortress Press, 2013), 207. In a similar vein, Ched Myers has located Jesus within "the tradition of the Hebrew prophets" as "a relentless interrogator of those in power." Ched Myers, "'I Will Ask *You* a Question': Interrogatory Theology," in *Theology Without Foundations: Religious Practice and the Future of Theological Truth*, ed. Stanley Hauerwas, Nancey Murphy, and Mark Nation (Nashville: Abingdon Press, 1994), 99.

54. John C. Haughey, S.J., "Jesus as the Justice of God," in *The Faith That Does Justice*, ed. Haughey, 270.

55. Ignacio Ellacuría, "The Political Nature of Jesus' Mission," in *Faces of Jesus: Latin American Christologies*, ed. José Míguez Bonino (Maryknoll, NY: Orbis Books, 1984), 82.

56. Walter Wink, "Jesus and the Domination System," in *Society of Biblical Literature 1991 Seminar Papers*, ed. Eugene H. Lovering (Atlanta: Scholar's Press, 1991), 268. For further discussions of some of these configurations of social relationship, see John S. Kloppenborg, "Alms, Debt, and Divorce: Jesus' Ethics in their Mediterranean Context," *Toronto Journal of Theology* 6, no. 2 (Fall 1990): esp. 185–189; William R. Domeris, "Leadership, Status and Position in the Early Jesus Community," in *A Democratic Vision for South Africa*, ed. Nürnberger, esp. 98–100; and Bruce J.

Malina, *The Social Gospel of Jesus: The Kingdom of God in Mediterranean Perspective* (Minneapolis: Fortress Press, 2001).

57. Lisa Sowle Cahill, "The Bible and Christian Moral Practices," in *Christian Ethics: Problems and Prospects*, ed. Lisa Sowle Cahill and James F. Childress (Cleveland: The Pilgrim Press, 1996), 9–11.

58. See Jon Sobrino, *No Salvation Outside the Poor: Prophetic-Utopian Essays* (Maryknoll, NY: Orbis Books, 2008), 82–88.

59. Sobrino, *Jesus the Liberator*, 162.

60. Sobrino, *No Salvation Outside the Poor*, 94.

61. Seán Freyne argues that Jesus' ethical vision was based on that of the prophets, whose foremost concern was with "righting social ills within Israel. This rather than worship of Yahweh in prayers, fasting and other religious and cultic practices was essential for a right relationship with Israel's God, who . . . had a strongly ethical character" ("The Ethic of Jesus," 48).

62. Wink, "Jesus and the Domination System," 271.

63. Ellacuría, "The Political Nature of Jesus' Mission," 86.

64. Sobrino, *Jesus the Liberator*, 80–81. See also Sobrino, *No Salvation Outside the Poor*, 22ff. For reasons that will become clear subsequently, I am not entirely comfortable with Sobrino's use of the term "dignity" here. Given its current usage, particularly in liberal social and political theory, I fear it is too easily grafted onto an understanding of moral worth in which particular capacities, such as rationality, serve as the criteria for moral standing. While a theological understanding of moral worth need not eschew the significance of such capacities, it is not their possession, but simply creation in God's image, with the attendant *need or ability to give and/or receive love*, that marks human beings as creatures possessing moral worth. "Sanctity" is perhaps a better word to capture theologically what Sobrino is after here. For important discussion of such matters, see Timothy P. Jackson, *Political* Agape*: Christian Love and Liberal Democracy* (Grand Rapids, MI: William B. Eerdmans Pub. Co., 2015), esp. Chapter 2, "The Image of God and the Soul of Humanity: Reflections on Dignity, Sanctity, and Democracy," and Chapter 5, "A House Divided, Again: Dworkin and Singer on Sanctity and Dignity."

65. See Sobrino, *Jesus the Liberator*, 88–93; Mott, *Biblical Ethics and Social Change*, 76–78; and Ellacuría, "The Political Nature of Jesus' Mission," 91.

66. See Wink, "Jesus and the Domination System," 269–271.

67. Sobrino, *Jesus the Liberator*, 173.

68. Gordon Lafer, "Universalism and Particularism in Jewish Law: Making Sense of Political Loyalties," in *Jewish Identity*, ed. David Theo Goldberg and Michael Krausz (Philadelphia: Temple University Press, 1993), 186.

69. Ibid.

70. For an argument defending love of enemies as present in the Hebrew Bible and subsequent Jewish literature, see William Klassen, *Love of Enemies: The Way to Peace* (Philadelphia: Fortress Press, 1984), Chapters 2 and 3.

71. Albert Nolan, *Jesus Before Christianity* (Maryknoll, NY: Orbis Books, 1978), 61.

72. On the significance of hyperbole for theology, see Stephen H. Webb, "A Hyperbolic Imagination: Theology and the Rhetoric of Excess," *Theology Today* 50, no. 1 (April 1993): 56–67.

73. Nolan, *Jesus Before Christianity*, 61–62.

74. For an excellent study of forgiveness in Jewish tradition, see Louis E. Newman, "The Quality of Mercy: On the Duty to Forgive in the Judaic Tradition," *Journal of Religious Ethics* 15, no. 2 (Fall 1987): 155–172.

75. While the *lex talionis* undoubtedly functioned to stay the excessively vengeful hand, it did not repudiate violence; indeed, it legitimated and counseled a proportionate violent response.

76. Timothy P. Jackson, *Love Disconsoled: Meditations on Christian Charity* (Cambridge: Cambridge University Press, 1999), 5.

77. David P. Gushee and Glen H. Stassen, *Kingdom Ethics: Following Jesus in Contemporary Context*, second edition (Grand Rapids, MI: William B. Eerdmans Publishing Co., 2016), 93.

78. Ibid., 96. See pp. 93–104 for the full discussion of such initiatives.

79. Wink, "Jesus and the Domination System," 279.

80. For further discussion of subversive aspects of this injunction, as well as of the associated injunctions to give up one's undergarment and to carry a soldier's pack a second mile, see Walter Wink, "Beyond Just War and Pacifism: Jesus' Nonviolent Way," *Review and Expositor* 89, no. 2 (Spring 1992): esp. 199–206. See also Wink, *Collected Readings*, Chapter 11, "Jesus' Third Way: Nonviolent Engagement."

81. Wink, "Jesus and the Domination System," 279.

82. Ellacuría, "The Political Nature of Jesus' Mission," 91.

Chapter 2

The Comforts of Home

Conventionalism and the Limits of the Prophetic Voice in Michael Walzer's Political Theory

WALZER, RELIGION, AND THE PROPHETIC VOICE

In *Interpretation and Social Criticism*, Michael Walzer enlists the Hebrew prophets as exemplars of his understanding of social criticism, as well as of his particularistic, community-oriented vision of moral and political philosophy, generally. Not only does he claim that the prophets were exemplary in their social criticism, he claims that "they were the *inventors* of the practice of social criticism."[1] Walzer's conception of social criticism is a central component of a broader argument that attempts to link a particularistic methodology, in which moral and political convictions are understood to arise out of and reflect the communities of which we are a part, with a theory of justice aimed at resisting domination, a participatory vision of politics, and an influential articulation of the just war tradition. Given the connections between this conception of social criticism and these other central elements in Walzer's political theory, it might seem that we have in Walzer's political philosophy a ready-made model of the contemporary shape of the prophetic voice.

The central place occupied by the prophets in Walzer's thought is hardly accidental. It is undoubtedly attributable, in part at least, to his own secular Jewish identity and the influence upon him of Jewish tradition. Though by no means a theological or confessionally religious thinker, his work clearly reflects the influence—"traces"—of Jewish theological and philosophical thought. Walzer's attention to justice is at least partly attributable to this influence. He locates a concern for justice at the center of the Jewish tradition, and argues that the insights of this tradition "must lead us . . . to a special concern with people who are poor or weak or oppressed."[2] Similarly, his defense of particularism, as well as of a limited universalism, resonates with core themes in Rabbinic Judaism. Discussing the political assumptions of Jewish Law, Gordon Lafer explains that "Rabbinic law describes a hierarchy of political obligation in which universalism and particularism are dialectically entwined, which seeks to formulate a particularist identity without dehumanizing outsiders, and conversely which recognizes limited universalist obligations without being fundamentally compromised by them."[3]

Despite these resonances, appropriating Walzer's thought as a model of how we might presently understand the prophetic voice encounters serious problems. One of the chief difficulties is that his appropriation of the Hebrew prophets, like so many of the examples that pepper his work, is *largely historical and illustrative*. He is less concerned with the distinctly theological dimensions of the prophets or the realist assumptions of prophetic commitments than he is with their role and function in ancient Israel, and how, in this particular context, they exemplify broader claims he wants to make about the practice of social criticism more generally. In forwarding this largely functionalist interpretation, Walzer is concerned with the prophets in largely descriptive terms and how they upheld and gave expression to the "cultural and historical products of groups of people."[4] He is concerned with what he calls the "shared understandings" and "common meanings" of a people, rather than with the nature or truth of the reality to which they witnessed. Indeed, a realist account of truth, which holds that reality exists independently of our apprehension of it, and that truth is measured in terms of some form of correspondence or adequation between our words and the world they describe or our ideas and the objects to which they refer, is rejected by Walzer in favor of a form of social conventionalism in which the political community is accorded pride of place. It is a realist understanding of truth, however, that an adequate contemporary understanding of the prophetic will take as axiomatic. On Walzer's account, by contrast, we are presented with prophecy without either theology or philosophy,[5] at least as each is traditionally conceived.

But can the prophetic remain content with interpreting a community's conventions, or does it have a stake in making more thoroughgoing claims about, alternately, what is true or real, right or just, in accord with God's will or contrary to it? Walzer's conventionalist understanding of the prophetic voice, and of moral and political philosophy more generally, leads to problematic understandings of some of its central claims and commitments. While Walzer's conventionalist understanding of the prophetic may be able to articulate coherently the commitments and meanings that are socially dominant in a community, without a commitment to realism, it is difficult to discern how it might be adequately responsive to those voices that are silenced or marginalized in the community and/or enjoin a social solidarity that transcends the boundaries of the community. This is seen most clearly in Walzer's understandings of justice and social criticism and in his discussion of just war theory. It is, on the contrary, precisely keen attention to those at society's margins and the articulation of an expansive understanding of social solidarity that defines the prophetic's ethical vision. Such a vision cannot coherently be upheld from a conventionalist standpoint, as I shall argue in this chapter.

COMMUNITY: THE INTERPRETATION OF SHARED UNDERSTANDINGS

Central to the whole of Walzer's philosophical and political project is his defense of particularism and connection in moral philosophy, and his concomitant rejection of detachment and aspirations to objectivity. This places community at the center of his work, for the meaning that is attached to particular moral and social goods is developed in and through community. At first glance, this might be thought to resonate with the claims developed in the last chapter that prophetic activity derives its logic and authority by appealing to, reiterating, and enacting the ancient religious traditions of Israel. Indeed, Walzer points to Israel's prophets as paradigmatic exemplars of his preferred path in moral theory, the path of interpretation. The ultimate difficulty with this conception of community, however, is that it falls into some of the same difficulties that many liberals worry plague other communitarians, more generally: namely, it bears with it (however unintentionally) exclusionary effects and it enshrines the conceits of a particular political community.

In the Preface to *Spheres of Justice*, Walzer makes the contrast between his approach and other approaches explicit. He writes:

> My argument is radically particularist. I don't claim to have achieved any great distance from the social world in which I live. One way to begin the philosophical enterprise—perhaps the original way—is to walk out of the cave, leave the city, climb the mountain, fashion for oneself (what can never be fashioned for ordinary men and women) an objective and universal standpoint. Then one describes the terrain of everyday life from far away, so that it loses its particular contours and takes on a general shape. But I mean to stand in the cave, in the city, on the ground. Another way of doing philosophy is to interpret to one's fellow citizens the world of meanings that we share."[6]

In articulating a particularist approach, then, Walzer's project, though not without precedent, breaks with the greater portion of the Western philosophical tradition.

Walzer notes that moral theory has traditionally been undertaken in one of two ways. It has been most commonly conceived, first, in terms of discovery. On this understanding, we are not morality's creators. Rather, we discover moral norms via divine revelation or rational reflection, for example.[7] Alternately, perhaps because they judge there to be no actually existing moral world or out of dissatisfaction of the actually existing moral world or our knowledge of it, some have attempted to invent morality. Walzer traces this second path at least as far back as Descartes, but it is most paradigmatically expressed in the moral and political philosophy of the early John Rawls, who asks readers to imagine individuals seeking to agree upon principles of justice by contracting behind a "veil of ignorance" in a state-of-nature-like "original position."[8] While on this and other similar procedures morality is invented rather than discovered, it does share with the path of discovery a key assumption that Walzer finds fundamentally problematic: moral knowledge is had through objectivity and detachment from particularity.

In contrast to these two dominant ways of conceiving the moral task, Walzer's particularist approach conceives of moral philosophy in a connected and interpretive mode. Moral argument is best understood in an interpretive mode because it is this path that gives "an account of the actually existing morality. That morality is authoritative for us because it is only by virtue of its existence that we exist as the moral beings we are." In contrast to the interpretation of lived moral existence, the paths of discovery and invention "are efforts at escape." Even if it is possible to articulate persuasively novel conceptions of discovered or invented morality—Walzer concedes that utilitarianism may be such a conception—this is generally a mark against them, for "the more novel these are, the less likely they are to make for strong or even plausible arguments." They fail to resonate with or speak to the already existing morality that *is* authoritative for us, morality that is the product of "time, accident, external force, political compromise, fallible and particularist intentions."[9]

Thus, for example, Walzer argues that Rawlsian decision procedures may provide us with a *modus vivendi*, a way of life, but it cannot provide us with a way of living. Taking the outcome of deliberations behind the original position as providing the substance of the moral life is akin to taking a "hotel room or an accommodation apartment or a safe house as the ideal model of a human home."[10] The arguably universal prohibitions generated through moral discoveries or through techniques of invention may provide us with a framework of minimal constraints, but they do not provide us with the sorts of substantive details that enable and comprise a moral culture. "It is not until" moral conversations "become continuous and the understandings thicken that we get anything like a moral culture, with judgment, value, the goodness of persons and things realized in detail."[11]

Our moral worlds, according to Walzer, are already familiar to us. We do not have to discover or invent the moral world "because we have always lived there." It "has a lived-in quality, like a home occupied by a single family over many generations, with unplanned additions here and there, and all the available space filled with memory-laden objects and artifacts. The whole thing, taken as a whole, lends itself less to abstract modeling than to thick description."[12] We are, it seems, all valuing creatures and we always find ourselves in someplace of value that demands to be interpreted. However unwittingly, this is seen, for example, in the appeal of some philosophers of invention to intuitions in constructing and/or testing their models of the moral life. We correct these intuitions "by reference to the model we construct out of those same intuitions, or we are to correct our more groping intuitions by reference to a model we construct out of our more confident intuitions. We move back and forth in either case between moral immediacy and moral abstraction, between an intuitive and a reflective understanding." But in this, we are not trying to understand divine decrees or objective moral principles; rather, what we are trying to understand is precisely "ourselves, our own principles and values."[13] Insofar as we are concerned to occupy and understand our moral worlds we cannot get beyond interpretation.

What get interpreted are just those communally common meanings and shared understandings that render our moral worlds familiar to us. The goods we value, the commitments we seek to uphold—in other worlds, all of the things about which we reflect, deliberate, and argue morally—are the result of social processes of creation. They are *social goods*, for they are not simply goods that I privately and idiosyncratically value, but, rather, goods that I value precisely as I have come, in a particular community, to share their meaning with others.[14] On the basis of such an account of morality, one can still plausibly explain the widespread influence of, and attention devoted to, many, if not all, conceptions of discovered or invented morality. The resonance of John Rawls' difference principle, for example, is due not to its derivation from an elegant device of invention, but, rather, to the fact that it accords well with other values that have widespread currency in American (and Western) society: values like equal protection, equal opportunity, political liberty, individualism, and the like. Community thus stands at the center or, perhaps more accurately, at the beginning of moral theory, Walzer contends, for it is the community and the historically formed and socially mediated commitments and meanings that comprise it that are the object of interpretation.

Walzer's approach to moral theory does seem to capture some of the essential elements of the role community plays in the prophetic voice. Like the Hebrew prophets, he affirms that we do not know morally by prescinding from the communities and traditions that shape us, but, rather, precisely by explicating and arguing about the commitments and meanings that constitute them. There is, however, a deep problem at the heart of Walzer's understanding of community. In short, the problem is that Walzer is so historicist and so constructivist that moral claims reduce simply and merely to how we, as a community, talk, to what our social conventions happen to be. From the standpoint of the prophetic voice, this problem compromises his account of truth, as well as his understandings of justice and of the legitimacy of political violence. Even if moral claims do not exist apart from some understanding of community—Walzer is right just this far—they are not reducible to it in the way he seems to hold.

TRUTH: CONVENTIONALISM AND THE REJECTION OF REALISM

In its weddedness to a distinct tradition and particular understanding of community, the prophetic voice may *seem* to attribute significance to community in the same way as Walzer. However, while the prophetic voice is formed in and through a particular tradition, and finds expression through communally embodied practices, it is not the tradition and its practices that are decisive, but the understanding of *reality* to which they give expression. Translating biblical assumptions into a contemporary idiom, the prophetic voice defended here assumes a realist standpoint with regard to questions of truth and moral value. Broadly speaking, realism claims that the truthfulness of a statement depends on a state of affairs existing independently (though not apprehended independently) of the speaker or her community. Depending upon how one understands the nature of reality, such statements may variously be understood to be true by virtue of their conformity to God's will, or human nature, or the demands of rationality, and so on. On this view, moral statements may be true irrespective of whether anyone believes them to be true.

Walzer's prescinds from such judgments regarding reality, however, and it is in this that the deepest problems for his account are rooted. He is interested in the (alleged) fact of shared understandings within a society, and not some deeper, fundamental reason(s) grounding that sharing. The important thing for Walzer is that members of a culture actually share culturally self-defining understandings, not that they share them for a particular reason—for example, because they are true or right or just or good or reflective of God's will. Insofar as actions or social institutions can be said to be "true," it is not because they correspond in some sense to a state of affairs that exists independently of speakers and their communities, but precisely because they give expression to the distinct understandings comprising a society's shared way of life. Realist considerations are, for Walzer, replaced by the task of discerning what is societally shared. Ultimately, he upholds not realism, but a form of social conventionalism.

In this conventionalism, although he seldom refers to them, Walzer is similar to some of his pragmatist and neo-pragmatist contemporaries, such as Richard Rorty. Brian Orend has noted that

> both Walzer and the pragmatists are sceptical about the discovery of objective truth, insisting that we stick with the beliefs we have and not subject them to contrived philosophical doubt if we do not actually doubt them in our everyday lives. Walzer, following the likes of Quine and Davidson, stresses the need to come up with coherent, powerful and persuasive interpretations of our existing 'webs of belief'. And, of course, both Walzer and the pragmatists are centrally concerned with how people are actually motivated to act in moral and political life. Drawing on these claims, pragmatists like Rorty, alongside Walzer, are convinced that we have no one else to turn to but ourselves—our own contingent beliefs, commitments and social arrangements—when it comes to seeking guidance in morality and politics. Ultimately, what matters most is what works best for us, what most fully realizes what we want out of life.[15]

For Walzer, as for pragmatists like Rorty, matters of justification and truth are wholly immanent constructions of particular historical communities. A robust realism seems precluded.

In this rejection of realism, Walzer's conventionalist approach to political theory may instructively be understood as a version of what Timothy Jackson has called the "lame" version of liberalism: liberalism as morally empty. Such an understanding of liberalism, in prescinding at the level of theory from (all but the most minimal) judgments regarding the human good, is characterized by an "extreme historicism and relativism." Truth and justification, as we have seen, becomes for Walzer "a matter of coherence with our clan's conventions," but this means that "ethico-political assertions cannot plausibly be thought to have any classical truth value at all. There is nothing objective to appeal to in order to adjudicate disputes; so, in the end, we whoop for our side and they whoop for theirs." With traditional claims about divine reality or moral truth bracketed in favor of the community's conventions, Walzerian prophets might seek to show how our practices have failed on their own terms and how they might be made more coherent on their own terms, "but there are no moral truths by which to measure those practices; there is no *reason*, for instance, to be inclusive and respectful of others."[16]

It might be suggested that Walzer *does* support a somewhat limited, but still rather traditional, philosophical defense of realism in the form of what he calls "moral minimalism." It is a common phenomenon of moral experience, one recognized by Walzer, that when individuals clamor for "peace" or "justice" or "human rights" in other parts of the world, even in places that seem to differ radically from our own, we understand what they mean and may even seek to join their cause in some way. Walzer does admit that there may be resonances among cultures regarding the minimal demands of such terms—this is Walzer's "minimal morality." These resonances, however, he claims, do not entail a substantive account of the nature, meaning, and/or foundations of those terms. The minimal, cross-cultural code to which Walzer avers, insofar as it exists, *arises out of* our thicker, maximal moralities. It does not reflect an objective, universal morality that we all share by virtue of deep facts about who we are as human beings or as children of God, but is, instead, "reiteratively particularist and locally significant, intimately bound up with the maximal moralities created here and here and here, in specific times and places."[17] As Orend nicely puts it, this "thin theory of minimal morality is universal *only* in the sense of the scope of those who endorse it. It is *not* the objective truth of morality, either discovered or invented; rather, it is nothing more (nor less) than that core set of values we find reiterated in every substantive moral and political code."[18] Walzer's minimalism, the point at which his thought might be thought to be straining toward a form of realism, is, finally, dependent upon and expressive of his conventionalism.

Conventionalism and the "Dangers" of Realism

Nevertheless, it must be noted that Walzer's conventionalism is motivated by laudable (if ultimately misplaced) normative concerns. A more substantive understanding of moral claims is not in the offing for Walzer, for a commitment to traditional moral realism (i.e., realism understood in terms of classical correspondence theory) is judged to have potentially high costs associated with it that he believes makes this modest, grounded approach more attractive. In addition to conceptual considerations regarding the nature and grounding of moral value, Walzer also forward pragmatic considerations regarding the potential dangers of truth talk. He worries that traditionally realist claims to truth could very possibly lead to manipulation and even violence. Insofar as realist moral reflection prioritizes and is most fundamentally interested in truth "out there," there is a danger that the door may be opened to authoritarianism and possibly manipulation or violence.

The problem with traditional philosophical aspirations to truth is that the philosopher removes himself from the community of ideas, from the rough and tumble politics of the city, in the interest of grasping it. In "Philosophy and Democracy," Walzer argues that, having discerned the truth, the philosopher will have "little taste for bargaining and mutual accommodation. Because the truth he knows or claims to know is singular in character, he is likely to think that politics must be the same: a coherent conception, an uncompromising execution."[19] Similarly, in *Interpretation and Social Criticism*, Walzer argues that detached critics, possessed of true and pure knowledge, too easily resort to "manipulation and compulsion."[20] Better, instead, to appeal to existing conventions and attachments, to affirm a more thoroughgoing democratic politics in which members of a polity respond, and are accountable, not to abstract truth, but to one another.

These ill effects are made all the more likely, Walzer would contend, by virtue of the fact that persons who adhere to a realist conception of truth are frequently governed by a singular conscience; they are likely to have a sense of self in which there is a unified, permanent center. However, Walzer argues that persons who identify "wholeheartedly" and "yield everything" to an overriding conception of reality have "dominated" or "tyrannical" selves. We most commonly associate such selves with religious or political fanatics who are "god-possessed or ideologically driven."[21] Such selves, Walzer contends, are not very good at self-criticism, and so we are better off understanding the self as being "as differentiated as the society in which it participates."[22] In modernity the self is properly understood as a plural self populated by "many internal critics," "a confabulation of critics," in which one is now "strong and consistent in this role or identity and then in that one," in which one acts "on behalf of this value and then that one."[23] Such a view of the self is better suited for the give and take of democratic politics

Realism and the Affirmation of Particularity

In response, one might point out that these essentially pragmatic considerations against realism are questionable on their own terms. Certainly, we are familiar with fanatics of the sort Walzer is worried about, persons who have sought to justify and defend their conception of reality by engaging in coercive action. But most of our culturally central moral exemplars—figures who have strenuously resisted the use of violence and manipulation—have themselves assumed the meaningfulness of realist talk. To suggest that such talk should be avoided altogether is ultimately morally and politically debilitating. In a response to Richard Rorty that applies to our consideration of Walzer here, Thomas McCarthy has noted that "whatever the sources, our ordinary, nonphilosophical truth-talk and reality-talk is shot through" with idealizations of various sorts. "We are heirs to centuries of distinguishing between appearance and reality, truth and opinion, prejudice and reason, custom and morality, convention and justice, and the like."[24] Of course, not every means of making such distinctions is worthy of endorsement. Some have been philosophically or theologically untenable, while others have been morally objectionable. But, as the examples of Jesus Christ, Martin Luther King, Jr., Dorothy Day, the Berrigan brothers, and others exemplify, robustly realist claims need not entail violence, and, as I will explain further shortly, they need not entail the rejection of our particularity, our groundedness in particular communities and traditions. This latter point, in particular, appears not to occur to Walzer. What we need to argue about, it seems, precisely *is* reality and the different ways we conceive of that reality—which conceptions are compelling, which are dangerous, which are constructive, which are destructive, and so on—but this cannot be done without assuming the meaningfulness of realist talk in the first place.

Further, we ought to question whether Walzer's characterization of the self animated by a strong commitment to truth is wholly accurate. Certainly, Jesus Christ, King, Day, and the Berrigans are rightly understood as having been "god-possessed" or animated by an understanding of reality to which they at least attempted to yield everything. But this seems to be an important aspect of moral courage. By virtue of their animating religious visions, such persons are morally articulate. They are, in Charles Taylor's term, "strong evaluators." As such, they possess a rich moral vocabulary that enables them to make evaluative distinctions according to which different desires, commitments, and values "are described as noble or base, integrating or fragmenting, courageous or cowardly, clairvoyant or blind, and so on."[25] It is through such frameworks that moral agents are motivated to act, and are sustained in their acting, particularly in the face of opposition or challenges to their moral commitments. Instead of thinking of these exemplars as having "dominated" or "tyrannical" selves, then, it is perhaps better to think of them as having well-ordered, coherent selves. Such a happy result is not a matter of necessity; it may well be the case that a particular, definitive conception of reality may fund, for example, a dangerous political or religious fanaticism. But, again, the key here seems not to be whether or not to affirm a realist posture, but, rather, *what* conception of reality it is we ought to affirm and how we ought to affirm it.

It may be unclear, however, how an affirmation of realism can go hand in hand with an affirmation of particularity. There seems to be an intrinsic tension between realist and non-foundationalist affirmations. For example, Timothy Jackson's earlier noted criticism of Walzer's political theory may appear to trade on some of the same bad habits of which Walzer rightly wishes to break us. In referring to "moral truths by which to measure" our moral practices and to something objective to which we can appeal in adjudicating disputes, Jackson may *seem* here, however unintentionally, to associate a realist posture in moral theory with the ability to make moral claims by standing outside of our particular histories and traditions (in actuality, he does not). If we admit, then, as I grant we must, that foundationalism is philosophically untenable and potentially morally problematic, how is realist talk possible? It may seem that we are caught on the horns of a dilemma: Either we assert the necessity for moral judgment of some extra-traditional claims about reality *writ large*, universally understood, and thereby effectively reject non-foundationalist insights, or we assert, from a non-foundationalist perspective, the necessarily and irreducibly traditioned nature of all knowledge claims, and thereby effectively reject a commitment to realism. This is a false dilemma, however.

Perhaps, the deepest problem present in Walzer's rejection of realism is that it assumes that a commitment to realism and a commitment to foundationalism go hand in hand. Yet, we do not and cannot have reality "raw," unmediated, as it is in itself. We can affirm with Walzer and the bulk of contemporary philosophers and theologians that foundationalism is an epistemological dead end and that all knowledge, because it is to be had only from within a limited perspective in a particular context, is fallible. As Jackson has rightly noted elsewhere, "To think that we can step outside of time and our limited perspectives for incorrigible revelations of reality is a species of pride."[26] But this need not entail that we have to let go of a commitment to alethiological realism, which concerns not the *justification* of truth claims, but their *meaning*. Alethiological realism holds that "the nature of truth is some form of correspondence or adequation between one's words and the world they describe, one's ideas and the objects to which they refer." The fallibilism entailed by a non-foundationalist epistemology, by contrast, holds not that truth so understood does not exist, but, rather, "that there are no indubitable tests for truth, no incorrigible evidentiary foundations on the bases of which other beliefs might be permanently or indubitably justified."[27]

It is thus conceptually coherent to claim that there is a truth to be known, that there is a reality "out there" to which our beliefs and practices ideally correspond, but also to claim, at the same time, that we can never know if we know that truth, that we can never be sure that we have actually "gotten" reality. For those who are religious this affirmation may be understood to be entailed by the recognition of human creatureliness, by the fact that human beings are not God. For others, it may be expressed more generally as a corollary of human cultural or historical situatedness. In making truth claims, then, including prophetic truth claims, we may affirm that we always make them from somewhere, from a particular perspective limited by time, history, and tradition, and that they are always subject to possible revision as they encounter challenges. Indeed, such willingness to revise our understandings has as its goal a clearer understanding, and greater approximation, of objective truth.

From a theological perspective, this affirmation that all of our truth claims, including prophetic claims, are traditioned and historically grounded is but a recognition that Christians are a *particular* people who uphold beliefs, forward claims, and seek to embody practices that make sense only from within a particular horizon of understanding. This is entailed by the very logic or "grammar" of Christian theology. In his defense and articulation of a realist conception of Christian faith and belief, Andrew Moore argues compellingly that, because God is the grammar of Christian faith, our religious claims and practices are not autonomous. Rather, it is *God* "who regulates our practices (including theological ones), teaches us their point, and thereby keeps our language in good order: God enables us to show his independent reality because he shows himself [*sic*] through the practices of faith."[28] The beliefs and practices of those prophets, ancient and contemporary, who are paradigmatic for the current account are just in this way regulated; they give expression to, they reveal, the reality and character of God, and, by extension, a vision of the proper shape of human existence.

When divorced from the particular understanding of reality which grounds them, religious practices and commitments lose their animating meaning and, in some cases, may become dangerously distorted, even turned against themselves. Paul's teaching regarding the Lord's Supper at 1 Cor. 11:17–34, for example, seems to be a clear example of what can go wrong when religious practices are divorced from attention to the reality that grounds them. Through their abuse of the poor and marginalized, the Corinthians constructed and imposed their own meaning on Eucharistic practices, and through this they decisively distorted these practices. Paul's point is to remind the Corinthian church "that the Lord's Supper was not invented by them: these practices have been given to the church; they were not invented by them. Forgetting these things God's people lose their sense of being one body loved, redeemed, and reconciled to God in Christ."[29] What the Corinthians lost was attention to that virtue that is central to the prophetic: justice understood in terms of solidarity with the marginalized, needy, and vulnerable. The form of justice the prophetic gives expression to is not fundamentally expressive of a community's shared understandings or meanings, but is, rather, a response to, and expressive of, God's character, God's steadfast love for humanity. We are to love because God loves, and it may well be the case that the love God models for us will be upsetting of widely accepted shared practices.

It might be argued, however, that all the foregoing considerations have provided is a description of the implications of the convictions of a particular religious tradition and not an affirmation of realism, in general. If the argument is limited in this way it may not seem to have much relevance for Walzer, whose mind is "theologically blank."[30] I am not sure, once we admit our situatedness and particularity, what such a general affirmation might look like, but some comments can be made toward such an end. Even a nontheological or nonreligious articulation of the sorts of convictions central to the prophetic has a stake in recognizing their grounding in realist claims or assumptions of some sort. Even in the secular case, mere conventionalism will not suffice.

One might attempt to argue, for example, that all we need to undergird a commitment to solidarity is some sort of concern to attend to the suffering and pain of others, but it need not matter what grounds that concern, or even if it is grounded at all. Yet, unless our commitment to the independent integrity of others is going to be reed-thin, we need to attend to *why* we ought to have affection for suffering others (a motivational issue) and *what* undergirds our concern for their pain (an issue of justification). There is an intrinsic connection between a commitment to human solidarity and some sort of realist affirmation of shared human worth. One cannot coherently refer, for example, to pain or humiliation or social domination as concerns that ought to have a claim on us without also admitting something like a shared conception of humanity. (Such a conception will, however, be shaped by a particular, historically mediated tradition of what it means to be human. The non-foundationalist accepts that our knowledge is mediated, but, in admitting this, she need not affirm that all one has access to is the mediation.)

It is certainly the case that a concern about pain, for example, about the sheer threat of pain and the humiliation that may accompany it, may provide one with self-sufficient reasons to attend to *one's own* pain or that of someone with whom one has an intimate connection. Walzer's position is certainly well-positioned to uphold this sort of attention to others. But it is difficult to see how that fact alone can provide one with compelling reason to care about, and attend to, the pain of *others* with whom one is not intimately connected, especially that of strangers or enemies or those to whom one is for some reason blind. Such a concern does not issue in the sort of nonexclusive social solidarity to which the prophetic gives expression. If aversion to pain or resistance to oppression or recognition of human worth are fundamental phenomena that unite us as human beings, and if concern for such matters is not merely contingent upon linguistic similitude or communal sharing with particular others, there must be something about human beings *qua* human that makes our pain the proper object of the concern of others, and their pain the proper object of our concern (whether actually recognized or not). A conventionalist understanding of morality will not suffice in such cases.

Put somewhat differently, we need to ask what real love, real respect, amounts to for the downtrodden, marginalized, or oppressed neighbor. What do we lose if truth is construed in a Walzerian manner? If it is only to shared understandings—what Richard Rorty, following Wilfred Sellars, calls our political culture's "we-intentions"[31]—that we refer in upholding a commitment to human dignity, then there is a good reason to question whether it is actually respect for our neighbor about which we are concerned. We can agree that "*we* have to start from where *we* are"[32] in discerning and articulating our moral obligations to our neighbor, but if what moves me to embrace her, to seek her well-being, is attention to our culture's shared understandings, this is less properly described as real respect for *her*, real attention to *her* moral worth than it is attention to the ostensible integrity of a common tradition and whatever worth *that tradition* happens to bestow upon her. When truth is construed in a Walzerian manner, in terms of shared understandings or common meanings, we lose connection to ways of understanding our obligations to others as something other than projections of our group's identity. We lose sight of how others are bearers of integrity and worth in themselves, an outcome contrary to any reasonable construal of the prophetic voice.

JUSTICE: CONVENTIONALIST BLINDNESS AT THE MARGINS

Whatever the merits of the foregoing arguments, it might be argued that Walzer's influential work on justice is an important counterexample that exhibits the nonnecessity of a realist posture in moral and political theory. Though arguing for the centrality of a society's common meanings and shared understandings, he seeks to uphold a conception of justice that is both egalitarian and focused on resistance to domination. Indeed, the prophets serve as the primary exemplars in his work of an engaged form of social criticism, exercised by and on behalf of those at the margins of society, which seeks to upset the dominance of social goods by one group, or a set of groups, over others. Perhaps conventionalism need not undermine solidarity with or commitment to those at society's margins, after all.

Indeed, one might argue that not only is there nothing more that prophets can do than to refer to shared conventions or understandings. The question, it may seem, is not about *whether* shared understandings are the substance of a conception of political criticism and social justice, but *how* they are so. From Israel's prophets to Jesus Christ to modern day prophets like Martin Luther King, Jr., what prophets do essentially is to reiterate and elaborate upon their society's shared understandings and commitments. In the latter case, for example, King routinely and self-consciously upheld American ideals about democracy and its constitutional tradition as central to social criticism. His social criticism, like that of Israel's prophets, was aimed at highlighting how a people failed to embody sufficiently their constitutive commitments, reminding them of their character, and enabling the envisioning of more inclusive understandings of those commitments.

While it can hardly be denied that King referred to such ideals, as the previous discussion of truth implies, it would be a mistake to *reduce* his message to them. Rather than understanding King as an interpreter of shared understandings, it is better and more proper to regard him as a sort of moral *bricoleur*[33] who discerned a great deal of congruity between elements of the American political tradition and his religious faith, but found in the latter the governing substance and basis for his message. Though his appropriation of the American political tradition was not merely strategic or rhetorical, the most fundamental basis of his message lay elsewhere. It was not most fundamentally from the American tradition of equality or liberty that he derived his account of human worth, for example, but from theological claims about human creation in the image of God.[34] These and other theological claims, though never articulated apart from an animating community, provided King with leverage for criticism of American society, especially when the shared practices and commitments of that society rang hollow.[35] Unlike Walzer, King never forsook a realist construal of moral meaning and value, and it was this that provided him with the ability to attend to society's margins and name injustice.

Walzer is right: *epistemologically*, we are all in the cave. All forms of human perceiving are inevitably shaped by culture and context, by the languages and stories that have currency *for us*. But the meaning or content of our moral concepts is not *reducible* to the contexts through which they are expressed, a point King recognized in his alethiologically realist conception of moral meaning and value. What Walzer's rejection of a realist account of moral meaning and value finally underwrites is a conventionalist conception of justice that exhibits what Seyla Benhabib has called "integrationist" characteristics.[36] Shared understandings and common social meanings are conceived in ways that assume and demand the presence of a well-defined and bounded coherence between moral and political communities, but this undermines the sort of attention to the marginal that is definitive of prophetic justice. Despite Walzer's best intentions, the limitations of a conventionalist position *are* clearly evident in his work on justice. Indeed, I will argue that a Walzerian reliance on shared understandings undermines resistance to domination by making exclusions on the margins inevitable.

Resisting Domination: Walzer's Account of Justice and Social Criticism

In keeping with his methodological commitment to particularity, Walzer eschews the articulation of general principles of justice that are to be applicable anytime, anywhere, in favor of a conception that roots such principles in the ways communities create and conceive of particular social goods. Social goods are not simply "found and then used";[37] rather, the meaning and manner of distributing such goods are the result of those social processes and interactions through which they come to have particular meanings for particular people. Distinct shared understandings, in different cultural or historical contexts, will thus yield distinct understandings of social goods. Distributions of such goods, then, are context-relative, and "are just or unjust relative to the social meanings of the goods at stake."[38]

More specifically, within particular contexts, different goods will themselves be distributed in accordance with different social meanings. "When meanings are distinct, distributions must be autonomous. Every social good or set of goods constitutes . . . a distributive sphere within which only certain criteria and arrangements are appropriate."[39] Each social good—community membership, money, political power, love, and so on—is distributed according to rules specific to that good. By attending to particularity in this manner, Walzer's position is both a response to, and an affirmation of, pluralism: "The principles of justice are . . . pluralistic in form; . . . different social goods ought to be distributed for different reasons, in accordance with different procedures, by different agents; and . . . all these differences derive from different understandings of the social goods themselves—the inevitable product of historical and cultural pluralism."[40]

The pluralism that underlies Walzer's theory of justice coheres with his rejection of a realist account of truth. As his many historical and anthropological examples attest, Walzer is struck by the utter diversity of human ways of being and doing, and the seeming impossibility of offering a singular explanatory framework within which these ways of being or doing can be understood. For Walzer, to recognize the facts of pluralism is to recognize as incommensurable the many cultures, practices, and ways of valuing found in the world. For Walzer, however, it is also important to note that this incommensurability exists at the level of societies or cultures. *Within a particular society*, he claims, it is possible to specify the goods that get distributed and the principles by which they are to be distributed.

Walzer's conception of justice upholds a vision of what he calls "complex equality." While broadly egalitarian in nature, complex equality is willing to countenance some inequalities because proper recognition of the plurality of distributive spheres will insure that it is restricted and not generalized throughout the social and political fabric. "Though there will be many small inequalities, inequality will not be multiplied through the conversion process. Nor will it be summed across different goods, because the autonomy of distributions will tend to produce a variety of local monopolies, held by different groups of men and women."[41] Differences in income, for example, are generally thought to be justifiable for a number of reasons—the desirability of particular forms of work, the difficulty of the work, the effort expended to enter a particular career, and so on. None of this is necessarily unjust, for the distribution of income in such cases is made in accordance with principles internal to the social meanings attached to work in a particular context.

What is unjust, however, is the dominance of social goods. Justice is essentially concerned with "the ability of a group of people to dominate their fellows. It's not the fact that there are rich and poor that generates egalitarian politics but the fact that the rich 'grind the faces of the poor,' impose their poverty upon them, command their deferential behavior."[42] Dominance is a form of social hegemony that occurs, for example, when the possession of money allows a person or a group of people to secure some other social good, as when one is able to "buy" a political office. "Dominance describes a way of using social goods that isn't limited by their intrinsic meanings or that shapes those meanings in its own image." It "is an elaborate social creation" through which "all good things come to those who have the one best thing. Possess that one thing, and the others come in train."[43] In resisting dominance, complex equality is primarily concerned to resist the convertability of one social good into another, a process Walzer believes would be largely maintained by "ordinary men and women within their own spheres of competence and control, without large-scale state action."[44]

Domination thus gives rise to social criticism, undertaken by ordinary men and women. Insofar as domination is successful, it is parasitic, one might say, on already existing social capital, and it is this already existing social capital that makes criticism of social hegemony possible. Social formations carry with them attempts at justification, but insofar as gaps exist between social reality and the ideals that it is to embody, space is opened for social criticism. "Every ruling class is compelled to present itself as a universal class."[45] In revealing the contradictions that exist in dominant ideologies—exposing, for example, "the larger meanings of equality, which are more mocked than mirrored in everyday experience"—the critic exposes the gap between the idealized picture rulers paint and "the lived reality of power and oppression."[46]

The "primary or natural language" of social criticism is that of "the folk."[47] Social criticism is "the educated cousin of common complaint. We become critics naturally, as it were, by elaborating on existing moralities and telling stories about a society more just than, though never entirely different from, our own."[48] One does not need to step outside of one's society to engage in social criticism; instead, social criticism is an immanent or connected activity, in which an individual or groups of individuals reflect critically on already present shared commitments and practices. The standards to which one appeals in engaging in social criticism are "social artifacts . . . embodied in . . . legal and religious texts, moral tales, epic poems, codes of behavior, ritual practices," and so on.[49]

While the social critic takes a society's shared understandings as the substance of social criticism, this is not a brief for a positivist reading of morality as it actually exists. For Walzer, existing ideals and commitments comprise the content of social criticism, but this content must be interpreted and interpreted well. The most "interesting parts" of the moral world are not simply described, but "'read,' rendered, construed, glossed, elucidated," and what is sought in an account of that world is not simply a reading that accounts for or summarizes all other readings, but a deep and inclusive, rather than shallow and partisan, reading of a society's social life.[50] Walzer is interested in the practice of what Benhabib has called a "normative hermeneutic," in which the understandings of social goods and practices are not measured simply in light of how they are currently, commonly understood, but in light of "better" understandings of these goods and practices.[51]

Much of my skepticism regarding Walzer's project concerns precisely the ability to specify in any definitive way what constitutes "better" understandings of a society's goods and practices. He asserts that though "we would argue about the best account, . . . we would know roughly what we were looking for and would have little difficulty excluding a large number of inadequate or bad accounts."[52] While he provides little concrete guidance regarding how to prioritize among, rank, and select from competing interpretations, he is optimistic about a community's potential in this regard. Indeed, as I will discuss later, he seems quite optimistic regarding the possibility of identifying, presumably after much argument, not just a range of "better" accounts of what a community's shared understandings entail in a particular case, at a particular time and place, but *the best* account of what they entail. As I will explain later, however, more sustained attention to the indeterminacy of interpretation calls the likelihood of this into question.

Whatever difficulties we might encounter here, Walzer contends that deep, normatively compelling readings of a society's shared understanding will clearly not be issued from the centers of power. It is at the centers of power that relations of domination are most likely to be produced and authorized. Power, Walzer urges, blinds one to those areas of society most in need of critical interrogation: "Criticism does not require us to step back from society as a whole but only to step away from certain sorts of power relationships within society. It is not connection but authority and domination from which we must distance ourselves." Power and ambition for power "are real obstacles to the practice of criticism, because they make it difficult to look with open eyes at those features of society most in need of critical scrutiny."[53]

Walzer argues that social criticism is thus a (relatively) marginal activity, an activity undertaken by, and often on behalf of, those at the margins of society. Social critics "come from some remote and neglected part of the country (Silone), or from an imperial colony (Camus), or from a declining social class (Orwell), or they are members of or choose to identify themselves with a lowborn, oppressed, or pariah group."[54] Martin Luther King, Jr. is a prominent American exemplar of a critic who both comes from and identifies with an oppressed group. Distanced from centers of power, social critics are marginal figures in their societies, but they are not detached from them. Good social critics have, Walzer urges, an antagonistic and ambiguous connection to their societies, but from *within and for* their societies. They stand "a little to the side, but not outside: critical distance is measured in inches."[55] So understood, social critics are not enemies of the societies they criticize,

Claudia,

I keep trying to find the words (see!?) for this note, but everything I write seems either too schmaltzy or too formal. So, I hope the book itself expresses adequately to you my profound Thanks for all you've done for me.

Best,

Chris

for they eventually want things to go well. They hope that, through their criticism and that of others, the idealism latent in the common meanings of their societies will be more fully embodied in practice.

Israel's prophets, Walzer argues, are particularly exemplary of this connected brand of social criticism, for it is precisely engagement with the everyday world and the constitutive commitments of their communities that characterizes the power of their work and messages. Walzer is less interested in claims regarding the psychological state of the prophet, or in obscure philological or historical details underlying the meaning of the prophetic texts, or in the theological assumptions of prophecy, than he is in prophecy as a *social practice*. He is concerned with the prophet's message and its reception. More specifically, he is concerned with the condemnations and proclamations of the prophets understood from within a moral frame, with those occasions when they give voice to "indignation," "provocations, [and] verbal assaults on the institutions and activities of everyday life."[56] Israel's prophets are particularly important for Walzer, as he wants to claim not only that they were social critics, but that "they were the inventors of the practice of social criticism."[57]

As expected, Walzer's heroes here do not discover or invent the morality they defend; they are its interpreters. As the previous chapter discussed at length, the prophets' messages depended on and assumed "previous messages . . . . For the most part, they disclaim originality, and not only in the obvious sense that they attribute their message to God. It is more important that they continually refer themselves to the epic history and the moral teaching of the Torah."[58] Once Moses climbed the mountain, it was not necessary for anyone to do it again. The law was not an esoteric teaching, but was now widely available and popular, it was "a social possession," and the prophets had only to "show the people their own hearts."[59] Although the prophet may interpret and revise the tradition in ways that enable him to connect better or more fully with his contemporaries, his activities are always parasitic on the persons who and messages that have preceded him.[60]

It is thus on the basis of their particular, inherited moral and religious traditions that the prophets engaged their paradigmatic task: "to judge the people's relations with one another (and with 'their' God), to judge the internal character of *their* society." Following Weber, Walzer argues that in this focus on the workaday world, Israel's prophets articulated a "resolutely this-worldly" ethic. They neither forwarded some vision of a prophetic utopia, an ideal political or religious regime, freed from all social and historical contingencies, nor did they take an interest in individual salvation or the perfection of their own souls. "They are not religious adepts or mystics; they never advocate asceticism or world rejection. Wrongdoing and rightdoing are alike social experiences, and the prophet and his listeners are involved in these experiences in accordance with the principle of solidarity, whether or not any given right or wrong act is their own."[61]

Prophets whose work is not rooted in the connections of shared traditions can do little more than speak in highly general terms, perhaps portending doom for those they condemn, but exhibiting little concern for a shared way of life. Thus, for example, unlike Amos or Micah, both of whom could refer to shared traditions in calling Israel to repent, Jonah prophesies doom in Nineveh as "an alien voice, a mere messenger, unconnected to the people of the city." His is "prophecy without poetry, without resonance, allusion, or concrete detail."[62] Without connection, it could have none of these things. Ironically, he is nonetheless successful, as the people recognize and "turn from their evil ways and from the violence that is in their hands" (Jon. 3:8). Social criticism of the sort Jonah engages in is then a permanent possibility, but it is of limited scope: Nineveh is guilty of breeches of "a kind of international law," crimes of violence against strangers and enemies. As in Amos' oracles against the nations, Jonah judges Nineveh "only for violations of a minimal code," violations that presumably were able to be reiterated[63] in terms of Nineveh's own internal, substantive commitments. But regarding the particulars of this "substantive social morality," Jonah "has nothing to say."[64] The successes present in the Jonah story importantly testify to Israel's confession of God's sovereignty over all of creation, but there is no substantive alternative conception of the moral world or social criticism at work here.

Conventionalism, Conflict, and (In)Attention to the Margins

Glimpses of the problems with Walzer's accounts of justice and social criticism are discernible in his treatment of the Hebrew prophets. In keeping with his treatments of religion generally, Walzer is not especially concerned to understand Israel's prophets in terms of the theological framework they assumed—not surprising given that his mind is "theologically blank"—but rather as exemplars of a general approach to understanding politics and the moral life that coheres with his own conventionalist approach.[65] In Walzer's hands, prophets serve as the voice of civil religion, calling the political community to fulfill its deepest hopes, and to critique it when it fails to do so. But is this radical enough?

It may seem relatively unproblematic for Walzer to depict the social function of Israel's prophets as the mediation of the political community's shared traditions because there was in that context an assumed coherence between the moral/religious community, on the one hand, and the political community, on the other. Such a situation is hardly surprising within a theocentric/theocratic context. Yet, such a situation did not hold in the New Testament period, as Jesus' activity, and that of his followers, opposed and often came into conflict with the occupying Roman political authorities. Walzer seems quite clearly, however, to assume a coherence of moral and political communities in modern, liberal democratic societies similar to that which held in ancient Israel. This is an assumption, as we will see, that presents considerable difficulties for taking his thought straightforwardly as a contemporary expression of the prophetic, for it harbors exclusions that imperil the prophetic voice's attention to those most marginal in the community.

Walzer apparently does not believe that there will be fundamental conflicts between the commitments of the moral community and those of the political community, even in modern liberal democratic states. William Galston has noted that although Walzer seems to offer two accounts of community, these are largely conflated in his work from *Spheres of Justice* forward. On one hand, as discussed earlier, he has a theory of moral community "in which individuals . . . are conjoined by their shared understandings of social goods." On the other hand, he also has a theory of legal community "in which individuals come together through specific acts of consent that create and delimit sovereign authority." These two conceptions are conjoined in *Spheres of Justice*, as Walzer assumes that the "moral and legal communities are congruent, that the community of shared meanings is also the sovereign nation-state."[66] Walzer thus writes, "The political community is the appropriate setting for this enterprise." It is "probably the closest we can come to a world of common meanings. Language, history, and culture come together (come more closely together here than anywhere else) to produce a collective consciousness. National character, conceived as a fixed and permanent mental set, is obviously a myth; but the sharing of sensibilities and intuitions among the members of a historical community is a fact of life."[67]

These assumptions are noticeable in subsequent works, as well. In *The Company of Critics*, for example, Walzer contends that social criticism is likely to be most effective when framed in the "national-popular" mode, that is, when it is national in form/idiom and popular in content/argument. The "ideal critic" is loyal to those most marginalized, but the nature of and solutions to the troubles of the marginalized are best seen "within the framework of national history and culture. Nation, not class, is the relevant unit." The social critic, then, is a sort of patriot, but she insists on a "deeper patriotism."[68]

As his comments on the myth of national character and his embrace of dissent make clear, Walzer does not intend here to issue a brief for some naive form of romantic nationalism or a parochial communitarianism. His general view of the state is, as Elizabeth Bounds puts it, "cautious."[69] The state must foster the associative activities of social groups, but social groups must also be strong enough to limit the power of the state. While communitarian themes pervade his work, Walzer's preferred political configuration here is quite clearly a liberal democratic state. This political configuration is a "social union of social unions," in which the state "presides over the pursuit and sponsorship [of the good life] but does not participate in either."[70] Given the facts of social pluralism and the central place occupied by resistance to domination in Walzer's thought, this desire on his part to carve out space for social groups to pursue the good life seems positively entailed by his most fundamental commitments. Bounds remarks that when she tries to envision Walzer's affirmation of pluralism within the context of the nation-state, she imagines "a neutral liberal state superimposed on a mass of organic traditions, cleaning them up. Walzer's communitarian correction of liberalism means that he tidies up, rather than throws out, historically rooted particular beliefs and experiences."[71]

Is this possible, however? It is worth asking if Walzer has an overly sanguine view of the "housekeeping" functions of the liberal democratic state. What about possible conflicts between particular moral, religious, or historical communities within the liberal state and the broader political community? One might well worry that Walzer's rather harmonious account of the liberal state obscures the possibility—indeed, the probability—of such social conflicts. In voicing worries of this sort, Robert Dahl argues that Walzer is insufficiently attentive to the fact that the larger political community may consist of smaller political communities, and that the good of certain of these smaller communities may not be identical with other ones or with the broader political community. This gives rise to the possibility of conflicts in social meaning at the level of these smaller communities, and to questions regarding how to resolve such conflicts.[72]

Walzer does recognize this possibility, but seeks to respond to it on his own terms. In *Spheres of Justice*, immediately after identifying the political community as the best locale for understanding common meanings, he concedes that

> sometimes political and historical communities don't coincide, and there may well be a growing number of states in the world today where sensibilities and intuitions aren't readily shared; the sharing takes place in smaller units. And then, perhaps, we should look for some way to adjust the distributive decisions to the requirements of those units. But *this adjustment* must itself be worked out politically, and its precise character *will depend upon understandings shared among the citizens about the value of cultural diversity, local autonomy, and so on.*[73]

So, disputes may arise, but if they do, "adjustments" can be made on the basis of other (more basic?) shared understandings. Here, although acknowledging the possibility of conflicts at one level, Walzer continues to evince a faith in the existence of basic, core principles or shared value commitments relative to which social conflicts may be successfully mediated.

Similarly, in a response to essays appearing in the *Journal of Religious Ethics*, he asserts the fundamental significance of "American" values to "multicultural" critics of his thought. Because multicultural insurgency is "directed to all Americans," it "draws its strength from understandings common to us all. The democratic state clearly is a world of meanings that we share—even if it is also, simultaneously, a world of conflict and domination." In giving voice to values like "equality and freedom, understood in a specifically American way," such critics assert the values that "we (Americans or most Americans) already acknowledge."[74] We see lingering here, again, a faith in the presence of shared underlying principles sufficient to mediate and, ultimately, resolve all disputes within a political community. Lawrie Balfour characterizes the vision assumed by Walzer in this essay as one of "an American landscape . . . dotted with bounded communities and held together by underlying principles."[75]

Walzer seems quite clearly to believe that the assertion of claims to equality and freedom by multicultural critics are communally/politically specific and content-full. They are "specifically American" claims. To invoke such terms in a particular context is to seek more than a certain degree of resonance with one's interlocutors. We can expect this of morality in its thin form, but we are dealing here with thick, culturally specific claims, and in this context we rightfully ought to expect much more. Walzer is thus quite serious when he claims that to invoke "equality" and "freedom" in such a context is to assert these values with such a degree of specificity that we do all already acknowledge them. Of course, what it is, specifically, that we already acknowledge about such terms may not be immediately apparent; it may take extensive argument and debate to reveal the specific contours and implications of claims to equality or other values in particular cases, but Walzer clearly contends that we can, in principle, come to resolutions on such matters. In particular hard cases, the values embedded in a political culture and their implications, can, in principle, be determined. In an exchange with Ronald Dworkin, he argues that, while decisions are always temporary, "*in a particular case, in a particular culture, there is, in principle, a right decision.*"[76]

But why have faith that shared understandings will exist at some other level? Why think that there will be sufficiently specific shared understandings about *these* matters, if they do not otherwise exist? In light of ongoing debates about multiculturalism, the Western canon, and "political correctness," for example, it is far from clear how shared understandings about cultural diversity, or even equality and freedom, despite Walzer's judgment to the contrary, could be the sources of resolution to such debates, for there simply do not seem to be any at the level of the political community.

To a large degree, the problems at hand are a corollary of the aspirations Walzer has for his preferred path in moral theory, interpretation. A closer examination of the nature of interpretation makes clear that interpretive decisiveness and specificity at the level of political community is not to be had, thus clarifying the difficulties with Walzer's responses to questions about the nature of conflicts between smaller communities within the broader political community. Social conflicts are frequently rooted in interpretive differences regarding social values and commitments. In the most significant and intractable cases of social conflict, it is not the case that conflicts between interpretations at the level of political community can either be dismissed as simply conflicts between a "shallow and partisan" interpretation and a "deep and inclusive" one, or resolved by reference to more basic principles. There may be, precisely as a function of the situatedness of interpreters and the multiplicity of factors considered in different interpretations, *competing deep and inclusive interpretations* of a particular social practice or norm. The adequacy of an interpretation depends upon whether it makes sense of a given practice or action in light of the broader context of meaning of which it is a part. The goal of a deep and inclusive account of social life is to achieve a holistic coherence between part and whole in which "the meaning of each practice, norm and arrangement of the society confirms our understanding of the whole and in which our understanding of the whole substantiates our understanding of each part."[77]

But understandings of the proper broader context within which particular interpretations take place will vary. Frequently, interpretive differences regarding value terms themselves stem from differences of judgment regarding the proper horizon of interpretation. These differences, in turn, stem from the fact that interpretation is always colored by the particular influences that have exerted themselves upon us: our particular concerns, interests, histories, normative judgments, and the like. The upshot of this is that our historical and social situatedness "imposes on our understanding the proper contexts for interpretation."[78] There is no way straightforwardly to "read" social meanings. Ambiguity, uncertainty, and dissensus attend all particular interpretations, and while we may do our best to determine the appropriate context of interpretation, and to interpret that context properly, it will characteristically be the case that there is no singular "way of understanding the evidence to which we appeal or, indeed, that we will agree on which evidence is relevant."[79] While this does not foreclose the possibility of rejecting some particular interpretations as shallow, it does raise the probability that there may be competing deep and inclusive interpretations of social meaning, each of which emphasizes "different practices, norms of action and institutions that place" them "within different historical contexts and frames of reference."[80] In light of such considerations, we do well to be suspicious of claims made on behalf of allegedly shared understandings in resolving political disputes, and of the normative attractiveness of a conventionalist account of morality more generally, for reference to such understandings will often have the effect of silencing voices, particularly those at the margins.

Social conflicts within a political community frequently arise in large part precisely because of interpretive disagreements that result when some voices do not figure or do not figure significantly in the construction of understandings that are widely shared in a society. Given that the construction of dominant, shared understandings is an historical affair, we should expect that they will reflect exclusions that have entered into their construction and/or that continue to find expression. Such historical exclusions may be largely overt, perhaps based on such factors as race, gender, or sexual orientation, or they may be less noticeable, due to alternative understandings suppressed or largely forgotten. Furthermore, even if some historically significant forms of exclusion have been formally prohibited, it may nonetheless be the case that they will continue to be significant, exerting exclusionary effects in a variety of subtle ways, as in the form, for example, of institutionalized racism or sexism. We must attend not only to distortions of power rooted in explicit physical, political, and economic coercion—such as when those in power distort the meanings of ethical ideals to suit their own ends—but also to the diffuse ways power may find expression in terms of ideological or psychological domination.[81]

These latter, more subtle forms of exclusion are particularly significant. Iris Young notes that the dominant understanding of oppression in political discourse—the use of overtly coercive power, in which one or a few ruthlessly impose their will upon others—is insufficient. We must also attend to subtle forms of oppression resulting not from the coercive effects of overt power, but from "the everyday practices of a well-intentioned liberal society . . . . Oppression in this sense is structural rather than the result of a few people's choices or policies. Its causes are embedded in unquestioned norms, habits, and symbols, in the assumptions underlying institutional rules and the collective consequences of following those rules."[82] Walzer *is* attentive to oppression and domination expressed in terms of overt coercive power. He notes, for example, that in the cases of slaves and masters, there are "no shared meanings. The two groups are simply at war."[83] He is less attentive, however, to oppression and exclusion in the more subtle forms Young highlights, and this blinds him to crucial ways in which some voices may be excluded from a society's "shared understandings."

These considerations, particularly, make it clear that *even if* it were plausible to contend that all members of a political community have "consented" to its norms and ideals, we could not thereby conclude that the voices of all are adequately represented, even in these cases. "Consent" to a social order or its values can mean and is often taken to mean that its members are actively committed to it, that they seek to preserve and advance its distinctive way of life. But it may also result "from combinations of fear, disinterest, narrow self-interest, a restricted sense of alternatives, or a strategic judgment about how to advance values not now embodied in the society." In such cases, it would be more proper to contend that individuals and groups do not really consent to their society's norms and ideals, but, rather, comply "with an order that embodies them."[84] This recognition should alert us to the ways in which even this key democratic concept may, in some cases, be more apparent than real, and therefore to the possibility, if not the likelihood, that the voices of some do not find adequate expression.

These considerations help to clarify the exclusionary implications of Walzer's focus on shared understandings. One of the tasks of a theory of justice is to give an account of justice: to say what undergirds justice, what it looks like, what would constitute a failure of it or departure from it, and so on. In Walzer's case, principles of justice are derived from the (ostensibly) shared understandings that give meaning to social goods within a culture. Though determining what these understandings are may take place through democratic and dialogical practices, when it comes to delineating an account of justice, the point is not simply to "keep the conversation going" in a pluralistic culture. Walzer's generally laudable democratic intuitions are here instead subordinated to the more problematic demands of theoretical construction, which requires the identification of shared understandings.

Whether or not such understandings can be identified, the problems for Walzer's theory are deep. However difficult it may be to achieve, let us assume, on one hand, that there is in fact an agreed-upon "best" interpretation of the shared understandings of a particular political society such as the United States. Walzer seems to assume this, and, if the principles of justice derived on his account are to be meaningful, there needs to be, for understandings have to be determinative enough to generate meaningful distributive principles. Such an account will be highly integrated and integrative, but, given the facts of pluralism and interpretive indeterminacy, it will not, because it cannot, be characterized by unanimity or consensus. Some voices will find themselves marginalized or will go unheard, and so the account will, *by necessity*, be *exclusionary*. If, on the other hand, there are in fact no shared understandings (I think a clearly more accurate picture), this does not lessen the need for some account of such understandings for Walzer's account of justice. In such a case, shared understandings and the distributive principles derived from them will have to be *imposed* by the majority culture. Indeed, as Will Kymlicka has argued, if conflicts between different historical communities within a political culture "must be settled by appeal to the (non-existent) shared meanings of all citizens, then they will in fact reflect, by default, the meanings of the majority culture."[85] In either case, though exclusion is not intended, it is inevitable.

The variety of ways in which Walzer's emphasis on shared understandings harbors unacknowledged and unintended exclusionary tendencies has been noted by a number of critics. Susan Moller Okin argues that Walzer's theory is insufficiently attentive to the nature and effects of gender hierarchy and domination. Those who have had a hand in the construction of understandings of gender in "'our' culture . . . have been almost uniformly male, and the culture and values they have affirmed have in a multitude of ways reflected the standpoint of men in gendered society . . . . [T]hey have defined a 'human good' that not only excludes women but depends upon this exclusion." Given this situation, Okin contends that "there are no shared understandings on this subject in our society, even among women."[86] In a similar manner, Lawrie Balfour contends that Walzer's account of connection is insufficiently attentive to the complexities that attend consideration of the significance of race. Drawing on the work of James Baldwin as a foil to Walzer's, she argues that Baldwin's work illustrates that race consciousness and other prejudices are as embedded in American society as the shared understandings upheld by Walzer. "Baldwin reminds his readers that the appeal to shared values . . . is always also susceptible to qualification or to doubt."[87] At the very least, these examples and the foregoing considerations disrupt Walzer's too-easy assurance that common values will be both readily acknowledged and, if only interpreted properly, morally benign. Because their historical formation may have included a number of exclusions, it may be the case that a tradition's core values are themselves vehicles of domination. Reliance on social convention alone, then, is an insufficient basis upon which to found justice.

The Comforts of Home

Balfour offers important insights into why Walzer fails to recognize the exclusionary implications of his reliance on shared understandings: She has detected in Walzer's particularist turn a "homeyness," a tendency to slide from arguments for embeddedness into moral confirmation, and it is this that in large part seems to blind him to the complexities that attend processes of interpretation and that are raised by voices of difference.[88] In several places this "homeyness" is quite explicit. Thus, as noted earlier, in his defense of connection in moral theory, Walzer asserts that the moral world is less like a sterile hotel room than the furnished homes in which we already live, contends that "moral philosophy is . . . a reflection upon the familiar, a reinvention of our own homes,"[89] and states that "the moral world has a lived-in quality, like a home occupied by a single family over many generations."[90]

This theme resonates throughout Walzer's writings on social justice and criticism, and is perhaps most problematically manifest in his understanding of political membership. The political community is like a home in that it is most fundamentally a place of sharing, a place in which one shares a life in common with others and is like them in relevant respects. In *Thick and Thin*, for example, Walzer contends that commitments by men and women to each other's equality and rights of free speech don't simply "leap from the philosopher's mind," but, rather, are the products of history. Such commitments "have been worked on, so to speak, for many generations; and they inhabit a society that 'fits' their qualities and so supports, reinforces, and *reproduces people very much like themselves*."[91] Similarly, in *The Company of Critics*, he contends that we come to recognize others not by seeing them as different, but by seeing them as similar to ourselves.[92] "It is not by comparison and classification that we acquire moral knowledge of other people; rather, we understand others by *reiterating our self-understanding*."[93]

With claims such as these in mind, Balfour thus argues that, in Walzer's account, the qualities and boundaries that define a community, that delimit and make meaningful particular sets of obligations and rights, are drawn in such a way that, notwithstanding "the disagreements that may occupy them on a day-to-day basis, the members of societies described by Walzer appear fundamentally alike." This, however, leaves "little room" for those whose membership is "fragile or incomplete," those whose interests and values have (at best) been marginal in the formation of the community's understandings or whose consent to the community has been assumed.[94]

The prophetic voice, however, is most concerned precisely with those whose membership in the community is fragile or incomplete. It is less concerned with home than it is with the homeless. It is less concerned with faithfulness to the community's conventions than it is with faithfulness to divine commands to attend to the needs of the stranger and to fostering peaceableness. Insofar as Walzer's account generally, and his account of the prophetic specifically, cannot attend to these voices sufficiently, it is a less than satisfactory model for a contemporary expression of the prophetic. But, in large part due to his conventionalism, in which the moral community is conflated with the political community, this is precisely what Walzer's account cannot do. A conception of justice and social criticism that is rooted in social conventions, due to their historical formation and interpretive complexity, inevitably harbors exclusions at society's margins. By identifying the nation-state as the primary locus of community and source of shared understandings, Walzer's account of justice and social criticism, despite its best intentions, obscures the conflicts and exclusions present within that rather broad context. The prophetic standpoint need not—indeed, it cannot—eschew a particularist orientation, but this will be an orientation that upholds a commitment to an understanding of justice that attends to the margins not by rejecting realism, but precisely through the articulation of a distinctive vision of moral truth.

VIOLENCE/NONVIOLENCE: CONVENTIONALISM AND THE PROBLEM OF "SUPREME EMERGENCY"

Walzer's rejection of realism and defense of a conventionalism in which the nation as political community occupies a central place also, perhaps not surprisingly, raises deep difficulties for his treatment of political violence. The same privileging of the political community seen in his understanding of justice and social criticism is evident in his treatment of political violence, and it, again, leads to problems. In adjudicating violent intercommunal conflicts, Walzer is generally guided by just war considerations, but he seeks to resolve the most difficult cases of conflict by elevating the political community to privileged status. From the prophetic standpoint, however, this is problematic, as it makes the political community an end in itself. The political community always stands under the judgment of ethical norms that transcend it.

In its broad outlines at least, Walzer's thought is largely consistent with many, perhaps most, theological treatments of political violence. Like most Christian theologians and ethicists who have reflected on the matter, Walzer is a just war theorist, *but only so far.* In his own unique manner, he upholds most of the central claims of the just war tradition. He recognizes that the moral chaos into which war throws us and the horrors with which it confronts us necessitates deeply critical thought about the moral limits that constrain decisions to go to war and that guide conduct in the course of prosecuting wars. Like others indebted to the just war tradition, he clearly hopes for peace beyond the violence. However, he defends just war theory in conventionalist terms, and it is this that presents the deepest problems for his account. This is seen most acutely in his defense of the doctrine of "supreme emergency."

The just war tradition is rooted in Christian tradition and theological reflection. While the prophetic witness of the Bible, viewed as a whole, is not univocal regarding the use of violence, it has never been possible for Christian theologians, precisely because of the character of Jesus' peaceable witness, to treat it lightly. Many—including most of the early church, a significant dissenting minority throughout Christian history, and a notable chorus of contemporary voices—view the use of violence as antithetical to the character of Christian discipleship. But even those who find it to be, on rare occasion, justifiable, recognize that the use of violence to respond to violence is always fraught with danger, and almost always morally ambiguous.[95] *If* violent means are to be used by governing authorities or their proxies, the bulk of the tradition has held, this violence is to be in service of ethical aims that give expression to core Christian theological convictions. Among other constraints on its use, this means that such violence must be defensive, and it may never be employed in a manner that directly targets the innocent. Yet a

Christian defense of a robust understanding of justice over a narrow account of peace may lead one to argue, coherently and consistently (though controversially) on Christian grounds, that "Christian violence may, *in extremis*, be the content of political love."[96] With the gravity of the events of World War II in mind, for example, Timothy Jackson argues that "it is not always possible to achieve justice, or perhaps even to be fully loving, without the use of some violence. To make true peace we may sometimes have to unmake unjust war by main force, even while refusing to hate those who are our enemies and for whom Christ died."[97] I will not address this debate internal to Christianity any further at this point (there will be opportunity to engage it again in treating the work of Stanley Hauerwas); it is enough for present purposes to recognize that *if* political violence is justifiable on prophetic grounds, its use is to be severely constrained, and it is licit only for the sake of securing true justice and true peace.

The just war theory that gradually emerged out of Christian reflection on the legitimacy and limits of political violence is affirmed by Walzer in its broad contours. Like the just war theorists who preceded him, Walzer treats both the conditions under which societies or states may licitly resort to war (*jus ad bellum*) and the moral rules that apply to conduct within war (*jus in bello*).[98] His treatment of *jus ad bellum* criteria fits more or less (he neglects the importance of declaration by public authority) within the mainstream of the just war tradition. However, he problematically allows departures from what is arguably the central *jus in bello* criterion, discrimination and noncombatant immunity, in his defense of a doctrine of "supreme emergency." To get a better handle on the difficulties here it is necessary to look more closely at the manner in which Walzer grounds his approach to just war theory.

With roots in the Christian tradition, just war theory has most commonly been grounded in substantive principles regarding individuals' rights to bodily integrity, political liberty, and the like. In short, it has generally conceived of moral value in realist terms. At points in his discussion of the ethics of war, Walzer seems to assume a similarly robust account of the principles which underlie just war thinking. In *Just and Unjust Wars*, for example, he claims that "aggression is a singular and undifferentiated crime because, in all its forms, it challenges rights that are worth dying for." On the following page, he claims that "individual rights (to life and liberty) underlie the most important judgments we make about war."[99]

Immediately following this latter statement, however, he asserts, "How these rights are themselves founded I cannot try to explain here. It is enough to say that they are somehow entailed by our sense of what it means to be a human being. If they are not natural, then we have invented them, but natural or invented, they are a palpable feature of our moral world."[100] Though Walzer does not provide a systematic justification of such rights in *Just and Unjust*

Wars, perhaps we can tease out what guides him here. On the next page, he writes that "the right of a nation or people not to be invaded derives from the common life its members have made on this piece of land . . . ."[101] And two pages later he asserts that the territorial integrity nations and their citizens assume "is a function of national existence . . . . It is the coming together of a people that establishes the integrity of a territory. Only then can a boundary be drawn the crossing of which is plausibly called aggression."[102]

These passages, in their references to "the common life" of a people, and "the coming together of a people" as the basis of territorial integrity, assume the sort of conventionalist understanding of morality explicitly articulated in his later works. Furthermore, the conventionalist underpinnings of Walzer's just war theory are explicit in his derivation of the substance of that theory from what he calls "the war convention." This consists not of a traditionally realist grounding of substantive moral principles, but, rather, of "the set of articulated norms, customs, professional codes, legal precepts, religious and philosophical principles, and reciprocal arrangements that shape our judgments of military conduct . . . ."[103] His method in *Just and Unjust Wars*, he explains, is to look to "historical cases and actual debates for those particular judgments that both reflect the war convention and constitute its vital force."[104] Here, then, he adopts the particularist and conventionalist methodology seen especially in *Spheres of Justice* and *Interpretation and Social Criticism*. The war convention is reflective of the "thin" or "minimalist" morality, discussed earlier, that is contingently shared cross-culturally. Just war principles for Walzer are not derived from some account of objective morality, but, instead, reflect the convergence of particular considered judgments of philosophical and theological reflection, as well as of legal and professional principles and practices, but, above all, of political communities.

The centrality, but ethically problematic nature, of this particularism is seen most clearly in his defense of the doctrine of "supreme emergency." When a political community's very survival is at stake it is confronted, Walzer argues, with a "supreme emergency." Threats which are both imminent and great—which promise to undermine "everything decent in our lives," in which "evil is objectified in the world"—constitute supreme emergencies.[105] In such a situation, the moral constraints of the war convention still do have a hold on us, but political leaders may do, for a time at least, whatever is necessary to rebuff the danger. Walzer suggests, for example, that the threat posed by Nazism during World War II was unquestionably great and, for a time, sufficiently imminent as to justify British terror bombing (aimed at the city center and residential areas, rather than military sites) of German cities. He argues that "It is not just that a [German] victory was frightening, but also that it seemed in those years very close; it is not just that it was close, but also that it was so frightening. Here was a supreme emergency, where *one might well be required to override the rights of innocent people and shatter the war convention.*"[106]

This is, he confesses, a hard doctrine, for it requires us to incur moral guilt by overriding the moral rules that otherwise properly govern conduct in wartime. "When our deepest values are radically at risk, the constraints [of rights] lose their grip, and a certain kind of utilitarianism imposes itself. I call this the utilitarianism of extremity, and I set it against a rights normality."[107] In a supreme emergency, in which the absolutism of rights is overridden by the necessity of utilitarian calculation, ethics is internally divided, as we paradoxically engage in so-called "morally defensible" acts of immorality.[108] Commenting on Walzer's doctrine, Timothy Jackson remarks, "We are faced in this case not with pure fatalism, à la Oedipus, but rather with moral fragmentation in which we can pick, in some sense, our poison. Ethics, that is, is *internally* inconsistent . . . ."[109]

Walzer has already chosen his poison, of course, because his conventionalism decides for him in favor of the political community, for supreme emergency arises, as he says, "when *our* deepest values are radically at risk." Indeed, given the centrality of the political community and the derivative nature of rights in his thought, it is hard to see how any other result is possible. In a remarkable passage, relevant not only to the present discussion but also to the foregoing arguments of this chapter, Walzer claims,

> When our community is threatened, not just in its present territorial extension or governmental structure or prestige or honor, but in what we might think of as its *ongoingness*, then we face a loss that is greater than any we can imagine, except for the destruction of humanity itself. We face moral as well as physical extinction, the end of a way of life as well as a set particular lives, the disappearance of people like us. And it is then that we may be driven to break through the moral limits that people like us normally attend to and respect.[110]

It is clear, then, that supreme emergencies are such precisely because Walzer ultimately attaches supreme value to the political community. From the perspective of the prophetic voice, the problems here are at least twofold.

The elevation of the political community in Walzer's thought is at odds with the prophetic subversion of all communities to a community-transcending realist conception of value. Walzer can resolve conflicts that fall under the rubric of supreme emergency only by elevating the status of the nation-state to a degree that is at odds with the prophetic voice. No political community, as, for example, Ezekiel's judgments against Israel and Amos' oracles against Israel and surrounding nations make abundantly clear, is an end in itself. From a prophetic standpoint, a community is always judged by the degree to which it fulfills the demands of justice and fosters peaceableness. The prophetic does not attach supreme value to the political community.

Rather, the hegemonic presumptions and assumptions of the majority or of those in power, particularly as they serve to legitimate the use of violence, are, prophetically speaking, always questionable and rightfully reigned in, especially in cases that would allow harm to be visited upon innocent others (as in cases of supreme emergency).

Finally, given the role of the political community in Walzer's thought, he cannot recognize adequately as a neighbor she who is also an "other," in particular those others who threaten us and our community, for it is "we" who stand at the center of his moral vision. This, however, is antithetical to a prophetic vision of moral concern, which enjoins a much more expansive solidarity than can be supported by Walzer's account. *If* violence may licitly be used, it is violence aimed not at self-preservation or even the preservation of one's own community, but at reconciliation, at the end of violence, at enabling the instantiation of a true and lasting peace. Walzer's enshrining of the supreme moral importance of the political community, by contrast, seems to offer, at least in a significant range of cases, particularly in a context such as the present in which terror has become almost routinized for some parties as a tool of war, the likelihood of the ongoingness, the ratcheting up, of political violence. This is perhaps most likely in cases where competing ethnic/political groups—such as Israelis and Palestinians—contend against one another, each claiming that their very existence is imperiled should the other side win.

CONCLUSION

Walzer is often counted among those political theorists labeled "communitarian." Though this label does not apply as neatly to Walzer as it does to, say, Alasdair MacIntyre—Walzer's thought is more clearly an admixture of liberal democratic and communitarian themes—it is finally communitarian themes that dominate and guide his thought. It is also, finally, Walzer's articulation of such themes that imperil his project from the standpoint of the prophetic voice. As a corollary of his non-foundationalist turn to community, Walzer rightly concedes that all knowledge is socially and linguistically mediated, but he does so in a manner that effectively *reduces* ethical knowledge to its communal mediation, and in this he departs from the guiding assumptions of the prophetic voice and imperils its normative commitments.

Though in his turn to community Walzer means to avert some of the very real pitfalls that he and others have identified with a commitment to realism, he actually undermines the ability of his position to realize its deepest normative aspirations. Walzer worries that such a commitment leads to forms of detachment and abstraction that may underwrite manipulation and violence, but the greater danger from the perspective of prophetic understandings of justice and peaceableness lies in what is lost when one lets go of such aspirations. Without a realist understanding of value, concern for the integrity and well-being of others, particularly those to whom one is not intimately connected or to whom one may otherwise be blind, lacks adequate grounding. Indeed, the problems here are clearly evident in the accounts of justice and political violence that Walzer derives from his emphasis on communal shared understandings. Despite his desire to place resistance to domination at the center of his account of justice, a concern that may seem to resonate with the prophetic concern for the most marginal, his conventionalist non-realism problematically contracts the range of moral vision such that the exclusion of those on the margins of community—those whose voices have figured little, if at all, in the construction of communal meanings—is likely, if not inevitable. Likewise, even if the prophetic commitment to peaceableness is compatible with just war theory, Walzer's conventionalist defense of the theory harbors a fundamental defect in the supreme value he attaches to the political community.

The task ahead, then, is to learn from Walzer's insights and his failures. He is right to emphasize non-foundationalist considerations about the mediated nature of knowledge, lest our claims underwrite manipulation and compulsion. What he seems not to realize, however, is that the affirmation of forms of non-foundationalism that let go of realist aspirations altogether constricts moral vision and thereby underwrites exclusion and marginalization. The danger cuts both ways, then, and an adequate contemporary construal of the prophetic voice will seek to avoid both pitfalls. An adequate contemporary construal of the prophetic voice will seek to uphold both non-foundationalist commitments *and* a realist construal of meaning and value, to uphold realist aspirations in and through formative community. As the next two chapters will help to clarify, articulating such a vision theoretically is challenging.

NOTES

1. Michael Walzer, *Interpretation and Social Criticism* (Cambridge: Harvard University Press, 1987), 71. Emphasis added.

2. Michael Walzer, "A Particularism of My Own," *Religious Studies Review* 16, no. 3 (July 1990): 196.

3. Gordon Lafer, "Universalism and Particularism in Jewish Law: Making Sense of Political Loyalties," in *Jewish Identity*, ed. David Theo Goldberg and Michael Krausz (Philadelphia: Temple University Press, 1993), 181.

4. Elizabeth M. Bounds, "Conflicting Harmonies: Michael Walzer's Vision of Community," *Journal of Religious Ethics* 22, no. 2 (Fall 1994): 366–367.

5. I thank Timothy Jackson for this felicitous phrasing.

6. Michael Walzer, *Spheres of Justice: A Defense of Pluralism and Equality* (New York: Basic Books, 1983), xiv.

7. Walzer, *Interpretation and Social Criticism*, 4–5.

8. See John Rawls, *A Theory of Justice* (Cambridge: The Belknap Press of Harvard University Press, 1971), 136–142.

9. Walzer, *Interpretation and Social Criticism*, 21, 20.

10. Ibid., 14–15.

11. Ibid., 25.

12. Ibid., 20.

13. Ibid., 17–18.

14. See Walzer, *Spheres of Justice*, 6–10.

15. Brian Orend, *Michael Walzer on War and Justice* (Montreal: McGill-Queen's University Press, 2000), 186–187.

16. Timothy P. Jackson, "Liberalism and *Agape*: The Priority of Charity to Democracy and Philosophy," *The Annual of the Society of Christian Ethics* (1993): 50–51. See also Timothy P. Jackson, *Political* Agape*: Christian Love and Liberal Democracy* (Grand Rapids, Mich.: William B. Eerdmans Pub. Co., 2015), 119–120.

17. Michael Walzer, *Thick and Thin: Moral Argument at Home and Abroad* (Notre Dame: University of Notre Dame Press, 1994), 7.

18. Orend, *Michael Walzer on War and Justice*, 32.

19. Michael Walzer, "Philosophy and Democracy," *Political Theory* 9, no. 3 (August 1981): 381.

20. Walzer, *Interpretation and Social Criticism*, 64.

21. Walzer, *Thick and Thin*, 99, 37.

22. Ibid., 37.

23. Ibid., 98.

24. Thomas McCarthy, "Private Irony and Public Decency: Richard Rorty's New Pragmatism," *Critical Inquiry* 16, no. 2 (Winter 1990): 360–361.

25. Charles Taylor, "What Is Human Agency?," in his *Human Agency and Language: Philosophical Papers 1* (Cambridge: Cambridge University Press, 1985), 19. Walzer and others (for example, Susan Wolf, "Moral Saints," *Journal of Philosophy* 79, no. 8 [August 1982]: 419–439) seem to worry that a unified self is one which denies ontological or axiological pluralism. On this view, all actions are to be done for the sake of a singular, overriding good. We are forced to choose, it seems, between an expansive pluralism, in which a seemingly infinite number of realities and goods may have a claim on us (a good thing, by their lights) and a reductive anti-pluralism, in which there is a singular value to which all other values must yield (a bad thing, by their lights). What Taylor and others highlight, however, is the possibility of a *rich, but well-integrated* moral vocabulary. This implicitly carves out a place for a form of pluralism—call it "conscientious pluralism"—that recognizes the multiplicity of moral goods and values, yet holds that they cohere within a system ordered and unified by a metavalue or hypergood, such as love or personal care. For further discussion of these forms of pluralism, see Jackson, *Political* Agape, 124–128.

26. Timothy P. Jackson, "Ambivalences About Nature and Naturalism: A Supernaturalist Response to Theodore W. Nunez," *Journal of Religious Ethics* 27, no. 1 (Spring 1999): 137–138.

27. Timothy P. Jackson, "Naturalism, Formalism, and Supernaturalism: Moral Epistemology and Comparative Ethics," *Journal of Religious Ethics* 27, no. 3 (Fall 1999): 481.

28. Andrew Moore, *Realism and Christian Faith: God, Grammar, and Meaning* (Cambridge: Cambridge University Press, 2003), 110.

29. Ibid., 115–116.

30. Walzer, "A Particularism of My Own," 195.

31. Richard Rorty, *Contingency, Irony, and Solidarity* (Cambridge: Cambridge University Press, 1989), 194–195.

32. Ibid., 198.

33. The term is derived from Jeffrey Stout, *Ethics After Babel: The Languages of Morals and Their Discontents* (Boston: Beacon Press, 1988), 74–77, 292.

34. See the discussion in John J. Ansbro, *Martin Luther King, Jr.: The Making of a Mind* (Maryknoll, NY: Orbis Books, 1982), Chapters 1 and 3.

35. See the discussion in Richard Lischer, *The Preacher King: Martin Luther King, Jr. and the Word That Moved America* (New York: Oxford University Press, 1995), 180–184.

36. Seyla Benhabib, *Situating the Self: Gender, Community and Postmodernism in Contemporary Ethics* (New York: Routledge, 1992), 76ff.

37. Tyler T. Roberts, "Michael Walzer and the Critical Connections," *Journal of Religious Ethics* 22, no. 2 (Fall 1994): 336.

38. Walzer, *Spheres of Justice*, 9.

39. Ibid., 10.

40. Ibid., 6.

41. Ibid., 17. On complex equality generally, see 17–20.

42. Ibid., xii–xiii.

43. Ibid., 10–11.

44. Ibid., 17.

45. Walzer, *Interpretation and Social Criticism*, 40.

46. Ibid., 43.

47. Michael Walzer, *The Company of Critics: Social Criticism and Political Commitment in the Twentieth Century* (New York: Basic Books, 1988), 9.

48. Walzer, *Interpretation and Social Criticism*, 65.

49. Ibid., 48.

50. Michael Walzer and Ronald Dworkin, "'Spheres of Justice': An Exchange," *New York Review of Books* (July 21, 1983): 43. See also Walzer, *Interpretation and Social Criticism*, 29–30.

51. Benhabib, *Situating the Self*, 79–80.

52. Walzer, *Interpretation and Social Criticism*, 28.

53. Ibid., 60. Elsewhere Walzer writes, "Political power is in two senses the end of criticism, first because the critic aims at the effectiveness that power makes possible, and second because, having attained power, he can no longer be critical of his own effects. Since these effects will undoubtedly require criticism, other men and women will have to take up the task, driven in turn by their own social connections, their own ambitions, and their own imitations of heroism" (Walzer, *The Company of Critics*, 23).

54. Walzer, *The Company of Critics*, 21–22.

55. Walzer, *Interpretation and Social Criticism*, 61.

56. Ibid., 70.

57. Ibid., 71.

58. Ibid. In his recent book on politics in the Hebrew Bible, Walzer continues to develop these themes: "The prophets became the representatives of God in the world, with no practical tasks except criticism. They spoke for the tradition: a history of miraculous interventions, a covenantal law divinely revealed." Michael Walzer, *In God's Shadow: Politics in the Hebrew Bible* (New Haven: Yale University Press, 2012), 87–88.

59. Walzer, *Interpretation and Social Criticism*, 74.

60. See Ibid., 82–83.

61. Ibid., 80–81.

62. Ibid., 77–78.

63. On reiteration, see Michael Walzer, "Two Kinds of Universalism," in *The Tanner Lectures on Human Value, XI*, ed. Grethe B. Peterson (Salt Lake City: University of Utah Press, 1990), 513ff.

64. Walzer, *Interpretation and Social Criticism*, 79.

65. Notice, however, the irony here. This approach fails to cohere with Walzer's guiding assumptions, for in understanding the prophets denuded of theological content, he fails to understand them in their own terms. His treatment of the prophets is not the sort of internal approach that he commends generally.

66. William A. Galston, "Community, Democracy, Philosophy: The Political Thought of Michael Walzer," *Political Theory* 17, no. 1 (February 1989): 120–121. See also Bounds, "Conflicting Harmonies," 359; and Brooke A. Ackerly, *Political Theory and Feminist Social Criticism* (Cambridge: Cambridge University Press, 2000), 89.

67. Walzer, *Spheres of Justice*, 28.

68. Walzer, *The Company of Critics*, 233–234.

69. Bounds, "Conflicting Harmonies," 359.

70. Michael Walzer, "The Communitarian Critique of Liberalism," *Political Theory* 18, no. 1 (February 1990): 16.

71. Bounds, "Conflicting Harmonies," 363.

72. Robert A. Dahl, *Democracy and Its Critics* (New Haven: Yale University Press, 1989), 304–5.

73. Walzer, *Spheres of Justice*, 28–29. Emphasis added.

74. Michael Walzer, "Shared Meanings in a Poly-Ethnic Democratic Setting: A Response," *Journal of Religious Ethics* 22, no. 2 (Fall 1994): 402–403.

75. Lawrie Balfour, "The Appeal of Innocence: Baldwin, Walzer, and the Bounds of Social Criticism," *The Review of Politics* 61, no. 3 (Summer 1999): 388.

76. Walzer and Dworkin, "'Spheres of Justice': An Exchange," 43. Emphasis added.

77. Georgia Warnke, *Justice and Interpretation* (Cambridge: MIT Press, 1993), 22.

78. Ibid., 26.

79. Ibid., 29.

80. Ibid., 26.

81. See Bounds, "Conflicting Harmonies," 364ff.

82. Iris Marion Young, *Justice and the Politics of Difference* (Princeton: Princeton University Press, 1990), 41.

83. Walzer, *Spheres of Justice*, 250n.

84. Joshua Cohen, "Book Review of *Spheres of Justice*," *Journal of Philosophy* 83, no. 8 (August 1986): 462.

85. Will Kymlicka, *Liberalism, Community and Culture* (Oxford: Clarendon Press of Oxford University Press, 1989), 223. See also Galston, "Community, Democracy, Philosophy," 121.

86. Susan Moller Okin, *Justice, Gender, and the Family* (New York: Basic Books, 1989), 66, 67. As I hope will be clear by the end of the book, understood properly and within the framework established by biblical texts, contemporary appropriations of the prophets will not serve as apologies for dominative and exclusionary power.

87. Balfour, "The Appeal of Innocence," 380.

88. Ibid., 379ff. Seyla Benhabib has voiced similar concerns, contending that situated criticism of the sort Walzer defends evinces "a nostalgia for home, for the certitudes of one's own culture." (Seyla Behabib, "Feminism and Postmodernism: An Uneasy Alliance," in Seyla Benhabib, Judith Butler, Drucilla Cornell, and Nancy Fraser, *Feminist Contentions: A Philosophical Exchange* [New York: Routledge, 1995], 28).

89. Walzer, *Interpretation and Social Criticism*, 17.

90. Ibid., 20.

91. Walzer, *Thick and Thin*, 12–13. Emphasis added.

92. Roberts, "Michael Walzer and the Critical Connections," 347. Roberts notes that this understanding of reiteration precludes structural criticism of the sort that would allow us to recognize the ways in which dominant traditions may serve as vehicles of domination and oppression.

93. Walzer, *The Company of Critics*, 67. Emphasis added.

94. Balfour, "The Appeal of Innocence," 384.

95. For instructive treatment of the historical background of Christian resistance to, and defense of, political violence, see Lisa Sowle Cahill, *Love Your Enemies: Discipleship, Pacifism, and Just War Theory* (Minneapolis: Fortress Press, 1994).

96. Timothy P. Jackson, *The Priority of Love: Christian Charity and Social Justice* (Princeton: Princeton University Press, 2003), 122.

97. Ibid. For a brief, but compelling, theological defense of political violence in light of recent events, see Jean Bethke Elshtain, "How to Fight a Just War," in *Strike Terror No More: Theology, Ethics, and the New War*, ed. Jon L. Berquist (St. Louis: Chalice Press, 2002), 231–235. For compelling and instructive discussion of the compatibility of love of enemy and the use of force on the battlefield, see Nigel Biggar, *In Defence of War* (Oxford: Oxford University Press, 2013), Chapter 2 ("Love in War").

98. For an excellent and detailed overview and evaluation of Walzer's just war theory, to which I am highly indebted, see Orend, *Michael Walzer on War and Justice*, Chapters 3–6.

99. Michael Walzer, *Just and Unjust Wars: A Moral Argument with Historical Illustrations* (New York: Basic Books, 1977), 53, 54.

100. Ibid., 54.
101. Ibid., 55.
102. Ibid., 57.
103. Ibid., 44.
104. Ibid., 45.
105. Ibid., 253, 252. Walzer further develops the doctrine in "Emergency Ethics," in his *Arguing about War* (New Haven: Yale University Press, 2004).
106. Walzer, *Just and Unjust Wars*, 259. Emphasis added.
107. Walzer, "Emergency Ethics," 40.
108. Ibid., 34–35.
109. Timothy P. Jackson, *Love Disconsoled: Meditations on Christian Charity* (Cambridge: Cambridge University Press, 1999), 208.
110. Walzer, "Emergency Ethics," 43.

Chapter 3

The Church versus Liberal Modernity

Communal Closure in Stanley Hauerwas' Postliberal Ecclesiology

POSTLIBERALISM VERSUS THE PROPHETIC?

Over the course of the last forty plus years, Stanley Hauerwas has established himself as one of Christianity's most compelling, provocative, and influential voices, chiefly by virtue of his claim that the church is a distinctive community whose *raison d'etre* is to give expression to Christian discipleship as it stands prior to, and as a standpoint for judging, all other communities and loyalties. Like Walzer, Hauerwas' work is community-focused, and it upholds an understanding of the necessarily socially mediated nature of knowledge. However, the primacy he accords to the church relativizes any and all commitments to other particular moral communities or configurations of ethical and political life—both epistemologically and axiologically. In Hauerwas, there is no Walzerian upholding of the nation-state as the primary locus of moral and political understanding and value. As Michael Quirk has noted, for Hauerwas, a "commitment to Christianity entails allegiance to a story which is inevitably alien to all forms of secular political institutions, however 'humanistic' they may be."[1] The first task of the church, for Hauerwas, is simply to be the church. But it is in doing so that the church is able to make what he would regard as a proper difference; indeed, it is precisely by standing as an alternative to all other social configurations that the church stands as a prophetic presence in society, or so Hauerwas claims.

Wittgensteinian philosophy and postliberal theology serve as key methodological and theoretical tools in Hauerwas' articulation of the significance of the church and the distinctiveness of Christianity. Hauerwas has said that Ludwig Wittgenstein ended for him "any attempt . . . to try to anchor theology in some general account of 'human experience,'" and his work taught him "that the object of theologians' work was best located in terms of the grammar of the language used by believers."[2] This influence readily leads to the adoption of a postliberal, "cultural-linguistic" understanding of religion. This understanding of religion denies the claims of liberal theologians that there "is some universal experience that all people have that can be characterized as religious," and claims, instead, that Christian theology is concerned with membership in "a particular community, formed by Christian convictions," whereby "an experience not otherwise available is made possible."[3] This is because, from a postliberal perspective, theology is understood as taking up "the ancient practice of absorbing the universe into the biblical world."[4] For Hauerwas, to understand Christianity as a distinct "form of life" is to understand it in a "cultural-linguistic" mode, in which its distinctive theological grammar and moral vision is defined especially in contrast to the assumptions and commitments of liberal modernity.

However, the more Hauerwas adopts such a position, the more he finds himself in trouble from the perspective of the prophetic voice. Specifically, Hauerwas' attempt to speak prophetically in a cultural-linguistic mode cannot match the dynamism of the biblical prophets' focus upon those at society's margins, a focus rooted in the core insight that God's identity and very character is intimately tied to "the least of these." His propensity to boundary-drawing, to distinguishing sharply the story or grammar of the church from all other stories or grammars, leads to blindness to the claims of those at the margins, and how they might render possible more complex understandings of truth, justice, and peaceableness. Even his recent work embracing radical democracy is insufficient in this respect. More sustained attention to the voices of "others" in the manner urged by many of his feminist critics offers crucial resources for resisting Hauerwas' conflation of the medium of truth (the church) with truth itself, his rejection of justice understood in terms of rights and liberation as a distorting concern of the Enlightenment, and his conflation of justifications for political violence with the idolization of the nation-state. Commitments to an adequate form of realism chastened by non-foundationalism, to a form of justice which prioritizes solidarity with the marginal and voiceless, and to an adequate conception of just peace require forms of humility, openness to challenge and change, and interpretive generosity not characteristically found in Hauerwas.

COMMUNITY: THE CHURCH AS A CULTURAL BUFFER AGAINST LIBERALISM

In discussing Michael Walzer, I noted that much of his resistance to modern forms of moral and political theory lies in their tendency to underwrite understandings of objectivity and truth that can foster coercion and violence.

I highlighted, however, problems with his rejection of realism in favor of a community-oriented particularism. I argued that an affirmation of particularity is compatible with an affirmation of realism, and that what we need to argue about is how we conceive reality, and what conception(s) might be most compelling. While Stanley Hauerwas does not follow Walzer in rejecting realism (whether his theological realism is sufficient in a matter I will address in the next section), he resonates with him regarding the problematic assumptions of much modern moral and political theory, and with his emphasis on particularism in moral and political theory. As a Christian theologian, however, Hauerwas upholds the church, rather than the political community, as the primary context within which one gains moral knowledge.

Liberalism and the Standard Account of Morality

Hauerwas' reflections on these matters are shaped by his understanding of modern liberalism. Arne Rasmusson notes that Hauerwas "tries to show the inherent tensions that characterize the structures, institutions and theories of liberalism and its conflicts with church and Christian faith and how the church can witness to different possibilities."[5] While Hauerwas' reflections on liberalism tend not to be systematically laid out—he has "tried to chip away" at it "one piece at a time"[6]—there are clearly discernible themes that recur in these discussions. Above all, he worries that liberal moral and political theory imagines persons to be unencumbered by their history or community, sharing no common history or good. This leaves them in a position where morality, politics, and public policy are about nothing more than aggregating and adjudicating, via abstract rules or procedures, the inevitably conflicting preferences of self-interested individuals.[7]

These problems are clearly discernible in what Hauerwas (along with David Burrell) has termed "the standard account of moral rationality." This understanding of moral rationality is typically liberal in that it yields an approach to normative thinking in which particularity and tradition are replaced by aspirations to abstraction and objectivity. In a world characterized by fragmentation and conflict we long for rational foundations for morality and social cooperation. This account, whether deontological or consequentialist in form, seeks to respond to this longing by promising "to secure for moral judgments an objectivity that would free such judgments from the subjective beliefs, wants, and stories of the agent who makes them. Just as science tries to insure objectivity by adhering to an explicitly disinterested method, so ethical theory tried to show that moral judgments, insofar as they can be considered true, must be the result of impersonal rationality."[8] This entails that any proper account of the moral life is fully detached from reference to, or reliance upon, particular relationships, communities, and traditions. "What

I am morally obligated to do is not what derives from being a father, or a son, or an American, or a teacher, or a doctor, or a Christian, but what follows from my being a person constituted by reason."[9] Hauerwas contends that there are at least two major problems with this approach to understanding morality.

First, he and Burrell argue that the standard account of moral rationality leads to a distorted understanding of the moral life because it places excessive emphasis on particular decisions or quandaries faced by the individual agent, apart from the broader context and history within which such decisions are faced.[10] With such a focus, ethics is construed in a manner that assumes judgments can be justified apart from the agent doing the judging. "The only intentions or reasons for our behavior that are morally interesting are those that anyone might have . . . . The 'personal' can only be morally significant to the extent that it can be translated into the 'impersonal.'"[11] However, this banishing of the personal point of view in favor of the impersonal has an alienating effect, as moral actions are separated from those projects and commitments that make such actions "ours" in the first place, pleasure and desire are excluded as aspects of doing the good, and the temporal character of the self is denied as our present is separated from our past.[12]

Furthermore, the standard account pictures the moral world as simply given, but this fails to attend to the role of what Hauerwas, following Julius Kovesi, calls moral notions. We do not know what moral terms such as "murder," "stealing," "abortion," "freedom," "justice," or "rights," and judgments that rely upon the usage of such terms, mean abstractly, but only and always from a particular narrative framework that gives such terms, and the judgments derived from them, intelligibility.[13] Thus, for example, what pro-life and pro-choice adversaries in the abortion debate often fail to recognize is that their disagreements stem not from a failure to acknowledge some range of brute facts—facts, for example, about when life begins or what constitutes personhood—but from the fact that the parties in the dispute possess different stories about "abortion" itself. "At least so far as 'abortion' is concerned," Hauerwas writes, "they live in conceptually different worlds."[14]

Second, in addition to these phenomenological distortions of the moral life, contemporary moral and political discourse, while seeking to provide a means of managing diversity peaceably, ironically threatens to foster the very sort of violence it is meant to quell. It is precisely when agents and the languages they employ are alienated or divorced from the broader institutions and narratives that provide the moral life with substantive content, Hauerwas argues, that moral fragmentation and the dangers it poses are most keenly felt. By imposing a false unity rooted in a problematic understanding of moral rationality, the "standard account of moral rationality" and the forms of liberal social and political theory associated with it essentially inscribe fragmentation into modern understandings of morality, thereby leaving moral agents alone, confronted with a moral vacuum that is too often filled by a longing for absolutes and security satisfied through violence.

When we live in a world in which moral fragmentation is assumed, Hauerwas contends, our desire for peace within ourselves and with our fellows is often expressed in the form of a "hunger for absolutes." In such a situation, with "no means to ensure that moral argument in itself can resolve our moral conflicts," we always stand on the brink of violence.[15] We fear the challenges inevitably posed to our own security, both physical and psychic, by the other. We claim to love peace, but what we really desire is order, and we are willing to use violence as a weapon against disorder. "We are peaceable so long as no one disturbs our illusions. We are nonviolent as long as no one challenges our turf." But our illusions and our turf *will* be challenged, so "violence becomes needlessly woven into our lives; it becomes the warp on which the fabric of our existence is threaded. The order of our lives is built on our potential for violence. What is true at the personal level is even more the case when we confront one another as 'societies' organized to protect and enhance our most cherished pretensions."[16]

From Decisions to Character, Community, and the Church

For Hauerwas, then, the task of ethics is not "to provide an account of reason that helps the agent make the right decision in a manner that" leaves her undetermined by her past. Rather, moral agency is but another name for "those skills necessary to make our past our own . . . . [O]ur moral lives are more properly constituted by retrospective rather than prospective judgments."[17] Character, rather than undetermined choice, "is the source of our agency, that is, our ability to act with integrity."[18] Who I have been formed to be is determinative of what I will do. This focus on character is, of course, closely allied and entwined with a focus on the virtues, those habitual dispositions which constitute our character and thus our agency.

Christian character is formed in reference to good exemplars, within particular communities. On Hauerwas' account of the moral life, moral character is thus not the achievement of independent, autonomous individuals, but, rather, is formed in and through the particular narratives of a particular community. Because "all existence, and in particular the human self, is narratively formed,"[19] we must attend to the communal contexts within which we become storied beings. While at times Hauerwas seems to make general claims about the inescapability of narrative for historical beings,[20] his overriding interest is not to articulate a sweeping anthropology, but to call attention to the significance of the qualifier "Christian" for Christian ethics.

In order to be properly oriented, it is necessary that we be immersed in and shaped by a narrative that is *truthful*, for only a truthful story can allow us to "face the limits and failures that are a part of human life without resorting to violence . . . . Only through a truthful narrative is one given the skills to live with integrity and consistency through the diversity of life's experiences and the limits of our historically particular traditions."[21] It is in response to, and imitation of, the truthful story of God in Christ that Hauerwas contends Christians find their proper orientation. "The form of the Gospels as stories of a life are meant not only to display that life, but to train us to situate our lives in relation to that life . . . . [W]e cannot know who Jesus is and what he stands for without learning to be his followers."[22] In turn, we do not know how to be Jesus' followers without those everyday saints who have preceded us and serve as exemplars of lives lived in conformity to Christ.

Insertion into and immersion in the narratives of the Christian community thus enable one rightly to envision the world; Christian ethics is an enterprise in learning to see rightly. "We do not come to see merely by looking, but must develop disciplined skills through initiation into that community that attempts to live faithful to the story of God."[23] Hauerwas is thus chiefly concerned with how the particular narratives of the biblical text and Christian tradition, embodied within the church and its practices, give shape to a person's identity and sense of agency. Shaped by the narratives of the church, Christians are provided with truthful moral vision whereby their understanding of moral terms and the nature of their moral judgments possess the sort of thickness Hauerwas argues is largely absent in contemporary moral discourse.

It is in this focus upon the narrative and communal constitution of Christian character and virtue in and through the church that the postliberal and Wittgensteinian aspects of Hauerwas' theology are seen most clearly. In arguing that moral vision is parasitic upon insertion into a particular community and its practices and language, Hauerwas upholds a characteristically postliberal understanding of the internal relation between discourse about, and knowledge of, the world. For Hauerwas, to learn how to be a Christian is not to comprehend the world *sub specie aeternitatis*, but from within the practices and beliefs of a particular form of life; it is to learn how to speak a certain sort of language. In his discussion of Lindbeck's influence on his work, Hauerwas echoes Lindbeck's claim that "religions, like languages, can only be understood in their own terms."[24] Similarly, Brad Kallenberg, in his study of the Wittgensteinian presuppositions of Hauerwas' thought, has explained that "since Hauerwas conceives language as internally related to world, Christian ethics begins and ends with a grammatical task; there is no way to describe the difference that Jesus makes without resorting to the language Christians have habitually employed. Moreover, it is precisely attention to this particular set of linguistic practices that train us to see the 'point' Christians have always claimed to see."[25] Thus, theological ethics for Hauerwas consists centrally of the "explication of the form of life of the actual community, which is to say, the grammar of Christian discourse."[26]

Above all, Hauerwas claims, the form of life the Christian community embodies is characterized by nonviolence. The vocation of Christians is to join Jesus "in the journey through which we are trained to be a people capable of claiming citizenship in God's kingdom of nonviolent love—a love that would overcome the powers of the world not through coercion and force, but through the power of this one man's death."[27] Christians are "to live without resort to violence" because in so doing, they "live as God lives. Therefore pacifism is not first of all a prohibition, but an affirmation that God wills to rule his creation not through violence and coercion but by love."[28] Peace is thus not something we simply hope for in the midst of a violent world, all the while continuing to make use "when necessary" of the tools of violence, for Jesus' resurrection is "God's decisive eschatological act," through which "we see God's peace as a *present* reality. Though we continue to live in a time when the world does not dwell in peace, when the wolf cannot dwell with the lamb and the child cannot play over the hill of the asp, we believe nonetheless that peace *has been made possible* by the resurrection."[29]

Practices of nonviolence and of those virtues allied with them—above all, forgiveness, patience, and hope[30]—require that we give up the illusion of control that Hauerwas contends so often underwrites our disposition toward violence. As followers of Jesus, "we must, like him, be dispossessed of all that we think gives us power over our own lives and the lives of others. Unless we learn to relinquish our presumption that we can ensure the significance of our lives, we are not capable of the peace of God's kingdom."[31] Christians are to be an eschatological people who "live out of control" by basing their lives upon the recognition that God has redeemed the whole of creation through Jesus Christ. "We live out of control in the sense that we must assume God will use our faithfulness to make his kingdom a reality in the world."[32]

In embodying such a communal life of discipleship, Hauerwas contends that the church stands as a distinct *political* presence in the world. His argument with modernity and liberalism is thus not simply a methodological quarrel regarding the nature of the moral life and the necessity of moral formation; it possesses as well a distinct political dimension. As Hauerwas says, "The gospel is a political gospel. Christians are engaged in politics, but it is a politics of the kingdom that reveals the insufficiency of all politics based on coercion and falsehood and finds the true source of power in servanthood rather than dominion."[33] Elsewhere, he advocates a "theological politics" in which the church's story is understood as a "'counter story' that interprets the world's politics."[34]

Indeed, Hauerwas contends, it is only through the church's embodied, nonviolent witness that the world knows itself to be world. The terms "church" and "world" in Hauerwas' thought do not designate ontological distinctions, but are, rather, relational terms that designate a "difference between agents," a difference in animating assumptions and commitments. The world is comprised by those, "including ourselves, who have chosen not to make the story of God their story. The world in us refuses to affirm that this is God's world and that, as loving Lord, God's care for creation is greater than our illusion of control. The world is those aspects of our individual and social lives where we live untruthfully by continuing to rely on violence to bring order."[35] The church, by contrast, relates all of the competing narratives of the world to, and reimagines them in light of, the peaceable character of God's dealings with creation.[36] The church rightly exists as a "counter-society" or "counter-*polis*" in the world, then, by serving as a sign, as first fruit, of the Kingdom inaugurated by God in Christ, witnessing to God's good and peaceable intentions for humanity.

The apparently prophetic nature of Hauerwas' thought is located here, in his articulation of the vocation of the church as a distinctive community in the world. His work can be instructively understood as a form of theological cultural criticism in which he seeks to expose the falsehoods and pathologies of regnant forms of social formation and organization, particularly those associated with liberal democracy, by contrasting them with the peaceable vision of creation that is embodied most especially in the church. "Because Jesus was who he was, Christians cannot help but be prophetic, since now their very existence is a prophetic sign of God's refusal to abandon creation. If the essential role of the prophet is to interpret the world in terms of God's providential care, then the church's very existence is prophetic, for without the church we could not know who we are or in what kind of world we exist."[37] It is through the particular witness of the church, which is the embodiment of the peaceableness that was Christ's life, that we can know how to name and resist the violence that surrounds us, and by which we are all too often defined. The church embodies an alternative consciousness, Hauerwas argues, whereby the false powers that rule us can be resisted.

The Church as a Cultural Buffer

As should be clear from the foregoing, Hauerwas' thought frequently trades on strong contrasts—overly strong contrasts, I shall argue—as he seeks to articulate the distinctive alternative offered by the church to a world otherwise owned by violence: Christian discipleship v. autonomous individualism, the peaceableness of the church v. the violence of modern liberalism, the renunciation of control v. the drive to control, and so on. This emphasis on the church as a distinct alternative is revealed in the titles of many of his books: As the embodiment of God's *Peaceable Kingdom*, the church is *A Community of Character*. It is a colony in the world as Christians live as *Resident Aliens* standing *Against the Nations*. Christians embody *A Better Hope* by confronting the pathologies of capitalism, democracy, and postmodernity and by *Unleashing Scripture* from captivity to the individualist and modernist assumptions of contemporary America. Hauerwas' work is a set of *Dispatches From the Front* as he addresses the challenges posted to the church as it engages the powers in its *Wilderness Wanderings*. The picture painted by Hauerwas, both conceptually and rhetorically, is thus of a church surrounded and under siege, but, nevertheless, standing firm as a distinct witness, resisting the alien forces that would seek to domesticate and undermine it. In his depiction of the church as a distinct culture or polity standing over and against or in contrast to competing social configurations, Hauerwas is aided by his appropriation of a postliberal theological standpoint, but the more strongly he adopts such a standpoint, the more his project is imperiled from a prophetic standpoint.

Kathryn Tanner's work on the variety of ways the concept of culture has found expression in theological reflection is instructive in highlighting some of the most fundamental problems lurking here. She has described the postliberal attempt to articulate Christian identity in terms of a cultural boundary that starkly distinguishes "a Christian way of life, on the one hand, from those of other religions or the wider secular society, on the other." Christian culture and other cultures stand relative to one another as "qualitatively discontinuous wholes," with the loci of Christian identity residing in "the spontaneous productions of the people concerned," such as the New Testament. The resulting "indigenous cultural productions—texts, rituals, peculiar symbolic forms, and patterns of behavior—are said to generate . . . their own world of meaning, a web of significance that is all their own." On this conception of Christian identity, one central concern, then, is to avoid "influences and alteration that might accrue to it by way of intimate involvement with other ways of doing, feeling, and understanding."[38]

While she does not address Hauerwas' work directly, one can see clear resonances between Tanner's description of postliberalism and Hauerwas' theological project. His conception of Christian identity is one in which the source of the community's identity resides not in the specification of generalized aspects of human experience, but, rather, in the articulation of a particular form of life, with its attendant vision and practices, that arises out of fidelity to a particular text. Christianity is a language that one learns to speak adequately only as a participating member of the Christian community, a community which, properly understood, derives its identity from fidelity to the narratives of God's actions and character as displayed in and through Jesus Christ.

A central contemporary threat—perhaps *the* central threat—to this identity is the modern liberal culture relative to which the church stands as a distinct alternative. As Hauerwas states in the Introduction to *Against the Nations*, his central statement of his postliberal commitments, "To recover a sense of how Christian convictions may be true (or false) requires a recovery of the independence of the church from its subservience to liberal culture and its corresponding agencies of the state."[39] Similarly, and perhaps even more tellingly, he has more recently defended what he calls "peasant Catholicism"—Christianity understood not primarily in terms of a set of beliefs or doctrines, but as a body-shaping and habit-determining communal way of being hierarchically governed and maintained—as a means of offering an "alternative to the endemic individualism and rationalism of modernity."[40] So understood, at least if the interpretation of Paul upon which Hauerwas relies is correct, the church as body is vulnerable to corruption: "Paul presumes the church is Christ's body so immorality is not like the body becoming ill or polluted, it is to make the body ill and polluted."[41] For Paul, then, it is crucial that the boundaries of the body/church be maintained. He thinks that "'the disguised presence within the church of a representative from the outside, from the cosmos that *should* be "out there," threatens the whole body. The body of Christ . . . may be polluted if its boundaries are permeated and an element of the cosmos gains entry into the body.'"[42]

Just to the extent, however, that Hauerwas offers such highly oppositional, tightly bounded accounts of Christian community, his project is problematically circumscribed from a prophetic standpoint. So understood, it has difficulty upholding a realist conception of truth, and it is denied important insights in addressing questions of justice and in articulating adequate Christian response to political violence, as I will now argue.

TRUTH: PERFORMANCE, REALISM, AND THE QUESTION OF REVELATION

Like Walzer, Hauerwas readily admits all knowledge is mediated. For him, this occurs in and through the church. Yet Hauerwas, of course, is a theologian and this is a difference of significance when it comes to his attitude toward realism. Though theology undertaken from a postliberal standpoint is concerned with the articulation of a distinctly Christian grammar, Hauerwas would contend that it does not give expression to conventionalism because Christian claims (and lives) are true; they are disclosive of reality. The difficulty here, however, is that it is not clear that Hauerwas' account of truth is wholly successful in overcoming the sorts of problems I have previously identified with Walzer's conventionalism. His position threatens to conflate the medium with the message by reducing truths disclosed through revelation to the church, the community through which that revelation is mediated.

Truth as Performatively Displayed

As discussed previously, Hauerwas has long contended that truth is not something known in the abstract; rather, it is communally disclosed through compelling practices. In this emphasis, Hauerwas' account is consistent with claims George Lindbeck makes in *The Nature of Doctrine*. Lindbeck claims that the norms of reasonableness of a religious tradition "are like the rules of depth grammar, which linguists search for and may at times approximate but never grasp. Thus reasonableness in religion and theology, as in other domains, has something of that aesthetic character, that quality of unformalizable skill, which we usually associate with the artist or the linguistically competent." The intelligibility of theological and religious claims "comes from skill, not theory, and credibility comes from good performance, not adherence to independently formulated criteria"[43]

With these sorts of considerations in mind, Hauerwas has long held that the primary test for the truth of a religious tradition resides in the quality of its performance, in the kinds of lives it produces. From early in his career, he has claimed that the question of truthfulness of Christian convictions "is most appropriately raised by asking how through our language and character they form and display our practical affairs." While metaphysical or ontological considerations are not thereby shunned, they are not primary in testing our theological convictions. We look instead to the lives produced by our convictions.[44]

Variations on this basic claim are found throughout Hauerwas' corpus. In response to concerns raised by Julian Hartt that even if positions such as Hauerwas' may help show the *internal coherence* of stories, they are inadequate to the task of showing whether the stories that shape lives are *true*, Hauerwas denies that it is possible "to distinguish between 'external' and 'internal' evidence" for the truth of Christian convictions because "the character of Christian belief requires the transformation of the self in order rightly to see the actuality of our world without illusion or self-deception." The stories found in the gospel, he readily admits, do involve metaphysical claims about the character of reality, but "the kind of truth entailed by the Gospels, the kind of demands placed on reality, cannot be separated from the way in which the story of God we claim as revealed in Jesus' life, death, and resurrection forces a repositioning of the self vis-à-vis reality."[45] And in more recent work, the connection between the truthfulness of lives and the truth of claims about reality is even clearer and more explicit. He argues that "truthfulness and worship of God are inseparable . . . . The truth is finally known in the showing." Drawing on Aquinas' and Luther's accounts of the Decalogue, he strives to show that "any attempt to tell the truth about God is unavoidably connected with our ability to speak the truth about the world. Truth about the way things are, accordingly, cannot be isolated from the kind of people capable of acknowledging the way things are. For the way things are, the God who creates the way the world is, is revealed by a people trained to be truthful."[46]

But how can we claim that the Christian story enables good performances? How does the Christian story shape lives in ways we might name as truthful? With David Burrell, he argues that, while understanding rationality in narrative terms denies us recourse to an abstract and objective standpoint in adjudicating competing claims, we are not devoid of criteria for judging among competing stories. Rather, "any story we adopt, or allow to adopt us, will have to display: (1) power to release us from destructive alternatives; (2) ways of seeing through current distortions; (3) room to keep us from having to resort to violence; (4) a sense of the tragic: how meaning transcends power." These criteria possess a pragmatic dimension insofar as they are meant to enable us to "envisage . . . the effect which stories might be expected to have on those who allow them to shape their lives."[47] If I understand Hauerwas correctly here, those narratives which display these features are in good working order, are superior to those that do not display them, and therefore rightly make claims to truthfulness. Thus, because the Christian narrative, at least as Hauerwas interprets it, fulfills these criteria, we have reason to affirm it, to allow it to shape our lives, and to utilize it in judging other competing narratives, such as that of liberal modernity.

Epistemological Sectarianism?

For many of Hauerwas' critics, however, it is precisely his unwillingness to distinguish between internal and external evidence for the truth of religious convictions that is problematic, for it seems to ensnare him in a form of sectarianism. The sectarian charge is one of the most enduring leveled against Hauerwas, and has been most influentially articulated by James Gustafson. He claims that the work of Hauerwas and others (Anders Nygren, D.Z. Phillips, Paul Holmer, and, especially, George Lindbeck) are fundamentally conservative reactions to the perceived threats posed by the "inexorable fact" of religious pluralism. Gustafson maintains that Hauerwas and his fellow travelers seek to erect a clear conception of Christian communal identity in the midst of ambiguity and uncertainty by isolating Christian theology and ethics from external criticism, but in so doing they thereby succumb to "the sectarian temptation."[48] While there are multiple dimensions to this charge, a second of which I will discuss later, a central claim made by Gustafson and others who level it is that sectarianism in theology imperils realism.

Sectarian forms of theology, Gustafson argues, have drunk too deeply at the wells of the followers of Wittgenstein and the sociologists of knowledge and too quickly accept that theology is "the result of a social construction grounded in a historically relative community."[49] Because the "Wittgensteinian fideists"[50]—postliberals among them—who succumb to sectarianism uphold an understanding of religion that gives pride of place to maintaining a distinctive language or culture, they are not concerned "to carry on an interaction with other ways of viewing the world with any openness to what these other ways might require as alterations of the religion's own way of construing the world. The 'Biblical mode' is not to be tampered with; rather one is to absorb 'the universe into the Biblical world.' The truth claims of theology are ignored, except insofar as they are *subjectively true* for persons socialized into the Christian culture and language."[51]

Critics who charge Hauerwas with such epistemological sectarianism worry that the theological assumption that we know God only in and through history, particularly in and through "the history of the Biblical people culminating in the events of Christ and their effects," seems to lead either to an understanding of God in which "there is only one community in the world that has access to knowledge of God because God has revealed himself only in the life of that community," or, worse, it seems to entail that Christian theology and ethics are not concerned with God so much as they are concerned simply to maintain "fidelity to the biblical narratives about Jesus."[52] In either case, insofar as these narratives are known only in and through the church, it is feared this leads to an idolatrous concern with the church, rather than God, as the focal point of Christian faithfulness. The object of the community's attention is not outwardly focused toward the God of the world, but turned inward. Hauerwas and others who have turned in a similar manner to the church as the locus of theological inquiry ultimately, it is argued, uphold a highly conventionalist understanding of theology and ethics in which *vox ecclesia* = *vox dei*.[53]

Hauerwas would deny that his thought harbors a conventionalism that subverts theological realism. He would claim that it is those who charge him with sectarianism who harbor untenable philosophical and theological assumptions. To those who claim that the church rather than God is the focus of his theology and ethics, he would likely respond that such a charge implicitly assumes that, *for Christians*, God can be known apart from the church, apart from the texts and practices that shape, and lives that give expression to, faithfulness in God. Knowledge of God, he claims, cannot be had in the abstract, in raw, unmediated terms. To claim otherwise assumes the ability to stand outside of history, but this is simply something we cannot do as the contingent, finite, fallible, particular creatures we are.

Hauerwas is thus inclined to say "church" rather than "God" when asked to say something theological because the church provides Christians with the grammar with which they are enabled to speak about God.[54] Thus, to claim, for example, that there is no salvation outside of the church is not to claim that only Christians are the beneficiaries of what they would call God's saving grace or that God is properly known only through the church, and so on. Rather, it is to make the claim that theological concepts are not foundationally given, but, rather, derive their intelligibility only as they are "historically learned and creatively employed within a particular social-linguistic form of life."[55] Thus Hauerwas contends that "Christian beliefs about God, Jesus, sin, the nature of human existence, and salvation are intelligible only if they are seen against the background of the church—that is, a body of people who stand apart from the 'world' because of the peculiar task of worshipping a god whom the world knows not."[56]

Notwithstanding this line of response, problems linger. Surely Hauerwas is right to affirm the mediated nature of knowledge and to highlight the manner in which Christian discourse reflects this, but it is not clear that this is a sufficient response to the concerns raised about the status of realism in his thought. We are still left with questions regarding the connection between *truthfulness*, which is concerned with internal or social reality—with the performative content, communal values, and patterns of behavior to which a narrative gives rise—and *truth*, which relates to the domain of external reality, and, in a realist perspective, is that against which social beliefs and practices are measured. Here, Hauerwas seems to fall into the all-too-common tendency to conflate matters of epistemology with matters of alethiology. He seems, in other words, to conflate the means of perception with the truth(s) to be discerned. Indeed, one sometimes gets the sense that Hauerwas wants to leave questions about external reality behind entirely.[57] But insofar as "God" names a reality that ultimately stands outside of our practices, judging and regulating them, even if only perceived and perceivable in and through those practices, we cannot neglect such matters.

Truth, Revelation, and Otherness

For Christians, affirmations of or claims to knowledge of external reality, of God, are characteristically understood in terms of revelation. The key question for Hauerwas, then, is whether and how claims about the truthfulness of sociolinguistic practices relate to claims about the truth of divine revelation. Samuel Wells has worried in an instructive way about these matters, arguing that

> Hauerwas' main problem in reaching external reality through social, linguistic and internal reality is a tendency to anthropocentrism . . . . Hauerwas' understanding of revelation corresponds with his antifoundationalist epistemology—what Hauerwas would call his ecclesiology. Resisting all temptation to found revelation on a prior phenomenology of existence, Hauerwas understands that the role of revelation is defined by Scripture and the Church (and is therefore narrative in character) rather than vice versa. The danger of this is that it retains God's prevenience as its starting point, but thereafter appears anthropocentric, since it concentrates on human language and society . . . . [I]n an effort to avoid foundationalism, Hauerwas can get so involved in the social and linguistic media of revelation that the sovereign power of the Revealer is neglected.[58]

In a similar manner, drawing on Karl Barth's threefold stratification of the Word of God, David Fergusson has worried that, while Hauerwas effectively captures "the self-involving nature of religious language" and "the ethical dimension of Christian confession," his account "seems to jeopardize the realist claim that truth is not of our own making." An adequate theological articulation of this seems to require that a distinction be drawn "between the linguistic practices of the community, the words of Scripture, and that to which these ultimately refer."[59]

But if we do not have unmediated access to the divine, how do we avoid anthropocentrism? Are we simply forever condemned to conventionalist affirmation of the practices of our own sociolinguistic community? In a footnote, Wells quotes Walter Brueggemann to suggest one way in which Hauerwas might profitably develop his thought in addressing such concerns.[60] Brueggemann writes,

> As concerns God, Barth has made clear that the God of the Bible is 'Wholly Other.' In conventional interpretation, the accent has been on 'wholly,' stressing the contrast and discontinuity. When, however, accent is placed on 'other,' dramatic interpretation can pay attention to the dialectical, dialogical interaction in which each 'other' impinges upon its partner in transformative ways. That is, 'otherness' need not mean distance and severity, but can also mean dialectical, transformative engagement with.[61]

What Brueggemann seems to advocate here is a way of understanding divine revelation, of construing our knowledge of God and of life lived in conformity to God, that avoids the pitfalls of both foundationalism and anthropocentrism through recognition of its inherently dialogical nature. Our particular construals of divine reality are always partial and never exhaustive of that reality, and so they must always remain open and be subject to further interrogation and rearticulation.

The fundamental problem here, then, is theological, as it concerns the adequacy of a perspective like Hauerwas' to speak of and apprehend God. In an instructive engagement with Hauerwas and postmodern a/theologian Mark C. Taylor that helps further to develop these themes, Tyler Roberts highlights the renunciative character of theology. Though theology gives expression to the desire to know God, it must also continually bear in mind "the limitations and inadequacies of human thought and imagination before God. Insofar as theologians renounce the goal of their thought in the process of seeking that goal, their renunciation takes on the dynamics of resistance: theological thinking resists itself."[62] A full recognition of the renunciative character of theology affirms that God, the object of theological reflection and inquiry, is ultimately beyond the grasp of human reason and imagination. All theological statements are relative, finite, and, ultimately, inadequate. Roberts writes, "Theology speaks of the comfort and empowerment that accompanies the belief that God has redeemed humanity once and for all. But it also must resist this comfort, glorifying God precisely in *keeping itself open to those painful events and voices that might otherwise be erased or suppressed by convictions about how the story ends*."[63] Implicit in Roberts' recognition that our apprehension of God and theological truth is always imperfect and so subject to revision is the affirmation that we come more fully to know God as we attend to those who suffer and live on the margins. As the biblical prophets recognized, the epistemological is entwined with the ethical, as our knowing, theologically, is parasitic upon our attention to those at the margins.

Though one finds elements of renunciation in Hauerwas' thought (as in his resistance to liberalism's autonomous individual and claim that our desire can be rightly trained only as we learn to renounce the obsessive drive for mastery), insofar as he upholds desire for the stability provided by a distinctive and bounded understanding of Christian narrative, he cannot avail himself of this option to a sufficient degree. In general, one finds little adjustment in Hauerwas' thought in response to challenges from other quarters. His characteristic response to most critics is to accuse them of misunderstanding him or harboring problematic, generally liberal-modern, assumptions. I will discuss instances of this and related problems more fully in the next section. This is not to say that Hauerwas does not engage non-Christian or marginalized voices, but when he does he does not characteristically do so in a manner that problematizes how he understands the nature and implications of the Christian story. In *The Peaceable Kingdom*, for example, he concedes that "Christian convictions must remain open to challenge from sources outside the Christian community, since those convictions presuppose that this is God's world—for example, Christians may well learn from other traditions that our attempt to justify violence in the interest of protecting the innocent is finally self-contradictory."[64] While this may seem to be an important concession, his example here is telling, for it does not constitute a genuine challenge to what Hauerwas takes to be the proper vocation and identity of the Christian church. Indeed, it does little more than confirm it. At best, it is a rebuke to those who fail properly to embody what Hauerwas already takes to be the scripturally established demands of discipleship.

These responses to otherness can be traced to Hauerwas' tendency to evince a self-assuredness about his interpretation of the Christian story, and a concomitant general unwillingness to reexamine or readjust it in light of challenges. Because he believes that "the interpretive framework of the Christian faith" is pragmatically effective, he believes that it has the power to be effective for others, as well, "and that it ought therefore to be defended" in conversations with other traditions "rather than adjusted or departicularized."[65] Hauerwas follows Lindbeck's suggestion that because "no world is more real" for the Christian community than the one created by Scripture, the scriptural world is "able to absorb the universe" rather than be absorbed by it. Scripture "supplies the interpretive framework within which believers seek to live their lives and understand reality."[66] Yet, as Hauerwas takes up this claim, it is difficult to discern how genuine conversation with "others" can take place, conversation that, at least potentially, could enable the church to critique itself prophetically, and therefore give fuller expression to a reality that ultimately transcends its human mediation. By upholding a highly bounded notion of Christian community that fails to attend adequately to such voices, Hauerwas not only imperils his ability to speak the truth about God, but also his ability to give adequate expression to a prophetic account of justice.

JUSTICE: LIBERALISM, CONSTANTINIANISM, AND ATTENTION TO THE MARGINS

Biblically understood, prophetic justice is an expression of, and response to, God's steadfast love (*hesed*) for humanity, a love concerned, above all, with the needs of those in the community who are most vulnerable or marginal. In imitating God's bestowal of love upon humanity, then, biblical justice/righteousness is more holistic than, and radically outstrips, the predominantly abstract, individualistic, and appraisive character of dominant forms of secular justice.

Such affirmations, it may seem, are troublesome for Hauerwas, who is the author of a book with a subtitle that characterizes justice as a "bad idea."[67] Though he is generally troubled by dominant approaches to justice and rights, the difficulty, he claims, is not that Christians have no good word to say to those who suffer from injustice, but, rather, that, in the context of liberal modernity, the terms set for discussions of justice and rights suffer from the same problems of abstraction that characterize moral discourse generally. The adoption of modern, liberal assumptions, and accounts of justice leads to forms of Christianity that are essentially undifferentiated from the surrounding culture. But as Christians adopt the terms set by culture and so accommodate the church to culture in "Constantinian" fashion, they lose sight of their distinctive voice and fail to live as faithful and prophetic witnesses, or so he argues.

However, while Hauerwas thinks the abdication by Christians of their distinctive vocation leads to a "Constantinian" accommodation of the church to culture, many of his critics claim that his position leads to a problematic withdrawal of the church from social responsibility, to a political form of sectarianism. Hauerwas' church, it is argued, cannot address adequately problems of justice and injustice. In response, Hauerwas claims, persuasively, that he does not advocate the withdrawal of the church from social and political life; the church is rightly engaged in the political realm, but it must be there on its own terms. He errs, however, in holding that, whatever else such political engagement might amount to, it will be defined in stark contrast to liberal modernity. Once again, his work is defined by the erection of a strong cultural divide between the church and that which he alleges lies outside of it. This leads him to reject important insights about the nature and tasks of justice, and so imperils his prophetic credentials.

Challenges to a Christian Conception of Justice: Constantinian Accommodation

In both theory and practice, the characteristic idiom of liberalism is that of justice and rights; indeed, justice is often conceived almost wholly in terms of rights by many liberals. The problem for Hauerwas with liberal talk about justice and rights, however, is that it reflects the problems with abstraction that plague dominant modes of contemporary normative thinking. Rights talk, like most recent talk about justice more generally, "tends toward individualistic accounts of society and underwrites a view of human relations as exchanges rather than cooperative endeavors. Contemporary political theory has tended to concentrate on the language of rights, not because we have a vision of the good community, but because we do not."[68]

While Hauerwas does not claim that talk about justice is in principle incoherent, liberal conceptions of justice, with their customary emphasis upon rights, are particularly problematic because they are fundamentally constructed for strangers, for people who share neither a common history nor common purposes. Given the dominance of such abstract ways of speaking of rights and justice, Hauerwas contends that Christians need a more substantive, theologically thick language for responding to matters of injustice. In this manner, Christians will be provided with some means to avoid having "their imaginations captured by concepts of justice determined by the presuppositions of liberal societies."[69]

Tragically, Hauerwas argues, the church has failed to serve as an adequate resource for resistance to the conceits of liberal societies because all too often it has identified itself with them. Following John Howard Yoder, Hauerwas laments this "Constantinian captivity" of the church. By this, he and Yoder mean to highlight what they see as the church's tendency to understand itself as having a stake in shaping definitively the ethos of society, even when this entails the use of violence, rather than (properly) understanding itself as standing in a critical, often oppositional, relationship to entrenched forms of power.[70]

While the apostolic church, defined by distinctive beliefs and practices, occupied a minority position within society, with the "Constantinian shift" (which, though bearing the name of the emperor Constantine [300–337], began around the year 200 and took another two centuries fully to unfold[71]), one witnesses the rise of Christianity as an imperial religion and a concomitant rise in political accommodationism and loss of Christian distinctiveness. Yoder summarizes the shift succinctly, stating that "before Constantine, one knew as a fact of everyday experience that there was a believing Christian community but one had to 'take it on faith' that God was governing history. After Constantine, one had to believe without seeing that there was a community of believers, within the larger nominally Christian mass, but one knew for a fact that God was in control of history."[72] After Constantine, the nature of Christian moral argument and political engagement shifts decisively. Perhaps, the most significant aspect of this shift is the assumption that the church's identity and significance is derived in large part from its association with the state. The church under this scenario becomes an agent of political efficacy, measured in terms of the prosperity of the regime.[73]

In the centuries following Constantine, the configuration of the relationship between the church and political power has taken on a variety of forms, but, Hauerwas argues, a persistent theme remains. Even if institutionally separate, the church continues to be identified morally with the ends of the state.[74] Hauerwas thus characterizes the primary theme of twentieth-century Christian social ethics in America as "the Christian's responsibility for societal affairs," which, from Rauschenbusch to the present, has been understood in terms of one agenda: "to show why American democracy possesses distinctive religious status."[75] Tragically, this has meant that a concern of much recent Christian ethical thinking has been to discern when and to show why violence may be legitimately employed in defense of democracy and its constitutive values, such as liberty or justice. Unless Christians give up their

Constantinian habits of mind and recover a sense of their identity as a distinct minority within the wider culture, Hauerwas urges, they will fail to develop those "skills necessary to see how deeply they have been compromised by the assumption that their task is to rule, if not the government, at least the ethos of America."[76]

Political Sectarianism?

For those who charge him with sectarianism, however, this response from Hauerwas doubles the problems faced by the church. Such critics not only charge his position with imperiling realism, they also claim that he effectively removes the church from any actual political engagement. Thus, James Gustafson argues that Hauerwas' sectarianism "isolates Christianity from taking seriously the wider world of science and culture and limits the participation of Christians in the ambiguities of moral and social life in the patterns of interdependence in the world."[77] Similarly, Wilson Miscamble claims that because he understands the mission of the church in terms of "standing apart from society and witnessing to it," Hauerwas upholds an ecclesiology that "is quite sectarian." He "effectively removes the church from the life and death policy issues of the human community." But to withdraw in this manner from the world "in order to give witness does not remove one's culpability for what takes place in the world. Hauerwas, effectively, runs from responsibility."[78] And Max Stackhouse charges that, in rejecting liberalism, Hauerwas repudiates the view that theology is properly concerned with responding "to the intellectual and social challenges of our times, especially economic and social realities."[79] Christian identity, in short, comes at the expense of political engagement and social justice.

Hauerwas' response to charges of political sectarianism is in keeping with his response to charges of conventionalism, discussed earlier. If there is no abstract, neutral, or universal starting point for, or conception of, knowledge, then "there is no universal society and/or knowledge from which the so-called sect can dissent."[80] "Society," "culture," "politics," "public discourse," "social responsibility," "justice," and the like are all "thick" concepts that have meaning *only* in relation to particular communities and traditions, not in the abstract. What one finds in Hauerwas' work, he would claim, is not sectarianism, as this implies the possibility of specifying in a neutral manner an account of society, culture, and politics from which the church can withdraw. Instead, what one finds is a different or alternative understanding of culture, society, and politics that stands in competition with regnant liberal accounts. Rightly understood, then, the church is a competitor to the modern liberal account that currently prevails and is too often mistaken as the embodiment of "how things really are."

As I have already noted, Hauerwas understands his own position as a form of theological politics, in which the church is a *polis*, a political society in its own right, with its own distinctive substance, ends, and culture that does not withdraw from political engagement, but, rather, attempts to articulate its own distinctive brand of politics. So, while it is correct to understand him as denying that Christians have a stake in supporting the American liberal democratic status quo, and as affirming that the first task of the church is to be faithful to its own theological commitments, as Nigel Biggar has noted, "this does not amount to irresponsible indifference to the fate of the world and disengagement from the task of promoting its good. On the contrary, as Hauerwas sees it, it is the only way in which the Church can serve the world properly."[81]

On this understanding, the question for Christians is not *whether* they will engage the public realm in seeking to address questions of social justice, but, rather, *how* they will address such questions.[82] Though Hauerwas does not think it is possible to articulate a universal theory of justice, this does not mean that he thinks "the church should avoid attempts to articulate concretely how this or that society should respond to the widow, the orphan, and the ill. What is needed, however, is not a theory of justice to secure that, but a people with the virtue of justice developed through the training of being part of a good community."[83] Furthermore, Hauerwas grants that Christians may rightly engage the institutions and policies of the state that seek social justice, insofar as they are compatible with Christian identity,[84] but they should not think about the alleviation of suffering or the meeting of peoples' needs only through the resources of state power. In articulating its understanding of the nature and demands of justice, the church should not have its imagination stifled by prevailing societal options. Indeed, if it "takes seriously its own integrity, it may well help the societies in which it lives to have alternatives that are not part of the current social and political agenda."[85]

If Hauerwas is taken straightforwardly here, these sorts of claims seem to undermine, at least to a degree, some of his strong language about the Constantinian captivity of the church. We see here cracks in the wall that separates Hauerwas' church from the liberal state. Surely Hauerwas is right that responsiveness to need and opposition to injustice need not find expression only through the resources of state power. Grassroots social movements, in which churches have traditionally participated, as well as denominational and local congregational efforts, are surely crucial, sometimes neglected, avenues for the expression of social engagement and political imagination. But insofar as he concedes that the church may rightly and faithfully engage state institutions and policies on matters of social justice, he admits the possibility of the sort of Christian engagement with the state that seems to be precluded by his generally oppositional ecclesiology.

In light of such considerations, it is far from clear how assuming responsibility for societal affairs or upholding in some sense the religious importance of democracy or even (at times and in a critical manner) identifying the church's vocation with some of the ends of the state necessarily entails the Constantinian captivity of the church, as he claims elsewhere. The church's witness is fragile and subject to distortion, and so such engagement can never be assumed, and when it is undertaken, it must be done so in a highly critical manner that finds authorization in Christian convictions. But the strong contrasts that Hauerwas' conception of the church and characterization of Constantinianism seem to assume weaken in light of these concessions. His characterization of Constantinianism is overstated in a way that occludes appreciation of how the church can legitimately engage and even endorse the activities of the state.

Hauerwas, Feminism, and the Character of Prophetic Justice

Might this mean that Hauerwas should recognize that claims about justice, rights, and associated concepts may be more resonant with Christian convictions than he is generally prepared to admit? While it should, he tends to resist such a conclusion. Hauerwas is not particularly helpful in articulating what a distinctly Christian approach to seeking justice looks like, as there is no extended, constructive treatment in his work of the nature of justice, theologically understood, and what it might entail in terms of responding concretely to the legacies of such injustices as racism, sexism, and poverty. Where he does discuss such concrete matters at some length, he tends to take one of two approaches, both of which are largely guided by his determination to resist the pathologies of liberalism. His feminist critics, however, offer insights that offer a more constructive path forward.

When his treatments of Christian exponents of, or movements for, social justice are affirmative, he tends to identify as most salutary those aspects that resonate with his own concerns about liberalism. Thus, for example, in an essay on Martin Luther King Jr. and liberalism, what Hauerwas finds most significant about King is the centrality of memory in King's life and work and his refusal to subordinate his religious convictions to the demands of liberalism. While Hauerwas affirms King's use of "the best of American civil religion," and appears, in referring to him as "the ultimate *bricoleur*" to affirm his critical and selective use of the resources of liberalism and the state,[86] the primary lessons King teaches us are ones Hauerwas wants us to learn. If one of the central deficiencies of liberalism is its detachment of persons from those histories and communities that enable them to forge meaningful lives, Hauerwas argues, it is one of the great virtues of King's life and work, notwithstanding a (false) cultural narrative that makes him the hero of abstract liberal "freedom" and "equality," that he "sought freedom for African-Americans as a people to remember slavery and the triumph over slavery offered by the black church."[87]

Negatively, and more characteristically, Hauerwas is concerned to show how many contemporary Christian treatments of justice reflect the sorts of dead ends his work aspires to help us avoid. Thus, for example, he argues that Gustavo Gutiérrez's account of liberation, particularly its characterization of liberated persons as artisans of their own destiny and its advocacy of freedom from servitude,[88] sometimes "sounds more like that of Kant and the Enlightenment than it does of the Kingdom established by Christ." Hauerwas argues, in contrast, that Christians rightly seek "not a life free from suffering, free from servitude, but rather a life that freely suffers, that freely serves, because such suffering and service is the hallmark of the Kingdom established by Jesus." Service, not freedom, is the hallmark of Christian discipleship, "for it is only by serving that we discover the freedom offered by God . . . . [F]reedom literally comes from having our self-absorption challenged by the needs of another."[89] Similarly, to those who would seek to articulate a Christian affirmation of rights by claiming that a proper recognition of human worth entails that persons should not be left to beg, Hauerwas claims that Christians, in fact, are creatures who beg. "Through prayer Christians learn how to beg from one another. Christians, therefore, can never be at peace with a politics or economic arrangements built on the assumption that we are fundamentally not beggars."[90]

These are, to be sure, rhetorically provocative statements, but that is perhaps the limit of their force. I have little doubt that we should affirm with Hauerwas the significance of communally borne memory, and it seems clear that any adequate conception of freedom cannot simply reduce to freedom from all constraint, but Hauerwas again problematically *juxtaposes* Christianity with concepts that he generally seems able to understand only in liberal-modern terms. In his nearly wholesale rejection of concepts he associates with liberal modernity, he also rejects affirmations that have theological authorization and are crucial for a Christian articulation of the prophetic voice. Conceptions of freedom, equality, and liberation not wholly discontinuous with, and often indebted to, liberal modernity—even rights talk, which Hauerwas seems to reject altogether—may be affirmed on Christian grounds in some form.[91] There are often tensions, to be sure, between Christian and Enlightenment trajectories of thought, but there is much overlap and mutual influence, as well. This should hardly be surprising, as Christianity is an animating source of a number of the central commitments of modern moral and political thought. Basic commitments to the moral worth of the individual, human rights, and democracy that are characteristic of modern moral and political thought are unthinkable absent the influence of Christianity.[92] Even if they are subject to distortion, such concepts cannot simply be chucked without undermining concerns proper to theology, in general, and the prophetic voice, in particular.

An understanding of the necessity of such affirmations, even for Hauerwas' own position, is made clear by questions raised by some of his feminist critics. Linda Woodhead and Gloria Albrecht are chief among those feminist critics who contend that Hauerwas' thought is reflective of an essentially conservative, socially relative challenge to the deficiencies of liberalism. While the sorts of claims Hauerwas makes in response to Gutiérrez and those who would uphold the legitimacy of traditional rights claims may have real critical force for someone who shares Hauerwas' social standing as a fully enfranchised, white, upper-middle-class male, how are they applicable, they wonder, when directed to those who do not share such privileges? What would it mean, Woodhead asks, "to tell a working-class mother whose days are spent earning money as a 'care-worker', and whose evenings are taken up with looking after her own children and elderly mother that 'freedom literally comes by having our self-absorption challenged by the needs of another'?"[93] Likewise, what would it mean to tell a person who can feed herself and/or her family only by begging that Christians are creatures who beg? Claims about nearness to Christ are likely at best to be false consolation to such persons. Because he conflates concern for such matters with his negative characterization of liberalism, Hauerwas seems largely blind to such questions, yet it is precisely such questions that a prophetic consideration of justice will prioritize.

Not surprisingly, Hauerwas argues that what he finds most troublesome about feminist (and, by extension, other forms of liberation) theology is that "it is so often liberal Protestant theology in a different key."[94] Feminist theology, in other words, is problematic for Hauerwas not because it is concerned with the well-being of women, but because he argues it swallows whole cloth the wrong turns characteristic of modern theology in general. It denies "the intrinsic authority of the received tradition in order to gain critical independence."[95] It is, in short, characteristically modern and liberal in its prioritizing of the abstract, unencumbered individual, in whom resides authority. For feminist theology, according to Hauerwas, the individual is central and formative tradition is of little importance, save as the object of critical scrutiny.

Even if there are some elements of some feminist and liberationist theologies that merit further interrogation, it is a gross mischaracterization to equate such theologies with unencumbered individualism. This, in turn, leads Hauerwas to fail to appreciate the critical questions such theologies pose to his thought and the crucial insights they offer for thinking about the normative commitments of Christianity. Aspects of feminist and liberationist theologies are frequently receptive to core assumptions of modernity and liberalism, but, at their best, they seek to build upon and go beyond such assumptions. What most theorists of liberation, secular and sacred, seek is to resist *both* forms of individualism that threaten networks of intimacy and relational care *and* forms of community that fail to attend to the integrity of individuals. Most charitably understood, we might understand such theorists as seeking to articulate visions of truly liberating, truly just communities. Seeking liberation from constraints or from servitude in the manner feminist and liberation theologians seek does not entail liberation from *all* constraints or limits. Indeed, most contemporary theological feminists actively resist liberal individualism, assume the centrality of community as a context for moral knowledge and sharing, and are keenly attuned to the disastrous results that come from denying limits and seeking control.[96] As Sharon Welch has explained, "In the work of liberation theology, in the women's movement, in the work for civil rights and an end to racism, it is not limits *per se* that are questioned, but the [unfair] differential effects of those limits on the lives of women and men, rich and poor, white and black."[97] In short, what feminist and other liberation theologians seek is liberation from the *differential effects of imposed constraint*.

Hauerwas would do well to take more seriously these concerns of feminists and liberationists. He is surely right that Christians are to serve their neighbors, but there is all the difference in the world between genuine service to the neighbor and servility, at least as these terms are straightforwardly understood. In his critique of Gutiérrez, the distinctions between these two terms are rather fuzzy; they are even arguably conflated. When Hauerwas says that Christians do not seek to be free but to be of use, that freedom comes from having our self-absorption challenged by others, and that Christians are creatures who beg, he seems to extol self-sacrifice and self-abnegation as ends in themselves. While the cross rightly occupies a central place in his thought, and while forms of self-renunciation are central to discipleship formed by the witness of the gospel, these are not ends in themselves, nor are they self-sufficient expressions of the Good News.

A central problem here, one to which feminists and liberationists rightly call our attention, as seen in Woodhead's question to Hauerwas, is that such a focus encourages victims of injustice to accept their lot and discourages them from recognizing their agency. Insofar as a person's "service" at least partly or implicitly presupposes her servility, she is unable to offer genuine service.[98] Genuine service presupposes genuine agency and genuine agency presupposes a sense of one's own self-worth. It entails the sort of self-respect that is frequently compromised, if not effaced, in those who live under conditions of oppression. Similarly, the Christ-like life of suffering is a life that *freely* suffers, that *willingly* gives of the self for the good of the other. Service is rightly given to others, suffering is properly borne, and sacrifices are to be willingly made by Christians, but these actions reflect a *form of power*—what Sarah Coakley describes as a kenotic "power-in-vulnerability"[99]—that flows from, and gives expression to, a well-developed sense of agency. For Christians, this form of power is seen paradigmatically in Jesus' own giving away of his life, which was "an expression of the fullness of his relationship with God and of God's love for the world. Jesus' death in love, therefore, was not an act of self-denial, but an act of fullness, of living out his life and identity fully, even when that living would ultimately lead to death."[100]

In seeking, with feminist and liberation theologians, the liberation and the freedom of those who are most marginal and vulnerable, and in affirming their moral worth, Christians do not, or do not necessarily, imbibe the worst of liberal modernity. Rather, they give expression to the demand for justice that is rooted in the steadfast love of God and that affirms the integrity and the fullness of the life of those who are most marginal. As the provisions of the Year of Jubilees illustrate, for example, God's justice is a justice that seeks to provide for the needs of those oppressed or marginalized in the community by redressing injustice in a manner that approximates equality. Indeed, as I discussed previously, without such a concern for justice, the integrity of Israel's religious life was brought into question, as justice is the very substance of religious faith. Likewise, in taking up his prophetic vocation, Jesus Christ unmasked and resisted the regnant domination system (in Walter Wink's terminology) by upholding Kingdom values in which the fundamental sanctity of all persons was affirmed. This finds concrete illustration, for example, in the parable of the great dinner, clearly a metaphor for the Kingdom of God, and in Jesus' miracles, which were aimed, at least in part, at the satisfaction of people's concrete material needs. Without affirmations such as these, talk of service, suffering, and sacrifice, though central to Christian discipleship, is hollow and dangerous.

The justice-driven concern for the liberation of the marginalized that motivates Hauerwas' feminist critics leads them to claim, by contrast, that what we need is not a community with clear boundaries that largely defines itself as a distinct alternative to liberalism, but, rather, a conception of a complex, differentiated community within which the voices of the least can be heard. The challenge such critics, as well as the prophetic voice, pose to Hauerwas is not to eschew the church as the primary locus from which Christians engage the world, but, rather, to reconceive the church so that its character might be truly liberating, so that it might be truly focused upon, and seek to be responsive to, those who are marginal. In this way, it will be possible not only to give fuller expression to prophetic commitments to justice, but also to be more fully open to those others who may help the church to hear more fully God's truth.

The Turn to Radical Democracy: A Way Forward?

In recent writings, the often hard contrasts between the church and the world that have long-dominated Hauerwas' thought seem to be somewhat softened. While remaining as skeptical as ever about the compatibility of liberal democracy and Christian convictions, he has written affirmatively about the compatibility of radical democracy and Christian convictions. Key elements of these later writings might be taken to comport nicely with the kinds of affirmations about justice I have suggested are necessary and the vision of the church as a differentiated community to which I just gestured. Could this turn by Hauerwas mark a development in his thought that both enables him to speak about justice and conceive the church in a manner that better comports with the prophetic voice? There are hopeful openings in Hauerwas' work here, to be sure, but there is, nonetheless, reason to worry that this radical democratic turn is insufficient.

Perhaps, the earliest explicit expression of this turn is a 2006 essay in a *CrossCurrents* symposium on "Theology, Democracy, and the Project of Liberalism"; it is most extensively developed in a book Hauerwas jointly authored with Romand Coles, *Christianity, Democracy, and the Radical Ordinary*. In both spaces, he is pushed to be more receptive to the generative, dialogical, and open character of radical democracy, a move that could pay dividends from the perspective of the prophetic voice.

In the *CrossCurrents* symposium, Peter Dula and Alex Sider challenge Hauerwas' circumscribed ecclesiology and suggest important resonances between radical democracy and a radical ecclesiology. Despite Hauerwas' fierce criticism of Rawls' liberalism, they note that both Hauerwas and liberal democrats like Rawls tend to view conflict as something to be expunged and overcome in favor of a unity defined from the standpoint of some privileged position: In the case of Hauerwas, "the role of the discerning *ekklesia* is repeatedly invoked but often eclipsed by the offices of pastoral authority," and in the case of Rawls a *unum* is forged out of the *pluris* only through the "careful education of the people, largely in terms of normalizing a set of exclusions (as in Rawls' banishing of 'comprehensive doctrines')."[101]

In response, Dula and Sider prescribe a kind of communal conversation as the "radical" remedy needed to avoid such privileging and exclusion. "If education is required it consists of communities in conversation, where there is an unscripted openness to the flexibility of the unforeseeable."[102] A truly radical democratic politics and a truly radical ecclesiology will thus place a premium on openness, generosity, trust, and mutuality as defining virtues. Of course, such conversations are power-ridden, and so they must be particularly attentive to those whose voices are most often silenced. The forms of exclusion and imbalance that are part of communal conversations are not glossed over by radical democratic practices; instead, they are brought to the fore, as they and their effects become part of the argument itself.[103] Influenced especially by the work of John Howard Yoder, and Romand Coles' engagement with Yoder's work,[104] Dula and Sider suggest that such practices are constitutive of Christian convictions and ecclesial practices. The Gospel incarnates practices of vulnerability that are incomplete absent encounter with, and clarification through, encounters with otherness.[105] "There is no way to know in advance whether and how each particular encounter will be revelatory. Hence, the church cultivates dispositions of patient listening. Instead of the fear that openness to outsiders might ruin the church, Yoder exhibits the awareness that deafness to outsiders will ruin the church."[106]

In the *CrossCurrents* symposium, Hauerwas, despite long-standing trajectories of his thought that stand in tension with such a position, essentially says, "Me, too!," and claims to advocate "some form of 'radical democracy.'"[107] Writing in response to Jeffrey Stout's challenge to take democracy more seriously and to avoid conflating liberal theory with democratic practice,[108] Hauerwas, like Dula and Sider, derives inspiration from Yoder (and Coles' appropriation of Yoder), particularly Yoder's claims that the sinfulness of the church "requires a stance of constant reformation," and his insistence that the church must "care for and listen to the 'weakest' member."[109]

This affirmation is developed more explicitly and at greater length in *Christianity, Democracy, and the Radical Ordinary*, coauthored with Coles. There, Hauerwas writes approvingly of Yoder's vision of a church with permeable boundaries. The church rightly engages and seeks voices outside of it, but it cannot do so from the perspective of some general theory or strategy of engagement that grants a false security, lest it reproduce Constantinian habits.[110] Such engagement, he clarifies in this later writing, is not opposed to justice, but intimately connected to it: "What the church contributes to radical democracy is . . . a people who seek not glory but justice. Such a people have been made possible because they have been formed through liturgical action to be for the world what the world can become."[111] The church, however, is not a radical alternative to the world but a present possibility for it. And this possibility is not restricted to the church. In addition to its various ecclesial expressions, the slow and patient work of justice and a receptive politics of gentleness is exemplified by the work of the L'Arche community and the activism of the Industrial Areas Foundation and Student Nonviolent Coordinating Committee. The embrace of finitude and the rejection of control is no longer, it seems for Hauerwas, the exclusive domain of the church. Revelation, he now seems to grant, comes in many forms and multiple voices, not all of them ecclesial. However, such justice and such politics, in whatever concrete form they find expression, will be irreducibly peaceable.

While these recent moves by Hauerwas are welcome, questions remain about their sufficiency. In response to Hauerwas, Coles raises questions that resonate with my earlier characterization of Hauerwas' affirmative treatments of social justice. There, I suggested that when Hauerwas speaks in such a manner about social justice, he identifies as salutary those aspects that resonate with his own understandings. As I noted, Martin Luther King, Jr. is helpful because King teaches us lessons Hauerwas wants us to learn. As Coles writes, "It remains unclear what you might be saying you have to learn from radical-democratic practices . . . . [O]ne could wonder, what and how does Hauerwas learn from radical democrats if what he learns is that Christians have always been, insofar as they were Christians, what could be called radical democrats?"[112] This underestimates the degree to which traditions distinct from Christianity might offer patterns of radical democratic practice and commitment different from, and even superior to, those found within Christianity.[113]

Additionally, some of the language Hauerwas uses continues to raise worries. In a footnote, he writes that he and Yoder are "theocrats. It is just very hard to rule when you are committed to nonviolence. But we are willing to try. 'Try,' however, means that politics is always a matter of persuasion."[114] This sort of language understandably evokes concern. It is language that seems to continue to harbor the conceit that the church rightly maintains a well-defined identity that provides a metanarrative able to outnarrate and incorporate all other competing narratives. It expresses a confidence, Coles notes, "that the church has within its history ample resources for every eventuality it faces." This, however, could easily have the effect of shutting "the door to other people's traditions and stories" from which Christians have much to learn. Ethical practice, Coles suggests, requires a "slackening" of the will to retain identity.[115]

A reasonable assessment of Hauerwas' recent "radical democratic" turn, then, seems to be that, while there are welcome gestures here to receptive generosity and an affirmative understanding of justice focused on the marginalized and excluded, he has not yet overcome some of the habits of mind and conceptual moves that limit the ability of his work to serve as an adequate contemporary expression of the prophetic voice. This is further underscored by his continued insistence that the church is defined by its pacifism.

VIOLENCE/NONVIOLENCE: CHRISTOLOGICAL PACIFISM V. THE NATION-STATE

Can violence ever serve the ends of prophetic justice? In the previous chapter, I circled around issues related to this question, but I did not address it directly, and so it remains unanswered. I argued that Walzer's conventionalist ethic upholds the centrality of the political community in a manner that is incompatible with prophetic commitments, as in its defense of "supreme emergency," but I did not argue that political violence is necessarily and always illicit. It is no longer possible to be silent on this question, however, for Hauerwas' work is centrally animated, as I have noted, by a particular vision of the church as a peaceable community that follows Christ by renouncing all resort to violence, even violence in defense of justice. While Hauerwas' vision of the peaceable vocation of the church is animated by his understanding of the person and work of Christ, it is also importantly shaped by his wish to resist the often violent character of the liberal nation-state and his worries about the church's Constantinian complicity with it. Unfortunately, particularly in light of the prophetic voice's concern for justice and its encompassing vision of peace, Hauerwas' account of peaceableness is overly narrow. A narrow reading of Scripture, a reading that is exacerbated through its coupling with a narrow understanding of the nation-state, underestimates the possibilities for, and responsibilities of, faithful participation in the political order. While nonviolence is generally preferable for a host of practical and theological reasons, it is possible, I will argue, to uphold highly circumscribed forms of violence, as in a just war, as faithful responses in responding to evil and seeking to secure basic justice and civic peace.

Christological Pacifism, the Nation-State, and Living "Out of Control"

As previously noted, Hauerwas claims that the defining characteristic of Christian community is its nonviolent character. Properly understood, living as a disciple of Christ entails pacifism. This "Christological pacifism"[116] is not rooted in philosophical presuppositions or arguments about the ineffectiveness of violence or the inherent rights of individuals not to be harmed, but, rather, in claims about the nature and demands of discipleship. Christians are called to be like Jesus, and Jesus, as the embodiment of God's peace, refused all recourse to violence, finding true power instead in God's forgiveness and mercy: "Through Jesus' life and teachings we see how the church came to understand that God's kingship and power consists not in coercion but in God's willingness to forgive and have mercy on us . . . Jesus challenged . . . the militaristic . . . notions of what God's kingdom required . . . by denying the right of violence even if attacked."[117] In refusing to resort to violence, Christians thus "live as God lives." Christian pacifism is above all "an affirmation that God wills to rule his creation not through violence and coercion but by love."[118]

Christians are able to refuse violence and follow Christ, Hauerwas argues, precisely because Christ has inaugurated a new history. This aspect of Hauerwas' Christological nonviolence is parasitic upon distinct eschatological claims. Jesus represents the inauguration of a new age in that he embodies, and makes present and possible to others, the reality of God's Kingdom.[119] "The eschatology of the New Testament rests not in the conviction that the kingdom has not fully come, but that it has. What is required is not a belief in some ideal amid the ambiguities of history, but rather the recognition that we have entered a period in which two ages overlap." These two ages exist simultaneously and each possesses its own distinct social manifestation. One, manifested by "the world," points backward to human history outside of Christ, while the other, manifested by the church as the body of Christ, points forward to the fulfillment of the Kingdom of God.[120] The vocation of the church, as the first fruits of the Kingdom realized in and through Christ, is to embody this latter history, a history radically different from that of the world. Jesus, then, is "God's decisive eschatological act," in whose resurrection "we see God's peace as a present reality." Though the peace envisioned in Isaiah 11 is not yet fully present in the *world*, Christians "believe nonetheless that peace has been made possible by the resurrection. Through this crucified but resurrected savior we see that God offers to all the possibility of living in peace by the power of forgiveness."[121] The primary task of the *church* is to witness to that peace.

Not surprisingly, these theological claims derive much of their force and intelligibility against the backdrop of what he judges to be problems that attend the liberal nation-state. "The world" and its deficiencies are manifested particularly in the liberal democratic nation-state and its assumptions. Even liberal democracies, Hauerwas contends, are dependent upon war not only for their ongoing existence in a threatening world, but for their very moral coherence. In a morally fragmented world, the nation-state derives much of its attractiveness, he claims, from that fact that it offers a context through which otherwise disconnected individuals may forge a common life together by telling stories about the goods they have come to share through the sacrifices of their forebears. In this context, war provides the citizens of nation-states with "a niche within an ongoing history. War is our ultimate comfort in a world without a history for it provides us with a story. To be sure it may be a hard and even gruesome story, but such a story is better than no story at all."[122]

Christian defenses of violence, even when couched in the terms of the just war tradition, are unfaithful, Hauerwas claims, because they assume a false history by making the nation-state and its legitimation of violence the center of history. It is not the nation, however, but the church, *properly understood*, that is able rightly to describe and respond to the reality of war. The history of the nation-state is finally a false history, "the history of godlessness." The church, by contrast, helps us to see war for what it is: "the desire to be rid of God, to claim for ourselves the power to determine our meaning and destiny[.] Our desire to protect ourselves from our enemies, to eliminate our enemies in the name of protecting the common history we share with our friends, is but the manifestation of our hatred of God."[123] Insofar as they lead to the adoption of violence, the conceits of the nation-state are fundamentally discontinuous with the nature and mission of the church, and the latter is obscured when it is identified with the former.

Though Hauerwas' rhetoric is certainly immoderate here, to a degree that may obscure his respect for Christian theologians who do uphold the possibility of justifiable political violence, it is clear that he believes that Christian defenses of war and violence fundamentally undermine the virtues he affirms as constitutive of the church as a peaceable community, and so finally represent a lack of faith, or at least a misplaced faith. Reflecting his concern with the Constantinian pretentions of the church, Hauerwas would claim that though such defenses of violence may be made in the name of a justice seeking a truer, more secure peace, it is not the job of Christians to secure peace, to make the world the Kingdom, for that has already been accomplished by God in Christ. Christians do not "seek justice from the barrel of a gun" because "God does not rule creation through coercion, but through a cross." As a people conformed to such a God, they must learn to "live out of control." This does not mean that Christians do not seek justice in the world, but they do not do so under the illusion of an omnipotence that assumes that their task "is to make history come out right."[124]

I have already noted that Hauerwas claims that the peaceable church is itself a polity; his pacifism is the content of his distinctly ecclesial politics. The patience and hope that lie at the center of such a politics affirm the importance, Hauerwas asserts, of the *gestural and trivial*, for it is through simple, everyday gestures and trivial practices (e.g., nurturing friendships, serving neighbors, patiently caring for those in need[125]) that the church learns and embodies its constitutive virtues and creates the time and space necessary for peace. He claims that

> nothing in life is more important than gestures, as gestures embody as well as sustain the valuable and significant. Through gestures we create and form our worlds. Through gestures we make contact with one another and share common tasks. Through gestures we communicate and learn from each other the limits of our world. In this sense, the church is but God's gesture on behalf of the world to create a space and time in which we might have a foretaste of the Kingdom. It is through gestures that we learn the nature of the story that is the very content and constitution of that Kingdom.[126]

In the same vein, by recognizing the sacredness of those sorts of ordinary, everyday practices that constitute a gestural politics the church can pose a "determinative *political* challenge to our culture."[127] By recognizing the significance of the seemingly trivial, we are given the power to reclaim our lives from the power of the "totalitarians" who would otherwise impose their claims upon us. Such recognition is a refusal of such claims that creates "the space and time that makes politics humane. Therefore, there is nothing more important for us to do" when confronted with threats to our existence "than to go on living—that is, to take time to enjoy a walk with a friend, to read all of Trollope's novels, to maintain universities, to have and care for children, and most importantly, to worship God."[128]

Love, Justice, and Political Violence

But it is the significance of just such seemingly trivial, everyday practices that may lead one to affirm not only the significance of the nation-state, but also the possible licitness of a just war. Jean Elshtain, for example, notes that she was reminded of the crucial purposes of government in the wake of the terrorist attacks of September 11, 2001. Her reflections are worth quoting at length here, for they are part of an argument that affirms the possibility of a just war, and thus stand in clear contrast to Hauerwas' central claims, but they resonate in important ways with his affirmations of the ordinary and trivial. "The shepherd," Elshtain writes,

> is charged with protecting the flock. None of the goods human beings cherish, including the free exercise of religion, can flourish absent a measure of civic peace and security. If evil is permitted to grow, good goes into hiding. Evildoers that lurk and plot in the darkness and secret, that operate stealthily, and that refuse to accept responsibility for wrongdoing perpetrate harm beyond the immediate violent event. It is they who would force good into hiding as we retreat behind closed doors. What good do I have in mind? The simple but profound good that is moms and dads raising their children, men and women going to work, citizens of a great city making their way on streets and subways, ordinary people buying airplane tickets in order to visit the grandkids in California, men and women en route to transact business with colleagues in other cities, the faithful attending their churches, synagogues, and mosques without fear. Make no mistake about it, this basic civic peace is a great good.[129]

This shepherd, of course, is the civil authority, the nation-state. Though the peace properly protected by the civil authority is not the peace of the Kingdom, it can offer this-worldly intimations of that just peace and so "is a good to be cherished and not to make light of."[130]

Elshtain upholds here a claim central to just war theory, namely, that the nation-state properly acts, sometimes in a violently coercive fashion, to build and secure justice and a basic civic peace. Hauerwas would of course demur here, but it must be asked, if Elshtain is right about the necessity of the civil authority to secure the basic peace that allows one to pursue those ordinary, but great, goods that he and she both affirm, whether he can reject the possibility of licit state violence without encountering problems.

The point here is not to fetishize the nation-state by making it the primary good in the manner Walzer does in his defense of supreme emergency, nor is it to uphold a Constantinian subversion of the church to the ends of the nation-state. No civil authority is due unquestioned, uncritical allegiance, and at their best Christian articulations of just war theory provide important leverage for criticizing the state, even while recognizing the goods it helps to secure. Christians properly resist the demands of the nation-state when they cannot be made to cohere with one's Christian commitments, as citizenship in the Kingdom of God possesses priority for the Christian over all other competing allegiances. We do, however, rightly recognize that though peace fully realized is marked by the absence of violence—this is always the ultimate end to which we should aspire—we insist upon nonviolence proximately "only so long as nothing of superior moral import (e.g., justice) is sacrificed."[131]

At their most theologically compelling, claims about the licitness of political violence are most fundamentally underwritten by considerations about the demands of love and justice for the neighbor in a fallen, conflictual world. First of all and most of the time, social goods and goals will be sought and secured through non-coercive forms of cooperation and/or negotiation. But the position Elshtain and most other theologians throughout the history of the Christian church defend is one that recognizes that political violence, properly motivated and limited, may be a legitimate tool of justice in defending innocent life from overwhelming threats. On this view, while states and their proxies are constrained in what they may do—among other things, they may never (*pace* Walzer) directly target innocent life, nor may they inflict harm that is disproportionate to the expected good to be achieved—we do properly endorse and participate in political violence if its use is the last available means for rebutting imminent threats to the well-being of innocent others, and if it can be done without hating our enemies. Indeed, in such cases, the use of violence is an expression of neighbor love.[132] Paradigmatic examples of this include the use of force (though not all particular justifications or instances of the use of force) by the allies in response to the horrors of Nazism during World War II, and by the NATO democracies in response to genocide in Kosovo in the closing years of the twentieth century. In such cases, the just war theorist argues, political violence aimed at rebutting barbaric pretensions may be justifiable both to protect innocent life against imminent threats and to establish true peace and justice, or at least to sow the soil for their seeds.

Hauerwas would likely claim that such arguments about civic peace are overstated, but, more importantly, he would claim that such Christian defenses of justifiable violence run aground because they are bad theology, for they fail to recognize the proper eschatological and Christological context of a Christian understanding of peace. This is, indeed, the fundamental issue at hand here, for it shapes how one reads and appropriates the scriptural witness. In her essay, Elshtain admits that the civic peace she defends "is not the peace of the kingdom promised by scripture. That awaits the end-time."[133] The vision of peace one finds summed up by the Old Testament understanding of *shalom*, in which swords are beaten into plowshares, in which the lion and lamb lie down together, in which enemies are reconciled to one another, is an eschatological vision that has yet to be realized. In the meantime, she observes, following Martin Luther, if we think the lion can now lie with the lamb, the lamb will have to be replaced frequently.[134]

We can grant, with Hauerwas, that the Kingdom is fully present and realized *in Christ*, and we can grant, further, that, *though imperfect and incomplete*, expressions of life in the peaceable kingdom are a present possibilities. We need not hold, as Reinhold Niebuhr does in some of his early work, that life in the Kingdom of God is an impossible ethical ideal that cannot be put into actual practice or approximated in this life.[135] Scripture, particularly the Sermon on the Mount, does clearly depict the Kingdom as fully realized in Christ. This should be clear from the discussion of the first chapter. But this exegetical claim does not settle the hermeneutical question of how that fact is to be appropriated by Christians seeking today to live as Christ's disciples. Hauerwas moves too quickly from a particular and not wholly rigorous reading of scripture[136] to prescribing and proscribing conduct. The church *does* rightly seek first of all to live peaceably. Forgiveness and reconciliation *are* often present possibilities that are ingredient to the church's temporal witness. Nevertheless, while it is through such commitments and practices that the church begins to establish temporally God's eschatological promises, in history the complete wholeness anticipated in the Hebrew vision of *shalom* and glimpsed in Christ ultimately eludes us.

The practical implication of Hauerwas' defense of pacifism is that he would permit the suffering and sacrifice of innocent lives for the sake of the purity of a religious vision. It is one thing to enjoin the acceptance of sacrifice and suffering for oneself, but another to assume such a fate for others. Elshtain asks, "Can I morally justify risking the lives of those not known to me—whether some of my fellow citizens or a group of foreigners who speak a different tongue, but are nonetheless children of God—in order to vindicate my principles?"[137] Her answer, and that of just war theorists, generally, is a resounding "No." In short, the costs associated with Hauerwas' appropriation of scripture are exceedingly high. This is not a merely practical judgment, concerned to measure and weigh the costs of competing options against one another. It is most especially a theological judgment that, in this time between the times, it would finally be *unloving*—out of step with the Christological demand to love one's neighbor *and* one's enemy[138]—to allow torment and abuse to be visited upon innocents, even if violent intervention is the only practicable means of rebutting that torment and abuse. Indeed, Hauerwas' thoroughgoing pacifism seems to entail either (1) an instance of free ridership as Christians unfairly takes advantage of others' protection of the civic peace upon which their practices depend, or (2) a fundamental threat to civic peace and stability as Christians absent themselves from the civil state and so "inspire fear in others not similarly at liberty."[139]

Lacking from Hauerwas' account is an adequate reckoning with the reality of sin, and how this shapes how the church serves as an agent of reconciliation in the world. In a recent critical engagement with the just peacemaking paradigm in Christian ethics, a paradigm that shares many common concerns with Hauerwas (and that I will discuss at greater length later in the final chapter), Lisa Cahill urges that a recognition of the sinfulness of humanity in the world must be interposed between that paradigm's commitment to a life of discipleship grounded in the life, death, and resurrection of Jesus and its commitment to further God's reign through the pursuit of justice. In seeking, out of Christian love, to protect the vulnerable, coercion may be necessary. Ideally, this will be achieved without physical violence, through such means as boycotts or economic pressure, but in cases of extreme and imminent threat (Cahill mentions genocide and terrorism), physical force may be necessary.[140] The dose of Augustinian/Niebuhrian realism commended here ought not to be understood as a concession of ethics to politics or as handing the demands of discipleship over to the realm of consequentialist calculation;[141] rather, it is simply meant to urge an awareness of the difficult fragility of engaging in the transformative work of love in the context of a sinful humanity.

This side of the fullness of the Kingdom, it is not possible, as Hauerwas seeks to do, to posit strict divisions between how "church" and "world"[142] or "church" and "nation-state" understand and engage or reject violent means. Our citizenship is dual and intermingled. Following Augustine, the progenitor of Christian thinking about the licitness of political violence, we can affirm that because Christians' ultimate citizenship is in the Heavenly City of God, they are "pilgrims" or "resident aliens" in their earthly cities, but "so long as the two cities are intermingled" they "make use of the peace of Babylon . . . . [T]he temporal peace of the meantime . . . is shared by good and bad alike."[143] We are returned, then, to considerations about how best to serve the neighbor under the fragile and fallible conditions of civic peace. While such peace is not the peace of the Kingdom, for it may at times call for the utilization of violent means in its defense, it "offers intimations of eschatological peace and is a good to be cherished and not to be made light of."[144] The demand to secure the civic peace as an expression of love and justice for the neighbor under such fallen conditions may sometimes permit the use of violence in her defense.

CONCLUSION

For Hauerwas, the church is central. It is *the* communal context that provides a unique standpoint through which a distinctive vision of truth can find embodiment and expression. On its face, this resonates in important ways with assumptions that underlie the biblical prophetic witness. Just as Israel assumed an organic connection between its understanding of God's character and activity in the world and its communal structures and practices, Hauerwas contends that the church, as the primary locus of Christian identity and practice, is defined by the truthful story that begins with God's dealings with Israel and finds its culmination in the life, death, and resurrection of Jesus Christ. Furthermore, in his resolute opposition of the church to liberal modernity, Hauerwas' thought may seem in its rhetorical structure to resemble the prophet versus king conflicts that often typify Old Testament expressions of the prophetic.

However, functionally, the church occupies a place in his thought similar to that of the political community in Walzer's. This leads him to defend what looks a lot like an identity politics that harbors an "incipient ecclesial triumphalism . . . that insists we have all the answers already."[145] In contrasting the church with liberalism in his characteristic manner, Hauerwas tends to articulate its identity in terms of a cultural boundary that stands in discontinuous relation with other forms of identity. It is through formation by the narratives and practices of the church, unsullied by the false stories of "the world," that one learns what it means to be Christian. This has the effect of heightening the distinctiveness of Christian communal identity and its linguistic practices, making a particular expression of Christian truth the primary object of Hauerwas' attention.

The danger, here, however, seen in his general unwillingness to revise or adjust his understanding of the church in light of competing understandings or criticisms, is that Hauerwas adheres to a notion of community focused upon reception, preservation, and repetition, rather than one that emphasizes a forward-looking standpoint, like that of the prophetic (recall Jesus' own revisions of his received religious tradition), that recognizes the need for ever fresh, though faithful, articulations of tradition, particularly as it encounters voices of "others."[146] While Hauerwas is surely right to emphasize the significance of the church in mediating and forming Christian identity and practice, a theologically adequate rendering of the prophetic will be concerned to guard against the identification of this social mediation of reality, the church, with reality itself, God.

His ecclesiology leads, in turn, to problems with the prophetic adequacy of his normative commitments. His characterization of calls for justice and liberation as reflective of modern corruptions of true Christian identity blinds him to how those on society's margins might be Good News for the church, challenging it in unexpected ways, offering to it new sources of revelation that call it out of itself, thereby expanding its practices to be more inclusive and just, in ways congruent with its true identity and mission, and more fully reflective of the reality that animates it. Similarly, while the peaceable thrust of Hauerwas' thought is powerful and resonates in some key respects with the peaceable thrust of the prophetic voice, his wholesale rejection of limited violence as a work of love and justice in defense of the vulnerable neighbor is problematic. Though Christians seek to be a peaceable presence in the world primarily through practices of forgiveness and reconciliation, true peace is eschatological. It follows from the doing of justice, which may *in extremis* require violent intervention to rebut torment and abuse.

Despite these problems, Hauerwas' attention to the church and its peaceable witness is significant. With him, we do well to recognize that a compelling contemporary theological expression of the prophetic voice *will* have an ecclesiological focus. This is because, as already noted, both the biblical witness and Hauerwas contend that responsiveness to God's character and actions properly finds communal expression and embodiment. Likewise, though Hauerwas' pacifism is problematic from the standpoint of the prophetic concern for justice and true peace, his resolute commitment to peaceableness does serve as a reminder that it is first of all and finally forgiveness and reconciliation that define Christian social witness.

NOTES

1. Michael J. Quirk, "Beyond Sectarianism?," *Theology Today* 44, no. 1 (April 1987): 79.

2. Stanley Hauerwas, *The Peaceable Kingdom: A Primer in Christian Ethics* (Notre Dame: University of Notre Dame Press, 1983), xxi.

3. Stanley Hauerwas, "Introduction," in his *Against the Nations: War and Survival in a Liberal Society* (Notre Dame: University of Notre Dame Press, 1992), 1–2.

4. George A. Lindbeck, *The Nature of Doctrine: Religion and Theology in a Postliberal Age* (Philadelphia: The Westminster Press, 1984), 135. For a good discussion of postliberalism, generally, and of Hauerwas as a postliberal, in particular, see William C. Placher, "Postliberal Theology," in *The Modern Theologians: An Introduction to Christian Theology in the Twentieth Century*, second edition, ed. David F. Ford (Oxford: Blackwell, 1997), 343–356.

5. Arne Rasmusson, *The Church as* Polis*: From Political Theology to Theological Politics as Exemplified by Jürgen Moltmann and Stanley Hauerwas* (Notre

Dame: University of Notre Dame Press, 1995), 248. For other interpretations of Hauerwas' work as framed by an opposition between liberalism, on the one hand, and the community of virtue called the church, on the other, see Todd Whitmore, "Beyond Liberalism and Communitarianism in Christian Ethics: A Critique of Stanley Hauerwas," *The Annual of the Society of Christian Ethics* (1989): 207–225; Christopher Beem, "American Liberalism and the Christian Church: Stanley Hauerwas vs. Martin Luther King Jr.," *Journal of Religious Ethics* 23, no. 1 (Spring 1995): 119–133; David Fergusson, *Community, Liberalism and Christian Ethics* (Cambridge: Cambridge University Press, 1998), Chapter 3; and Douglas Harink, "For or Against the Nations: Yoder and Hauerwas, What's the Difference?," *Toronto Journal of Theology* 17, no. 1 (Summer 2001): 167–185.

6. Stanley M. Hauerwas, "Creation, Contingency, and Truthful Nonviolence: A Milbankian Reflection," in his *Wilderness Wanderings: Probing Twentieth-Century Theology and Philosophy* (Boulder, CO: Westview Press, 1997), 197 n7.

7. For representative discussions, see Hauerwas, "Introduction," *Against the Nations* and Stanley Hauerwas, "The Church and Liberal Democracy: The Moral Limits of a Secular Polity," in his *A Community of Character: Toward a Constructive Christian Social Ethic* (Notre Dame: University of Notre Dame Press, 1981), 72–86.

8. Stanley Hauerwas (with David Burrell), "From System to Story: An Alternative Patter for Rationality in Ethics," in his *Truthfulness and Tragedy: Further Investigations into Christian Ethics* (Notre Dame: University of Notre Dame Press, 1977), 16.

9. Ibid., 17.

10. Here, they follow Edmund L. Pincoffs, *Quandaries and Virtues: Against Reductivism in Ethics* (Lawrence: University Press of Kansas, 1986), esp. Chapter 1, "Quandary Ethics."

11. Hauerwas, "From System to Story," 18.

12. Ibid., 24.

13. Ibid., 21.

14. Ibid., 22.

15. Hauerwas, *The Peaceable Kingdom*, 5–6.

16. Ibid., 144.

17. Stanley Hauerwas, "Going Forward By Looking Back: Agency Reconsidered," in his *Sanctify Them in the Truth: Holiness Exemplified* (Nashville: Abingdon Press, 1998), 93.

18. Ibid., 95.

19. Hauerwas, *The Peaceable Kingdom*, 35.

20. See, for example Ibid., 36–44.

21. Gloria Albrecht, *The Character of Our Communities: Toward an Ethic of Liberation for the Church* (Nashville: Abingdon Press, 1995), 44.

22. Hauerwas, *The Peaceable Kingdom*, 74.

23. Ibid., 29–30.

24. Hauerwas, "Introduction," *Against the Nations*, 5. See Lindbeck, *The Nature of Doctrine*, 129. For instructive discussion of the relationship between Lindbeck and Hauerwas, see Samuel Wells, *Transforming Fate Into Destiny: The Theological Ethics of Stanley Hauerwas* (Carlisle, UK: Paternoster Press, 1998), 52–61; and

Emmanuel Katongole, *Beyond Universal Reason: The Relation Between Religion and Ethics in the Work of Stanley Hauerwas* (Notre Dame: University of Notre Dame Press, 2000), 203–213.

25. Brad J. Kallenberg, *Ethics as Grammar: Changing the Postmodern Subject* (Notre Dame: University of Notre Dame Press, 2001), 221.

26. Ibid., 230.

27. Hauerwas, *The Peaceable Kingdom*, 76.

28. Stanley Hauerwas, "Pacifism: Some Philosophical Considerations," *Faith and Philosophy* 2, no. 2 (April 1985): 99.

29. Hauerwas, *The Peaceable Kingdom*, 88–89. Emphasis added.

30. On these virtues, see Hauerwas, *The Peaceable Kingdom*, 89, 103; and Stanley Hauerwas, "Peacemaking: The Virtue of the Church," and "Hope Faces Power: Thomas More and the King of England," both in his *Christian Existence Today: Essays on Church, World, and Living In Between* (Durham, NC: The Labyrinth Press, 1988), 93–94, 201.

31. Hauerwas, *The Peaceable Kingdom*, 86.

32. Ibid., 105.

33. Ibid., 102.

34. Stanley Hauerwas, "Introduction," in his *In Good Company: The Church as* Polis (Notre Dame: University of Notre Dame Press, 1995), 6.

35. Hauerwas, *The Peaceable Kingdom*, 100–101.

36. Philip D. Kenneson, *Beyond Sectarianism: Re-Imagining Church and World* (Harrisburg, PA: Trinity Press International, 1999), 87.

37. Stanley Hauerwas, "The Pastor as Prophet: Ethical Reflections on an Improbable Mission," in *Christian Existence Today*, 158.

38. Kathryn Tanner, *Theories of Culture: A New Agenda for Theology* (Minneapolis: Fortress Press, 1997), 104–105.

39. Hauerwas, "Introduction," in *Against the Nations*, 6–7.

40. Stanley Hauerwas, "The Sanctified Body: Why Perfection Does Not Require a 'Self,'" in *Sanctify Them in the Truth*, 79, 80.

41. Ibid., 82. In his discussion of Paul on the embodied nature of the church, Hauerwas relies upon Dale Martin's, *The Corinthian Body* (New Haven: Yale University Press, 1995).

42. Ibid., 83. Hauerwas is here quoting Martin, *The Corinthian Body*, 170. For a recent instructive discussion of Hauerwas' ecclesiology and its constrastive nature, see Nicholas M. Healy, *Hauerwas: A (Very) Critical Introduction* (Grand Rapids, MI: William B. Eerdmans Pub. Co., 2014), esp. Chapters 2 and 3.

43. Lindbeck, *The Nature of Doctrine*, 130–131.

44. Stanley Hauerwas, "Introduction," in *Truthfulness and Tragedy*, 9.

45. Stanley Hauerwas, "Why the Truth Demands Truthfulness: An Imperious Engagement with Hartt," in *Why Narrative? Readings in Narrative Theology*, ed. Stanley Hauerwas and L. Gregory Jones (Grand Rapids, MI: William B. Eerdmans Publishing Co., 1989), 304–305. Passages slightly rearranged. For Hartt's critique, see his "Theological Investments in Story: Some Comments on Recent Developments and Some Proposals," in *Why Narrative?*, esp. 286ff.

46. Stanley Hauerwas, "The Truth About God: The Decalogue as Condition for Truthful Speech," in *Sanctify Them in the Truth*, 43, 44.

47. Hauerwas, "From System to Story," 35–36.

48. James M. Gustafson, "The Sectarian Temptation: Reflections on Theology, the Church and the University," *Proceedings of the Catholic Theological Society of America* 40 (1985): 83–84.

49. Ibid., 92.

50. For this characterization, see Ibid., 85.

51. Ibid., 86.

52. Ibid., 92–93.

53. Timothy A. Beach-Verhey, "Exemplifying Public Discourse: Christian Faith, American Democracy, and Martin Luther King Jr.," *Journal of the Society of Christian Ethics* 24, no. 2 (Fall/Winter 2004): 121.

54. Stanley Hauerwas, "On Keeping Theological Ethics Theological," in *Against the Nations*, 43. The reference here is to Gustafson's 1981 Nora and Edward Ryerson Lecture, "Say Something Theological!" delivered at the University of Chicago on April 28, 1981.

55. Katongole, *Beyond Universal Reason*, 254.

56. Hauerwas, "On Keeping Theological Ethics Theological," 42.

57. For an instructive, if not entirely charitable, discussion of these matters, see Scott Smith, "Hauerwas and Kallenberg and the Issue of Epistemic Access to an Extra-Linguistic Realm," *The Heythrop Journal* 45, no. 3 (July 2004): 305–326.

58. Wells, *Transforming Fate into Destiny*, 79–80.

59. Fergusson, *Community, Liberalism and Christian Ethics*, 70–71.

60. Wells, *Transforming Fate into Destiny*, 80 n44.

61. Walter Brueggemann, *Texts Under Negotiation: The Bible and the Postmodern Imagination* (Minneapolis: Fortress Press, 1993), 106 n19.

62. Tyler T. Roberts, "Theology and the Ascetic Imperative: Narrative and Renunciation in Taylor and Hauerwas," *Modern Theology* 9, no. 2 (April 1993): 182.

63. Ibid., 193–194. Emphasis added.

64. Hauerwas, *The Peaceable Kingdom*, 120.

65. Terrence P. Reynolds, "A Conversation Worth Having: Hauerwas and Gustafson on Substance in Theological Ethics," *Journal of Religious Ethics* 28, no. 3 (Fall 2000): 408.

66. Lindbeck, *The Nature of Doctrine*, 117. See Hauerwas, "Introduction," *Against the Nations*, and *The Peaceable Kingdom*, 98.

67. Stanley Hauerwas, *After Christendom? How the Church is to Behave if Freedom, Justice, and a Christian Nation Are Bad Ideas* (Nashville: Abingdon Press, 1991).

68. Stanley Hauerwas, "On the 'Right' to be Tribal," *Christian Scholar's Review* 16, no. 3 (March 1987): 238. See also Stanley Hauerwas, "Should Christians Talk So Much About Justice?," *Books and Religion* 14, nos. 5–6 (1986): 14. Stephen Macedo, "Hauerwas, Liberalism, and Public Reason: Terms of Engagement?," *Law and Contemporary Problems* 75, no. 4 (2012): 161–180, argues that Hauerwas' treatment of liberalism is a caricature that is more misleading than helpful. "Just as he seeks to

understand Christianity at its best, I would say that we owe the same treatment to liberalism. Both, after all, are complex traditions of thought and practice informed by high moral aspirations and terrible actual failures" (168). This lack of charity toward liberalism blinds Hauerwas to constructive resources within that tradition that I will highlight later. It is also worth noting that Hauerwas' tendency to uphold an idealized vision of the church blinds him to some of its very real deficiencies.

69. Hauerwas, *After Christendom?*, 68. See also Hauerwas, *The Peaceable Kingdom*, 112–113.

70. See John Howard Yoder, "The Constantinian Sources of Western Social Ethics," in his *The Priestly Kingdom: Social Ethics as Gospel* (Notre Dame: University of Notre Dame Press, 1984), 135–147. Hauerwas' reliance on Yoder is explicit in "A Christian Critique of Christian America," in his *Christian Existence Today*, 180ff.

71. See Rodney Clapp, "Practicing the Politics of Jesus," in *The Church as Counterculture*, ed. Michael L. Budde and Robert W. Brimlow (Albany: State University of New York Press, 2000), 15. Clapp's helpful summary of "Constantinianism" is indebted to Yoder's characterization of the phenomenon and resonates in all crucial respects with Hauerwas' treatment of it.

72. Yoder, "The Constantinian Sources of Western Social Ethics," 137.

73. Ibid., 136–141.

74. Ibid., 143.

75. Hauerwas, "A Christian Critique of Christian America," 173, 177.

76. Ibid., 183.

77. Gustafson, "The Sectarian Temptation," 84.

78. Wilson D. Miscamble, "Sectarian Passivism?," *Theology Today* 44, no. 1 (April 1987): 73, 74.

79. Max L. Stackhouse, "Liberalism Dispatched vs. Liberalism Engaged," *The Christian Century* (October 18, 1995): 962.

80. Stanley Hauerwas, "Will the Real Sectarian Stand Up?," *Theology Today* 44, no. 1 (April 1987): 88.

81. Nigel Biggar, "Is Stanley Hauerwas Sectarian?," in *Faithfulness and Fortitude: In Conversation with the Theological Ethics of Stanley Hauerwas*, ed. Mark Thiessen Nation and Samuel Wells (Edinburgh: T & T Clark, 2000), 142–143.

82. Hauerwas, "Will the Real Sectarian Stand Up?," 89. See also Stanley Hauerwas, "Epilogue: A Pacifist Response to the Bishops," in Paul Ramsey, *Speak Up for Just War or Pacifism: A Critique of the United Methodist Bishop's Pastoral Letter "In Defense of Creation"* (University Park: The Pennsylvania State University Press, 1988), 178; and Hauerwas, *The Peaceable Kingdom*, 104–106.

83. Hauerwas, "Will the Real Sectarian Stand Up?," 89. See also Hauerwas, *The Peaceable Kingdom*, 113–114.

84. Hauerwas writes, "I do not see why the position for which I have argued forces the church to withdraw from public policy matters . . . unless . . . public policy always involves questions of violence and/or coercion. I simply do not believe that." Hauerwas, "Will the Real Sectarian Stand Up?," 90.

85. Ibid., 89.

86. For both of these affirmations, see Stanley Hauerwas, "Remembering Martin Luther King Jr. Remembering," in his *Wilderness Wanderings*, 228.

87. Ibid., 230.

88. See Gustavo Gutiérrez, *A Theology of Liberation* (Maryknoll, NY: Orbis Books, 1972), 91.

89. Hauerwas, *After Christendom?*, 52, 53–54; see generally, 50–58.

90. Stanley Hauerwas, "Postscript: A Response to Jeff Stout's *Democracy and Tradition*," in his *Performing the Faith: Bonhoeffer and the Practice of Nonviolence* (Grand Rapids, MI: Brazos Press, 2004), 240–241. Here, Hauerwas is responding to Jeffrey Stout's characterization of rights (following Annette Baier) as "an unwillingness to beg" (see Jeffrey Stout, *Democracy and Tradition* [Princeton: Princeton University Press, 2004], 204–209). There are many possible expressions of such a position within Christian thought. See, for example, Nicholas Wolterstorff, "Christianity and Social Justice," *Christian Scholar's Review* 16, no. 3 (March 1987): 211–228. In this article, reflecting on the South African *Kairos Document*, Wolterstorff affirms, with authors of the document, that a reasonable understanding of a person's rights means that "*other things being equal*, oppressed people should claim their rights, not beg for them . . . . [S]ervitude in the oppressed is wrong" (216).

91. For a recent attempt to ground rights talk in biblical and theological considerations, see Nicholas Wolterstorff, *Justice: Rights and Wrongs* (Princeton: Princeton University Press, 2008). For instructive discussion of the limits of Hauerwas' treatment of rights, see Timothy P. Jackson, *Political Agape: Christian Love and Liberal Democracy* (Grand Rapids, MI: William B. Eerdmans Pub. Co., 2015), 262–265.

92. See, for example Max L. Stackhouse, *Creeds, Society, and Human Rights: A Study in Three Cultures* (Grand Rapids, MI: William B. Eerdmans Publishing Co., 1984); John W. DeGruchy, *Christianity and Democracy* (Cambridge: Cambridge University Press, 1995); Michael L. Westmoreland-White, "Setting the Record Straight: Christian Faith, Human Rights, and the Enlightenment," *Annual of the Society of Christian Ethics* (1995): 75–96; and Wolterstorff, *Justice*, Part I.

93. Linda Woodhead, "Can Women Love Stanley Hauerwas? Pursuing an Embodied Theology," in Nation and Wells, eds., *Faithfulness and Fortitude*, 179. See also Albrecht, *The Character of Our Communities*, esp. 108–112.

94. Stanley Hauerwas, "Failure of Communication *or* A Case of Uncomprehending Feminism," *Scottish Journal of Theology* 50, no. 2 (1997): 234; see also Stanley Hauerwas, "Where Would I Be Without Friends?," in Nation and Wells, eds., *Faithfulness and Fortitude*, 327. For a discussion of Hauerwas and his feminist critics that seeks to be both feminist and highly sympathetic to Hauerwas' project, see Debra Dean Murphy, "Community, Character, and Gender: Women and the Work of Stanley Hauerwas," *Scottish Journal of Theology* 55, no. 3 (2002): 338–355.

95. Hauerwas, "Failure of Communication," 234 n11.

96. See, for example, Sharon D. Welch, *A Feminist Ethic of Risk*, revised edition (Minneapolis: Fortress Press, 2000).

97. Sharon Welch, "Communitarian Ethics After Hauerwas," *Studies in Christian Ethics* 10, no. 1 (1997): 82–83. In this respect, much contemporary rights discourse is reflective not of the abstract, individualistic assumptions and arguments of the Enlightenment-liberal tradition (even of its contemporary exponents, such as Rawls, Dworkin, and Nozick), but of the experiences of struggle for recognition among particular peoples and groups in the second half of the twentieth century. On

this characteristic of contemporary rights discourse, see Westmoreland-White, "Setting the Record Straight," 84–86.

98. For a now-classic discussion, see Thomas E. Hill, Jr., "Servility and Self-Respect," *The Monist* 57, no. 1 (1973): 87–104.

99. Sarah Coakley, *Powers and Submissions: Spirituality, Philosophy, and Gender* (Oxford: Blackwell, 2002), 3–39. Coakley writes that the kenotic self-emptying which she has in mind "is not a negation of self, but the place of the self's transformation and expansion into God." It is "the *willed* effacement to a gentle omnipotence." (36, 37, emphasis added). For instructive overview of recent feminist work on the power to be found in Christ's suffering, see Elizabeth A. Webb, "Power in Weakness: Feminist Reclamations of the Suffering of Christ," *Religious Studies Review* 38, no. 4 (December 2012): 199–205.

100. Gail O'Day, "The Gospel of John," in *The New Interpreter's Bible*, vol. 9, ed. Leander Keck (Nashville: Abingdon Press, 1995), 734.

101. Peter Dula and Alex Sider, "Radical Democracy, Radical Ecclesiology," *CrossCurrents* 55, no. 4 (Winter 2006): 486. "The dominant (though by no means the only) mode of imagining conflict in Hauerwas' writing is as an insinuation into the church's life, one that originates elsewhere and, as such, is essentially foreign to the gospel" (495).

102. Ibid., 488.

103. Ibid., 489–491.

104. See Romand Coles, "The Wild Patience of John Howard Yoder: 'Outsiders' and the 'Otherness of the Church,'" *Modern Theology* 18, no. 3 (July 2002): 305–331.

105. Dula and Sider, "Radical Democracy, Radical Ecclesiology," 497.

106. Ibid., 498.

107. Stanley Hauerwas, "Democratic Time: Lessons Learned From Yoder and Wolin," *CrossCurrents* 55, no. 4 (Winter 2006): 537.

108. See Stout, *Democracy and Tradition*, esp. Chapters 5 and 6.

109. Hauerwas, "Democratic Time," 541.

110. Stanley Hauerwas, "A Haunting Possibility: Christianity and Radical Democracy," in Stanley Hauerwas and Romand Coles, *Christianity, Democracy, and the Radical Ordinary: Conversations between a Radical Democrat and a Christian* (Eugene, OR: Cascade Books, 2008), 22–23.

111. Ibid., 26.

112. Romand Coles, "Letter of July 17, 2006," in Hauerwas and Coles, *Christianity, Democracy, and the Radical Ordinary*, 35.

113. Ibid., 36–37.

114. Hauerwas, "A Haunting Possibility," 22, n5.

115. Coles, "Letter of July 17, 2006," 42. Passages rearranged.

116. For this characterization of his position, see Hauerwas, "Epilogue," 159.

117. Hauerwas, *The Peaceable Kingdom*, 85.

118. Hauerwas, "Pacifism," 99.

119. See Hauerwas, *The Peaceable Kingdom*, 81ff. See also Hauerwas, "Epilogue," 159ff. This text seems to reveal unresolved tensions in Hauerwas' work regarding the character of Christian nonviolence. In describing the new aeon God

has inaugurated in Christ, Hauerwas, following John Howard Yoder, characterizes Jesus as "God's agape—self-giving, nonresistant love" (159). On the following page (160), he writes that "Christian nonresistance is a form of discipleship to Jesus not in a legalistic way but rather 'as he is, so are we in this world' (1 John 4:17)." In these passages, Hauerwas appears, quite straightforwardly, to identify pacifism not simply with nonviolence, but with a thoroughgoing nonresistance, a position that seems clearly to entail the withdrawal of Christians from social and political affairs in the manner many of his critics fear. If this is his considered position on such matters, Hauerwas would have to eschew even the nonviolent active resistance of a Martin Luther King, Jr. as in keeping with Christian discipleship, a position that would make difficult, if not impossible, the sort of work for justice he otherwise (though in problematically underdeveloped form) generally affirms. Such a position would lend real credence to the charge of political sectarianism commonly leveled against him. A few pages later, however, Hauerwas seems to defend a more moderate position. He views as incorrect Paul Ramsey's "characterization of Jesus' teaching and life as one of absolute 'nonresistance'" because, he says, "Jesus' cross was a confrontation with powers that was meant to defeat those forces that hold us to the presuppositions of the old age. He did not restrain from fighting them and that includes their embodiment in Rome—but rather refused to fight them on their own terms" (177). Here, his position seems to be in keeping with that outlined earlier, namely, that Christians rightly engage in social and political struggles for justice, though they must do so on their own terms. A position such as this is able to render intelligible Hauerwas' claim that the church—precisely by being an active, though nonviolent presence—may be a difference in the world. The ambiguity lingers, however, as Hauerwas seemingly fails to recognize the tensions here, let alone offer some means of resolution. My sense is that the latter passage is more in keeping with Hauerwas' considered position, as it remains compatible with his commitment to nonviolence, while shoring up his long-standing contention that his thought does not entail the withdrawal of the church from public affairs.

120. Stanley Hauerwas, "Should War Be Eliminated?," in his *Against the Nations*, 194. See also Hauerwas, "Epilogue," 159–160.

121. Hauerwas, *The Peaceable Kingdom*, 88–89.

122. Hauerwas, "Should War Be Eliminated?," 185; see generally, 183–186. See also Stanley Hauerwas and William H. Willimon, *Resident Aliens: Life in the Christian Colony* (Nashville, TN: Abingdon Press, 1989), 35.

123. Hauerwas, "Should War Be Eliminated?" 196.

124. Hauerwas, *The Peaceable Kingdom*, 104–106. Quoted passages slightly rearranged.

125. Stanley M. Hauerwas, "The Gesture of a Truthful Story," in his *Christian Existence Today*, 105.

126. Ibid., 106.

127. Stanley Hauerwas and Will Willimon, "Why *Resident Aliens* Struck a Chord," *Missiology: An International Review* 19, no. 4 (October 1991): 424.

128. Stanley M. Hauerwas, "Taking Time for Peace: The Ethical Significance of the Trivial," in his *Christian Existence Today*, 256–257.

129. Jean Bethke Elshtain, “How to Fight a Just War,” in *Strike Terror No More: Theology, Ethics, and the New War*, ed. Jon L. Berquist (St. Louis: Chalice Press, 2002), 232.

130. Ibid., 233.

131. Timothy P. Jackson, *The Priority of Love: Christian Charity and Social Justice* (Princeton: Princeton University Press, 2003), 119.

132. For a compelling and sophisticated defense of this position, see Nigel Biggar, *In Defence of War* (Oxford: Oxford University Press, 2013), Chapters 2 and 3.

133. Elshtain, “How to Fight a Just War,” 232.

134. Ibid., 233.

135. See Reinhold Niebuhr, *An Interpretation of Christian Ethics* (San Francisco: Harper and Row, 1963), Chapter 4 (Originally published in 1935). Elsewhere, particularly in his discussions of the relationship between love and justice, Niebuhr seems to be more nuanced. See Reinhold Niebuhr, *The Nature and Destiny of Man, Volume II: Human Destiny* (Louisville: Westminster John Knox Press, 1964), Chapter 9 (Originally published in 1943).

136. See, for example the discussion in Biggar, *In Defence of War*, 17–20.

137. Jean Bethke Elshtain, “Review Essay: Theology and Political Life,” *Modern Theology* 12, no. 3 (July 1996): 372–373.

138. On the latter, see Jackson, *The Priority of Love*, 124.

139. Ibid., 117.

140. Lisa Sowle Cahill, “Just Peacemaking: Theory, Practice, and Prospects,” *Journal of the Society of Christian Ethics* 23, no. 1 (Spring/Summer 2003): 201–202.

141. This is how Richard Hays interprets Reinhold Niebuhr’s defense of violence. See Richard B. Hays, *The Moral Vision of the New Testament: A Contemporary Introduction to New Testament Ethics* (San Francisco: HarperSanFrancisco, 1996), 219.

142. For instructive discussion of why there is good reason to be wary of such distinctions, see Jackson, *Political* Agape, 9–19.

143. St. Augustine, *City of God*, book XIX, Chapter 26.

144. Elshtain, “How to Fight a Just War,” 233.

145. Charles T. Mathewes, “Appreciating Hauerwas: One Hand Clapping,” *Anglican Theological Review* 82, no. 2 (Spring 2000): 345.

146. On the creative, prospective character of theology, see, for example, Rowan Williams, *On Christian Theology* (Oxford: Blackwell, 2000), 131–147.

Chapter 4

Prophets, Pragmatism, and Politics

Cornel West's Democratic Domestication of the Prophetic Voice

SOCIAL AMELIORATION AND INTELLECTUAL ECLECTICISM

Both Michael Walzer and Stanley Hauerwas are frequently regarded as exemplary spokespersons for the communitarian orientation that has infused many recent expressions of political theory and theological ethics. And for both, it is their treatment of community that renders their respective projects problematic from the standpoint of the prophetic. Walzer's thought is finally dominated by a conventionalist communitarianism that yields what Seyla Benhabib has called a highly "integrationist" political theory, and Hauerwas' thought is finally dominated by a highly bounded ecclesiology that yields a closed, even authoritarian, understanding of theology. For both, these dominating themes make difficult attentiveness to the voices of the marginalized and render problematic their very different treatments of violence and nonviolence.

While Cornel West also emphasizes community, his "prophetic pragmatism" is primarily concerned not to articulate the constitutive self-understandings of either a political or religious community, but with the conditions under which we may corporately be enabled "to let suffering speak, let victims be visible and let social misery be put on the agenda of those with power . . . . [T]he life of the mind is inextricably linked with the struggle of those who have been dehumanized on the margins of society."[1] Social amelioration, not communal self-description, is the defining and orienting concern of West's thought. It is precisely in this commitment to the marginalized and suffering that one most clearly discerns resonances between West's project and the concerns of the biblical prophets.[2] In articulating this project, he draws inspiration particularly from (1) the example of the biblical prophets, who sought to bring "urgent and compassionate critique to bear on the evils of their day,"[3] and (2) the tradition of American pragmatism, which places a premium on social transformation and a non-systematic, non-dogmatic approach to knowledge that is less interested in traditional philosophical or theological aspirations than it is in drawing from any available resources in seeking to achieve practical goals.

But how successful is West's eclectic project in taking up the torch of the biblical prophets? Though his references to Israel's prophets as moral exemplars and his own self-identification as a Christian may seem to provide some hope that we have here a compelling contemporary manifestation of the prophetic, matters here, like West's thought, are somewhat complex. The basic problem is that it is often difficult to determine what is fundamentally authoritative for West's normative project, apart from a general commitment to social amelioration. His thought is, more to the point, characterized by real ambivalence regarding truth, an ambivalence captured in the term "prophetic pragmatism." Insofar as seeks to be prophetic he cannot swallow whole cloth some of the assumptions he identifies as central to pragmatism, and insofar as he affirms certain assumptions of pragmatism he is prevented from serving as a meaningful exemplar of the prophetic.

West skirts the tensions that exist in his thought with regard to truth through the affirmation of radical democratic commitments, which give expression to the concern for social amelioration shared by both pragmatism and Christianity. However, while such an affirmation is certainly not discontinuous with prophetic Christian commitments, West's articulation of them is too underdeveloped to give sufficient expression to the "thickness" of those commitments. These problems are discernible not only in his treatment of issues of justice, but also in his rather ambiguous treatment of issues relating to the legitimacy and use of political violence.

COMMUNITY: STRUGGLING FOR HUMAN MEANING AND FREEDOM IN MODERN AMERICA

Whatever the difficulties that might ultimately attend West's thought, he is clearly motivated by laudable concerns. His project is fundamentally an attempt to respond to the challenges to meaning and freedom that he claims characterize our age. In a manner that resonates explicitly with the concerns of the biblical prophets for those suffering at society's margins, he attempts "to understand and respond to the guttural cry that erupts from the depths of the soul of each of us. The existential quest for meaning and the political struggle for freedom sit at the center of [his] thought." He seeks to delineate the ways in which people "grapple with concrete and universal issues of life and death, oppression and resistance, joy and sorrow."[4] At one level, then, general questions about the human condition drive his thought, but, at the same time, these questions are always situated for him within the particular (post)modern context of contemporary America. His work is motivated by three interrelated questions: What does it mean to be human? What does it mean to be modern? What does it mean to be American?[5]

In situating his work around these three questions, West's concern for community becomes most apparent. While he affirms, like Walzer and Hauerwas, the communally mediated nature of knowledge and belief, he is concerned with community less for general epistemological insight than for the way in which the moral challenges he is concerned to address—suffering, oppression, meaninglessness—are experienced and embodied. His work is communal primarily in the sense that it is contextual, and it is contextual in the sense that he is concerned with fundamental existential challenges that confront particular people at particular times and places. He is, first and foremost, though not exclusively, concerned with the existential meaningless and despair that African Americans and other oppressed people have experienced and continue to experience in America. There is a communal crisis in America, particularly black America, today, and whether we might respond to it adequately remains an open question.

Drawing inspiration from a wide array of literary figures (such as Sophocles, Shakespeare, Kafka, Beckett, and, especially, Chekov), philosophers and theologians (such as Kierkegaard, Schopenhauer, Montaigne, and Pascal), and musicians (especially John Coltrane), West is fundamentally concerned to confront head-on the "sense of the tragic" that characterizes life: "the irreducible predicament of unique individuals who undergo dread, despair, disillusionment, disease, and death *and* the institutional forms of oppression that dehumanize people."[6] Such basic human concerns are originative for his thought. In an interview with George Yancy, West explained his attraction to Kierkegaard as follows:

> I think early on I was just in some sense seized by a certain kind of terror that struck me as being at the heart of things human and a profound sadness and sorrow that struck me as being at the core of the human condition. And so in reading Kierkegaard from the Bookmobile, and here was someone who was seriously wrestling with a certain level of melancholia, I was struck by his very honest and candid . . . encounter with what he understood to be this terror, this suffering and this sadness and sorrow. It resonated deeply with me. Prosser Hall Frye used the wonderful phrase "the tragic qualm" to describe this encounter. It is a kind of vertigo, a dizziness, a sense of being staggered by the darkness that one sees in the human condition, the human predicament.[7]

Or, as he says elsewhere: "To be human is to suffer, shudder and struggle courageously in the face of inevitable death . . . . [It] is to encounter honestly the inescapable circumstances that constrain us, yet muster the courage to struggle compassionately for our own unique individualities and for more democratic and free societies."[8] West's thought, then, while not existential*ist*, in the sense of offering a systematic body of thought à la Sartre, is clearly, even "preeminently," *existential* in its focus on ordinary people wrestling with "death, dread, despair, disease and disappointment" and the necessity of radical choice in the face of such absurdity to sustain hope and hold at bay cynicism and despair.[9]

For West, the most significant absurdities and challenges to hope that confront persons today are rooted in the pathologies of modernity. While the defining mark of modernity for West consists of the employment of critical intelligence in seeking to "challenge the prevailing authorities, powers and hierarchies of the world"—most characteristically by engaging with others in fallible dialogue—this essentially democratic thrust of modernity is also clouded by its "night side."[10] The Enlightenment focus on natural reason and Romantic focus on imaginative expression and transformation gave rise to or crystallized much of what we positively associate with modernity, particularly the affirmation of individual dignity and rights, and the democratic accountability of social institutions to "the people."[11] These high points of modernity notwithstanding, its legacy is highly ambiguous. The achievements of modernity have often also been associated with forms of exclusion and domination that have been rooted in, or given rise to, racism, sexism, homophobia, environmental degradation, and so on. In the case of Africans in the New World, particularly, modernity is beset by an "ignoble paradox": the flourishing of democracy for white, especially propertied, European men "alongside the flowering of the transatlantic slave trade and New World slavery."[12] Given this legacy and its lingering effects, the promises of modernity have yet to be realized.

For West, this paradox is particularly notable in America, for a chief characteristic of the American experiment with democracy is that ethical significance is given to the future "by viewing the present as terrain capable of transcending any past and thereby arriving at a new identity and community . . . . American culture accentuates what is to come, what is not as opposed to what is and what has been."[13] Ironically, African Americans, those who have been most victimized by American democracy, have been among those who have most fully glimpsed what a transformed future might look like, as they have struggled valiantly in the name of a more democratic America. But hope that we might yet grapple *collectively* with the dark side of modernity in the American context is tempered by American tendencies toward sentimentality, to downplay history, and to overlook the dark legacies of the past that continue to haunt the present. Such amnesia will ill serve us, West urges, for the very meaning of democracy is imperiled by the legacies of our history.

If America is to realize its promise, it must continually "raise the frightening democratic question: What does the public interest have to do with the most vulnerable and disadvantaged in our society?"[14]

The challenges the vulnerable and disadvantaged currently pose to democratic aspirations are perhaps best captured in West's discussions of "black nihilism." While West is concerned with domination and exclusion in all of its forms, he has written most extensively about the nature and effects of racial domination and exclusion. While recognizing that traditional liberal (focusing on structural constraints) and conservative (focusing on behavioral impediments) approaches to the plight of African Americans contain some truths, West contends that both camps fail to address "the most basic issue now facing black America: *the nihilistic threat to its very existence*."[15]

West is not concerned here with a philosophical understanding of nihilism, which claims that there are no standards of authority or values, but, rather, with what might be called "existential" or "walking" nihilism, which focuses on "*the lived experience of coping with a life of horrifying meaninglessness, hopelessness, and (most important) lovelessness*." Such nihilism owes its existence to the legacies of white supremacy—economic breakdown, the abdication of political responsibility, and patterns of personal behavior—but its most immediate cause is the deterioration of cultural institutions and resources of support. The result of such hopelessness is "a numbing detachment from others and a self-destructive disposition toward the world."[16] Its effects are manifested in drug addiction and its associated social pathologies, pervasive homicide, increasing suicide rates among African Americans, alcoholism, and the general "gangsterization" of culture, in which the immediate fulfillment of desire rules.[17]

While hope is hard to come by for many, it has not died for West. His hope, however, is more than a facile form of optimism or positive thinking; it is a critical and "combative spirituality," which holds out for the possibility of change, all the while knowing that utopia will never be fully realized and that any progress that is achieved will require much work and patience. Belief in a "utopian impulse, where you try to project a whole different and better society that could be realized and actualized,"[18] is illusory for West. "When you talk about hope, you have to be a long-distance runner. This is . . . very difficult in our culture, because the quick fix, the overnight solution, mitigates against being a long-distance runner in the moral sense, the sense of fighting because it's right, because it's moral, because it's just."[19] Such hope, however, is not self-sustaining; it must be tied to social vision and a critical temper. Of particular importance in this regard for West are sources of normative engagement, especially those provided by Christian tradition. Unfortunately, the constructive insight that might be provided by such sources is imperiled by West's ambiguity regarding the nature of truth claims.

TRUTH: "RORTIAN" OR "KIERKEGAARDIAN"?

West claims that an adequate response to the social suffering which he so acutely identifies requires a sustaining moral vision. For many, this seems to entail the affirmation of a realist perspective with regard to truth and value. Given that West professes to be a committed Christian who is trained as a philosopher and has spent the bulk of his professional career teaching in schools of theology and departments of religious studies, it might be thought that such a perspective is readily forthcoming in his thought. However, although indebted to a range of philosophical and theological texts and thinkers, West strongly resists traditional understandings of philosophy and theology, as he is deeply suspicious of the approaches and aspirations which dominate these disciplines. Indeed, at times—particularly when under the influence of Richard Rorty—he seems to reject realism altogether, a move that threatens to undermine his normative commitments. At other times, however, he seems to affirm a realist conception of truth, though claiming that it is never known apart from particular, communally mediated practices. Finally, West's understanding of truth is elusive, both for his readers and himself.

"Rortian" Anti-Realism?

When West was first formally introduced to philosophy as an undergraduate at Harvard, it struck him "as being very interesting and full of intellectual curiosities," but he found it "too far removed from [his] own issues," issues related to the problem of evil, of misery and suffering, and how to struggle and maintain joy and courage in light of such realities.[20] Insofar as philosophy is concerned with matters of reality, truth, goodness, justice, and so on, understood abstractly, apart from attention to the particular social and historical contexts within which these terms are concretely instantiated, it is, West contends, a dead end, intellectually and existentially.

West does not reject philosophy or theology altogether, however, for he finds in pragmatism, that distinctly American brand of philosophy (which has also infused much recent theology), an approach to thinking critically that is neither disengaged nor abstract. According to West, in pragmatism we find philosophy redefined "as a form of cultural criticism in which the meaning of America is put forward by intellectuals in response to distinct social and cultural crises."[21] Rather than aiming at knowledge as such, abstractly and ahistorically understood, pragmatism has the virtue of understanding knowledge in relation to action. Pragmatism is philosophy on the ground, engaged with the world.

Pragmatism's chief virtue, for West, is that it has as its practical purpose the amelioration of social suffering. "The distinctive appeal of American pragmatism in our postmodern moment," West claims, "is its unashamedly moral emphasis and its unequivocally ameliorative impulse." Although "a diverse and heterogeneous tradition," it has as its "common denominator . . . a future-oriented instrumentalism that tries to deploy thought as a weapon to enable more effective action. Its basic impulse is a plebian radicalism that fuels an antipatrician rebelliousness for the moral aim of enriching individuals and expanding democracy."[22] All other things being equal, such emphases and impulses are all to the good, and are likely to be ingredients in any normatively compelling account of social amelioration.

In addition to its politically engaged nature, pragmatism also importantly *evades* the unwarranted and antiquated assumptions of traditional, "epistemology-centered philosophy" (hence the title of his *The American Evasion of Philosophy*) and theology. "Three theses," West tells us, "are basic" to pragmatism:

> (1) antirealism in ontology, so that the correspondence theory of truth is called into question and one can no longer appeal to Reality as a court of appeal to adjudicate between conflicting theories of the world; (2) antifoundationalism in epistemology, so that one cannot in fact invoke noninferential, intrinsically credible elements in experience to justify claims about experience; and (3) detranscendentalizing of the subject, the elimination of mind itself as a sphere of inquiry.[23]

Here, then, we have a seemingly straightforward rejection of realism with regard to truth. Of particular note here is West's linking of such anti-realism with epistemological anti-foundationalism. For West, in this passage, as for many other non-foundationalist philosophers, the rejection of the quest for foundations regarding how we might know truth is closely associated with, and may even be thought to entail, the rejection of realism regarding the nature of truth itself.

In "The Political Intellectual" West identifies his characterization of the central theses of pragmatism with the thought of Charles Sanders Peirce, William James, and Dewey. Elsewhere, however, it is clear that the post-modern neo-pragmatism of Richard Rorty, which builds upon the triumvirate of Willard V.O. Quine, Nelson Goodman, and Wilfred Sellars, is at least as influential. "The great contribution of Richard Rorty," he writes, "is that he constructs a powerful narrative history of modern North Atlantic philosophy in light of the Quine-Goodman-Sellars contributions and boldly draws the threatening implications for philosophy as a discipline." His "provocative and often profound meditations impel philosophers to examine the problematic status of their subject-matter—only to discover that modern North Atlantic philosophy has come to an end."[24] This important narrative, West argues, is precisely that of "the emergence, development, and decline of the correspondence theory of truth, the notion of privileged representations, and the idea of a self-reflective transcendental subject."[25]

Like Rorty, West is motivated here not only by conceptual considerations, but also moral ones. He is clearly concerned with the absolutist cast of many accounts of truth and our apprehension of it. Foundationalist epistemologies, especially, often resemble forms of fundamentalism, as they promise clear answers by eliminating doubt and asserting claims with absolute certainty. Like the fundamentalist preacher who dispenses true wisdom to his flock which only he, through God's revelation, knows, the foundationalist philosopher is "a cultural overseer who knows everyone's common ground—the Platonic philosopher-king who knows what everyone else is doing whether *they* know it or not, because he knows about the ultimate context (the Forms, the Mind, Language) within which they are doing it."[26] The assertion of certitude in this way—as a history littered with wars of religion and terrorism rooted in religious fundamentalism has taught us—has often mutated into violence and harm visited upon those who disagree or who do not possess the "Truth."

These themes are clear in West's attitude toward much of the traditional conceptual apparatus of theology. He associates the traditional tasks of theological inquiry with rendering "the dogmas and doctrines, insights and intuitions of the Christian tradition" in a systematic, coherent, consistent, and epistemically valid manner.[27] Theology, when understood in this sense, West argues, is characteristically concerned with upholding forms of realism in which metaphysical and ontological inquiry is undertaken "in the grand mode" or "old sense," concerned to articulate in an abstract, timeless manner "the way the world is or the legitimate grounds of knowledge."[28] However, such claims to knowledge are neither innocent nor intellectually disinterested. They are frequently put forward, West claims, by religious realists from the standpoint of the alleged authority of a particular ecclesiastical or personal perspective and without regard "*their role and function in one's life*,"[29] thus serving to obscure the sources and operations of power and authority prevalent in society. Similarly, he finds "all notions of providence" problematic because they can be too easily "manipulated by unaccountable elites who 'know' how and where history is going."[30]

This rejection of realism leads West to uphold, at times, a conventionalist account of truth and its apprehension. In "Nietzsche's Prefiguration of Postmodern Philosophy," for example, West suggests that the rejection of realism entails the acceptance of such an account of truth.[31] Underpinning the basic theses of pragmatism (and neo-pragmatism), he tells us elsewhere, is the claim that social practices "lie at the very center of knowledge," for "knowledge is produced, acquired, achieved."[32] Indeed, West writes that he agrees with the Derridean claim that "there is *nothing outside social practices*: intertextuality is a differential web of relations shot through with traces, shot through with activity. For a pragmatist, that activity is always linked to human agency and the context in which that agency is enacted."[33]

West applies these considerations to moral claims directly and most explicitly in *The Ethical Dimensions of Marxist Thought*. There, he defends a radical historicist approach to ethics that calls into question the notion that there are "criteria, grounds, or foundations" for our ethical claims that "carry the weight of rational necessity and/or universal obligation."[34] In rejecting such grounds, West claims that ethical claims are founded only in the "contingent, community-specific agreements people make in relation to particular norms, aims, goals, and objectives."[35] The conventionalist dimensions of this position are soon made even clearer: from a radical historicist perspective, the point is "to immerse oneself more deeply into history by consciously identifying with—and digesting *critically* the values of—a particular community or tradition."[36] For West, then, the denial of foundations for ethical knowledge is taken here to entail the absence of a realist account of moral claims. Claims refer not to an objective reality that undergirds universal obligation, but only to contingent, community-specific agreements.

If West is an anti-realist and conventionalist cut from much the same cloth as Walzer, as these statements seem to imply, then his project is in serious trouble, for it lacks an adequate ground to support the commitments to solidarity and social amelioration that are otherwise so central to it. Like Walzer, absent the affirmation of a resolutely realist account of value, West finally cannot provide an adequate account of the commitment to solidarity that is so central to his project.

"Kierkegaardian" Realism?

West is not so straightforwardly interpreted, however. At other significant points in his work he appears to recognize both the insufficiency of a conventionalist standpoint and many of the problems that attend the rejection of realism. Passages from two essays are particularly instructive here. In "Afterword: The Politics of American Neo-Pragmatism" and "Nietzsche's Prefiguration of Postmodern American Philosophy," essays in which he elaborates and, to all appearances, straightforwardly defends the central methodological commitments of neo-pragmatism, he ends by worrying about the ethical and political deficiencies of neo-pragmatism. In the former essay, he contends that Rorty's project "remains too broad, too thin—devoid of the realities of power; his ethnocentric posthumanism is too vague, too nonchalant—and unmindful of the decline of liberalism," and it possesses "relativist, even nihilist" implications.[37] In the latter essay, he worries that the claims forwarded by those such as Rorty and Thomas Kuhn "leave postmodern American philosophy hanging in limbo, as a philosophically critical yet culturally lifeless rhetoric *mirroring* a culture (or civilization) permeated by the scientific ethos, regulated by racist, patriarchal, capitalist norms and pervaded by debris of decay."[38]

In these passages, which are found in essays that otherwise devote considerable space to affirming the central commitments of neo-pragmatism, West is clearly urging for something more than a more politically self-conscious form of neo-pragmatism in keeping with the "classical" pragmatism with which it otherwise shares much. His worries about the nihilist and relativist implications of neo-pragmatism point to the need for some conception of objective truth, some realist account of value, and his worries about its tendency to merely mirror a culture point to the necessity of a more substantive moral vision than conventionalism will provide.

Beyond these considerations, the general trajectory of West's thought points in a realist direction. He believes, and clearly believes that others should likewise believe, that racist, sexist, and homophobic practices and discourses are unjust, and therefore untrue, and he clearly contends that wholly private and politically quietistic interpretations of the Christian gospel are false.[39] In short, he urges us to care about various forms of social suffering and injustice because they are *wrong*—not wrong from the standpoint of a particular community or tradition, but simply wrong. It is *true* for West that people should be treated with dignity and respect, that they should be recipients of justice. Mark David Wood is surely right to argue that West's social program assumes a realist standpoint "to the extent that it assumes . . . that reality and claims about it are distinct from each other and that it is possible to distinguish the relative truth values of claims made about reality through the process of empirical research, theoretical analysis, and practical engagement."[40]

More to the point, there are passages in his corpus in which West makes claims that have little cogency apart from the affirmation of a realist account of truth, albeit one chastened by recognition of our status as fallible, historical beings. In a 2001 commencement address at St. John's College (Santa Fe), West asserted, "I'm not a relativist, I'm a fallibilist. I think I'm right, but I recognize I could be wrong."[41] And in *The American Evasion of Philosophy* he claims that though it is not possible to forward defenses of one's faith that verify its veracity, "the fundamental philosophical question remains whether the Christian gospel is ultimately true. And, as a Christian pragmatist whose focus is on coping with transient and provisional penultimate matters yet whose hope goes beyond them, I reply in the affirmative, bank my all on it, yet am willing to entertain the possibility in low moments that I may be deluded."[42] It is difficult to see how to make sense of either of these statements without assuming the meaningfulness of a realist account of truth.

Some purchase on how West may be understood in realist terms may be had by considering how his work resonates with a reading of Søren Kierkegaard's understanding of these matters. There are, I believe, real congruities between a "Kierkegaardian" and a "Westian" realism, congruities all the more instructive because of West's high regard for the Dane. In a recent essay, C. Stephen Evans argues that though some of his postmodern readers interpret Kierkegaard as upholding anti-realist claims, he is best understood as a realist of a rather distinctive stripe. One of the difficulties with many contemporary anti-realists (like Richard Rorty), Evans notes, is that they falsely believe that realism only makes sense if one has some sort of direct access to reality such that "we can compare our ideas with a reality that is known independently of those ideas."[43] Evans argues that Kierkegaard upholds realism while rejecting this demand for objective certainty by affirming the "approximative" character of knowledge. Our knowledge is never complete and always fallible, but there is an ideal to be approximated, an ideal understood as "an accurate representation of the object of knowledge."[44] He emphasizes, that is, "the tentative, never-final character of empirical inquiry, which is rooted both in the complexity and flux-infused character of what is known as well as the finitude and uncertainty linked to the temporal character of the knower." He does not, then, reject correspondence to reality as an ideal after which our claims strive—indeed, he seems to assume that no other ideal makes sense—though he does object to "any claim that the ideal can be finally and fully actualized." This is not, Evans notes, an anti-realistic claim, but, rather, rests on a defining tenet of realism (a tenet I gestured to in chapter 1, in the distinction between alethiology and epistemology), namely, "the radically non-epistemic character of truth. It is just because reality is ultimately independent of human minds that human attempts to know that reality must always be approximations."[45] For Kierkegaard, these considerations apply particularly to claims about moral and religious truths. As Evans explains, he held that "human existence mirrors human knowing, but with what might be called a reverse directionality. In knowing we attempt to 'reproduce' or reduplicate reality, and though we speak of some of these attempts as knowledge and regard knowing as a case where our thought accurately mirrors reality, Kierkegaard says that such efforts are never final but always approximate and tentative."[46]

Something very much like this position, I want to suggest, is found in West's lengthiest and most systematic discussion of the nature of truth and truth claims, "A Philosophical View of Easter." Here, he offers a more adequate framework for resisting the difficulties inherent in Rorty's denial of realism, and for giving expression to his own normative concerns. He begins his essay by forwarding claims that may seem at first glance to be straightforwardly conventionalist and anti-realist. He claims that the commonsensical view of truth, in which a claim correlates directly with a set of experiences or observations, is false, for the truth values of claims "can be determined neither in isolation from other sentences nor by a particular set of observation." Instead, he asserts, "the truth-value of our claims about the self, world and God are determined by marshalling evidence for or against the descriptions, versions or theories of which these claims are a part."[47] When we claim to "know" that a particular claim is true, what we are doing is identifying ourselves with some "particular group of people, community of believers or tradition of social practices."[48]

Some of West's interpreters have been troubled by these claims. George Yancy, for example, has rightly noted that for West there is no "way that we can *know* that the Christian narrative has the relational or representational force of 'having gotten the world right.' There is no way to establish externally (that is, outside of Christian social and historical practices) whether one's Christian beliefs correspond to some given metaphysical, transcendent, or ahistorical divine referent."[49] However, if this is true, Yancy worries, we are "condemned to bear witness to mere cultural idols, existential fissures, and our own deepest ontotheological projections."[50] For Yancy, a credible account of religious truth requires precisely what West's account lacks, namely, a way of *ascertaining* whether a particular religion is true (in the correspondence sense).

West's claims only pose problems, however, if claims about the nature of truth are conflated with claims about how we know truth. This is a difficulty that, at least on Evans' reading, Kierkegaard's insights can help us to get beyond. Thus, in his understanding of the approximative character of our knowledge claims, Kierkegaard (at least on Evans' reading) recognizes that, though we can never extricate ourselves from our embodied, historical existence, this does not condemn us to a simple, uncritical parroting of our clan's conventions. We need not simply be bounded by our cultural and historical facticity. Our truth *claims*—our *talk* about truth—may not be independent of our particular cultural and historical standpoints, but this does not entail that all those claims refer to, or seek to refer to, are those standpoints. A similar recognition is discernible in West. Implicit in West's account in "A Philosophical View of Easter" essay, I would argue, is just this recognition of the distinction between how we *speak of* truth (i.e., the nature of our truth *claims*) and truth *itself*, in its fullness. Reality can serve as a "pull" on our contextually articulated claims, leading us to revise them in ways that are more accurate, more fully reflective of the truth.

This is precisely the sort of position that is subsequently borne out in the "Easter" essay. This is seen especially in the following passage, in which he elaborates upon what it might mean to say that a Christian description of the self, world, or God is true:

> As a self-avowed Christian, it seems redundant to say that a particular Christian description of the self, world and God is true. But, more important, it is misleading to say this. Christians believe in various Christian descriptions that do not claim their descriptions are true, but rather that these descriptions are acceptable and possibly sufficient for their aims. Christian descriptions hold that our fallenness will never permit our Christian descriptions to grasp the Truth. This is so because, for Christians, Jesus Christ is the Truth, and Jesus Christ always rests outside our particular Christian descriptions.[51]

In this pregnant passage, West clearly affirms truth as an ideal (indeed, truth is the ideal that finds fulfillment in Jesus Christ) but denies, precisely because we are finite, fallen, and sinful beings, that our particular claims—our particular descriptions—ever fully reflect that truth. While, on this reading, West would contend that we may have glimpses of the truth, he would also contend that we can never grasp it fully.

It seems that, for West, it is misleading to say that particular Christian descriptions of God, self, and world are true because such a claim may be taken to entail the sort of exact and exhaustive one-to-one correspondence between the knower and the known that our status as historical beings denies us. Though such descriptions may be acceptable or sufficient within a particular context or in response to particular problems, questions, or needs, implicit here is the claim that such descriptions may need to be revised, or possibly even abandoned, as we attempt through them to give ever more adequate expression to the reality to which they refer. Truth is, as Joerg Rieger rightly notes, "always unfinished and in progress, not systematic or complete."[52] Thus, writes West, from the perspective of Christian convictions, "Truth [in its fullness] is not a characteristic of a description, not even of a Christian description. Rather [in Kierkegaardian fashion], Jesus Christ is the Truth or Reality and can only be existentially appropriated by fallen human beings caught in their finite descriptions."[53] Understood in this manner, "Truth" or Christ is, for West (as for other liberation theologians), that reality that is most meaningful and real, but always fundamentally elusive. It is always before us, regulating our beliefs and practices, calling us, but it is also that which we fail adequately or fully to understand or appropriate.

West gives clear expression to this basic claim on more than one occasion. Toward the end of the "Easter" essay he claims that for Christians

> the primary test for the "truth-value" of particular Christian descriptions . . . is their capacity to facilitate the existential appropriation of Jesus Christ. This means that any "true" Christian description makes the Reality of Jesus Christ available, that it promotes and encourages the putting of oneself on the line, going to the edge of life's abyss and finding out whether the Reality of Jesus Christ, though understood through one's finite Christian description, can sustain

> and support, define and develop oneself in one's perennial struggle of becoming a fuller and more faithful self in Christ.[54]

In the following passage from *Prophesy Deliverance!* this standpoint is perhaps even more clearly upheld:

> For Christians, truth is not a property, characteristic, or attribute of a theory, portrayal, and description, not even a Christian description. Rather, Jesus Christ is the Truth, a reality which can only be existentially appropriated (not intellectually grasped) by fallen human beings caught in ever-changing finite descriptions . . . . [W]e are inscribed within the hermeneutical circle with a dim hope for awareness, but with no intellectual access to it.[55]

West continues, after a passage echoing the one from the "Easter" essay just quoted: "For Christians, 'truth talk' precludes disinterest, detachment, and distance because the reality of Jesus Christ continually performs such tasks; that is, Jesus Christ is literally the Truth, the Truth which cannot be intellectually reified but rather existentially appropriated by finite human beings with urgent needs and pressing problems."[56] Our particular claims about God, self, and the world find their measure, then, in their ability to give expression to the lived implications of the reality of Jesus Christ. For West, that is a reality that necessarily calls us to seek ever more adequate forms of response to suffering others. Insofar as our claims about the self, the world, and God fail to elicit such a response, they are presumptively false.

While the pragmatic function of religious belief is central here for West, on this reading, it seems clear that religious belief is not reduced to utility (*contra* George Yancy[57]), to what it can do for us. It is fairer to West, at least on the present reading, to interpret him as claiming that, since religious belief deals with that which is most true and most fundamental, it will naturally and necessarily engage the sorts of existential questions and issues that his concern with human suffering leads him to highlight. Thus, while we can be provided no guarantee of the truthfulness of those beliefs that enable coping, sustenance, transformation, for example, such outcomes give us good presumptive reason to affirm their truth.

Skirting Tensions

If this realist reading of West is compelling, then there are, to be sure, real tensions at the heart of his work. How ought we to understand these tensions and does West offer any resources for resolving them? Particularly in light of those essays discussed earlier, in which West appears to uphold both realist and anti-realist claims, it might be suggested that West evinces an ambivalence regarding truth. This is not a self-conscious ambivalence, however, with West struggling, but finally failing to reconcile the tensions that exist between these two positions. Indeed, he seems to vacillate from one position to the other, seemingly unaware of the tensions that exist.

The reason for this, I suggest, is that the tensions that exist here are in effect resolved—and obscured—*for West* through his adoption of radical democratic commitments as the substance of his normative thought. Both pragmatism and Christianity, at least as West interprets them, have similar aims and share common ground in their concerns for social transformation and amelioration. For both, radical democratic principles and practices can give effective expression to this emphasis. In short, I suggest, as he seeks to maintain an anti-systematic, anti-dogmatic position, West's adoption of radical democratic commitments as the normative center of his thought effectively skirts the tensions that exist between these two positions. Such a standpoint is compatible with the essentially pragmatic claim that "history only goes where we take it,"[58] but it also lends concrete expression to the Christian recognition of the dignity of the individual. In doing so, however, the theological contours and substance of his normative thought are rendered rather vague. Finally, even when "theologically dressed up" the normative dimensions of his thought are too thin and underdescribe the sorts of commitments and claims that are necessary for a contemporary Christian construal of the prophetic voice.

JUSTICE: HUMAN DIGNITY AND THE PRIORITY OF DEMOCRACY

If truthful Christian claims are those that existentially appropriate the Truth that is Jesus Christ, then we must ask, "Who is Jesus Christ?," according to West? In "The Historicist Turn in Philosophy of Religion," West states that the moral vision and norms he accepts "are derived from the prophetic Christian tradition" and that he follows "the biblical injunction to look at the world through the eyes of its victims, and the Christocentric perspective that requires that one see the world through the lens of the Cross—and thereby see our relative victimizing and relative victimization."[59] Christology and attentiveness to suffering and victimization are of a piece for West. In short, the Truth that is Jesus Christ is inextricably bound up with attentiveness to the marginalized, the victimized, those who suffer. The difference that the existential appropriation of Christ makes in lives is properly understood not solely in terms of the salvation of individual souls, but also, crucially, in terms of its this-worldly possibilities. West's understanding of salvation "insists upon both this-worldly liberation and otherworldly salvation as the proper loci of Christianity."[60] He turns to democracy to give normative content to this liberating expression of Christianity in an anti-dogmatic, anti-systematic manner. Yet, in doing so, his theological claims become problematically deflated of much of what would be their distinct and substantive content.

Christianity, Human Dignity, and Democracy

In *Democracy Matters*, West asserts, "In the face of callous indifference to the suffering wrought by our imperialism, we must draw on the prophetic." Central here is the "prophetic commitment to justice," a central element of all three of the great monotheistic religions, and "one of the great moral moments in human history . . . . Prophetic witness consists of human acts of justice and kindness that attend to the unjust sources of human hurt and misery. Prophetic witness calls attention to the causes of unjustified suffering and unnecessary social misery. It highlights personal and institutional evil, including especially the evil of being indifferent to personal and social evil."[61] The goal of prophetic justice "is to stir up in us the courage to care and empower us to change our lives and our historical circumstances."[62] For West, this prophetic emphasis on the marginalized is rendered normatively substantive through the expression of democratic commitments, which are based on the dual recognition of the dignity and depravity of humanity.

The moral core, the "first and fundamental norm," of the prophetic Christian gospel, according to West, is an affirmation of the dignity of the individual. This affirmation rests on the claim that all human beings possess an inherent dignity bestowed upon them by God. This radically egalitarian norm holds that "every individual regardless of class, country, caste, race, or sex should have the opportunity to fulfill his or her potentialities" within community. "A transcendent God before whom all persons are equal . . . endows the well-being and ultimate salvation of each with equal value and significance."[63] This affirmation of the dignity of all persons is a crucial source of West's social hope because it upholds "their ability to contradict what is, to change and be changed, and to act in the light of that which is not-yet."[64]

This affirmation of human dignity is, however, chastened by the recognition of human depravity, of the proclivity of persons "to cling to the moment, to refuse to transform and be transformed." The Christian gospel acknowledges that the ability to contradict and transform existing conditions is always "circumscribed by human imperfection."[65] This realism, along with its resolutely moral content, clearly distinguishes Christianity from grand theoretical versions of Marxism and is a chief characteristic of its social significance. Like Marxism, Christianity promotes a Promethean temper that seeks the transformation of prevailing realities. However, dominant understandings of Marxism, West judges, are too entwined with the valorization of scientific method, and disclose "the will to power which rests at the center of European modernity: the will to cognition and control, manipulation and mastery."[66] The Christian understanding of the depravity of human beings, by contrast, introduces a chastening and humane skepticism regarding the possibilities of social transformation. "Human history dooms human beings to problems and problematics, obstacles and obstructions, to relative achievements and relative accomplishments." All liberation is "penultimate liberation."[67]

The dialectic between dignity and depravity issues in democracy as West's second fundamental norm. West's defense of democracy is twofold. First, negatively, he argues that human depravity necessitates that democratic "accountability—of institutions to populace, of leaders to followers, of preachers to laity—be the center of any acceptable social vision. This accountability exists when people have control over the leaders and institutions that serve them." Second, positively, he contends that actualization of the dignity of the individual is best realized through democratic participation and processes of decision-making. West's affirmation of individuality and democracy are thus "inseparable. The former rests upon the moral core of the Christian gospel, the latter upon its historical realism."[68] West's affirmation of the dialectic between dignity and depravity, and his defense of democracy as reflective of the realism of the Christian gospel, echoes Reinhold Niebuhr's claim that humanity's "capacity for justice makes democracy possible; but [its] inclination to injustice makes democracy necessary."[69]

For West, in the context of policies and practices of domination, subordination, and marginalization, a democratic politics that embodies the affirmation of the dignity and equality of all human beings and enables their self-realization will, ideally, serve to enhance and give expression to both love of self and love of others. For example, with regard to the challenges posed by the legacy of race in America, this claim is aptly illustrated in West's essay, "Nihilism in Black America," as well as by other closely allied pieces. Nihilism cannot be overcome by arguments and analyses, but by a model of democratic politics—West calls it "a politics of conversion"[70]—that gives expression to love and care for those who suffer and are downtrodden.[71] Nihilism is tamed as one comes to affirm one's own worth and identity, an affirmation that is "fueled by the concern of others." West asserts that love and care are not simply "sentimental feelings or tribal connections," but, rather, real, material forces that have political significance in their ability to generate "a sense of agency among a downtrodden people . . . . Self-love and love of others are both modes toward increasing self-valuation and encouraging political resistance in one's community." This is largely a local project, one that takes place "in those institutions of civil society still vital enough to promote self-worth and self-affirmation."[72]

This affirmation of oneself and one's identity need not issue in the denigration of others and their identities, however. Racial and other forms of justice are predicated on a strong affirmative sense of one's own identity, but they are likely to be realized only as one works with and affirms the identity of others, as well. While identity politics are "inevitable," West worries that, taken alone, they are too limited and limiting. One will naturally begin the fight for social justice by focusing on those sources of suffering that have most scarred oneself,[73] but West contends that "the fundamental transformation of American society toward more egalitarian distribution of goods and resources" is predicated on ultimately reaching some sort of "overlapping consensus regarding the way in which . . . various systems of oppression operate."[74]

In addition to a self-love generated by the love of others, he thus also advocates a form of coalition politics whereby persons of different identities and groups work together toward realizing common goals and the common good. With regard to the particular problem of liberation from white supremacist institutions and practices, West contends that "instead of a closing-ranks mentality," a prophetic framework of racial reasoning encourages a morally engaged and oriented "coalition strategy that solicits genuine solidarity with those deeply committed to antiracist struggle."[75] West does not deny that claims rooted in racial, gender, sexual, or other forms of identity have legitimacy, but he wants to encourage a capaciousness that attends to the complexity of fighting for social justice, "with the aim of enabling different groups to at least tolerate each other as they pursue common *and* different ends."[76]

It is precisely this inclusive, socially engaged, ameliorative understanding of Christianity that many of West's readers find so attractive. For West, to be a prophetic Christian is to love one's way through the tragedies and absurdities of the world, seeking for oneself and others more just, more humane communities. As James Cone notes, "justice, faith, love, hope, and courage shape West's theological perspective." Importantly, this is not a static and dogmatic, but inclusive and dynamic perspective in which "justice is defined as fairness among people in society. It involves analyzing and transforming unjust social, political, and economic structures. There can be no successful achievement of justice without critical analysis of the structures of power and the willingness to fight injustice wherever it raises its ugly head."[77] Similarly, Josiah Ulysses Young contends that, for West, "personal liberty and justice-for-all define Christian hope, socialist ethics, and the Lord's identity . . . West's revolutionary Christianity . . . ponders the Lord's identity as a *private agony* born from suffering" that underwrites a commitment to the dignity of all.[78]

While a compelling articulation of Christianity divorced from social engagement is unthinkable for West, this is not, he would claim, a reduction of faith to a merely political program. On the reading presently under consideration, while democracy may be seemingly more central in West's thought than, say, eschatology or soteriology or the doctrine of God, he would contend that his normative vision is parasitic on a *prior* commitment to particular theological understandings. He is, he tells us, "a Bible-thumping, Sunday-school-attending evangelical believer."[79] He speaks "as a Christian—one whose commitment to democracy is very deep but whose Christian convictions are even deeper. Democracy is not my faith. And American democracy is not my idol."[80] Nevertheless, though he does not *intend* to subordinate his Christianity to democracy, this is, I shall argue, what he effectively does.

The Democratic Domestication of Christianity

West's assertions about the primacy of his Christian faith notwithstanding, with some frequency and at key places, West reduces theological considerations to democratic ones, such that Christian convictions appear, at best, to serve as a motivational influence. They do not shape his understanding of the prophetic in a distinctive way, however. Specifically, his treatments of justice and democracy are characteristically highly generalized, and his theology is thin, such that the connection between the former and the latter seems to be tenuous at best. Despite his intentions, it is questionable, finally, whether his constructive normative thought, as articulated, can fulfill its intention to give expression to the Truth that is Jesus Christ.

This tendency seems to have its source in West's anti-dogmatic, anti-systematic dispositions. One clear virtue of West's thought is his desire to be inclusive in his construal of the prophetic. He thus rightly allows that prophetic pragmatism can find expression in a range of political and religious movements: "feminist, Chicano, black, socialist, left-liberal," and so on. It is, he says, "possible to subscribe to prophetic pragmatism and belong to different religious and/or secular traditions . . . ."[81] This is in keeping with West's own intellectual eclecticism and capaciousness. However, while he is right to resist forms of ethical discourse that are absolutist in character, he seems to harbor a reticence toward overtly theological claims, thereby denying himself insights and resources that would most naturally enable him to offer a theologically robust articulation of the prophetic voice. West tends to reduce social and political expressions of the prophetic to highly generalized forms of democratic practice that fail to render his own theological account of the prophetic voice with enough thickness to show how it can resist incorporation into dominant forms of political discourse, some of which can veer in anti-prophetic directions.

Much of his reticence about overtly theological claims is rooted in understandable concerns about their possibly divisive, violent, and idolatrous character. In essays published in the early to mid-1980s, writing out of his location in the black church, in the context of the burgeoning influence of the Religious Right on American politics, and evincing a concern for the tendency of public discourse to become heated and even violent, West argues for a decentering of authoritarian religious beliefs systems in order to create crucial public space for civil discourse in pluralistic societies comprised by clashing creeds and ideologies.[82] More recently, in *Democracy Matters*, he worries about the deleterious effects of Christian fundamentalism on American politics. Such forms of Christianity give expression to an authoritarian, intolerant, and imperialist Constantinianism that marginalizes the love and justice that properly stand at the center of Christian identity.[83] For West, such Constantinian distortions of Christian faith are a perennial danger, an ever-present and idolatrous temptation. In an exchange with Judith Butler, while questioning the secularization thesis and Weberian claims about the disenchantment of the world, West worries that in the modern world religious faith seems to have lost much of its proper focus. Too often, we worship "the market or its accompaniments and accoutrements." We "end up with idolatrous worship of a lot of profane things."[84]

Despite such concerns, West clearly does not want wholly to evacuate the public square of religion. In *Democracy Matters*, he criticizes not only the public marginalization of religion one finds in the liberalism of John Rawls and Richard Rorty, but also the alleged flight of religion from the public square advocated by Stanley Hauerwas and John Milbank. He laments Rawls' failure to appreciate the compatibility between a commitment to constitutional and civic ideals and the prophetic Christianity of Martin Luther King Jr.[85] And while he resonates with Rorty's fears about the authoritarianism of the religious Right, he accuses him of having a secular faith that is "too pure" and of engaging in a "too rigid" "secular policing of public life." Secularism can also devolve into dogmatism and authoritarianism, foreclosing dialogue and debate. "Democratic practices—dialogue and debate in public discourse—are always messy and impure. And secular policing can be as arrogant and coercive as religious policing."[86] By contrast, recapitulating charges of political sectarianism discussed in the last chapter, he asserts (somewhat problematically) that Hauerwas flees from the public square to find "solace only in a prophetic ecclesiological refuge that prefigures the coming kingdom of God."[87]

However, when West does write explicitly about the constructive role of religion in public life he tends to envision it as (1) expressing broadly shared normative commitments and/or (2) functioning in a largely motivational capacity. The first understanding is seen, for example, in writings from the 1980s in which, largely due to concerns about the religious Right, he affirms secularization as a good thing and claims that in their public and political interventions Christians "must speak the common moral language of the society as a whole: namely, the language of rights."[88] The motivational dimension is seen, for example, in West's affirmation, in *Democracy Matters*, of the crucial role played by "values engendered by Christian belief" in driving early Americans to engage in nascent democratic projects and to resist the abuses of the British Empire.[89] It is also seen a few pages later in his recognition that "loyalty to constitutional and civic ideals may have religious motivations."[90] In either case, the broad tendency in West's thought is to depict the prophetic voice as largely undifferentiated from and coterminous with democratic commitments and discourse.

Examples of this general tendency are abundant. In a conversation with Eva Corredor in which she asks West to explain how his affirmation of the prophetic can be reconciled with concepts—like philosophical certainty and eternal truth—that he rejects, he distances himself from traditional understandings of its grounding assumptions in a manner that seems to give expression to the reservations about religious realism discussed earlier. His conception of the prophetic is, he says, "peculiar" because it is "not one in which one speaks from on top, which is continuous with the great and grand Jewish and Christian traditions of the prophetic that I know of, in which 'Thus says the Lord' or 'Eternal truth speaks from on top.'" Instead, and here he returns once again to generalized talk about democracy and moral conversation, he asserts that his notion of the prophetic "is a democratic one in which, in the midst of the quotidian, the commonplace, in the midst of the messy struggle in which one's hands are dirty, that one is holding on to moral convictions and tries to convince others that they ought to be accepted even though these moral convictions themselves can still be subject to criticism and change in vision and what-have-you."[91]

In his more recent work, the conflation of the prophetic and democracy is perhaps even more forthright. In *Democracy Matters*, he is concerned with forging "a new democratic Christian identity in America."[92] While West finds inspiration for this defense of democracy in, and believes it to be fundamentally compatible with, prophetic religious visions (Jewish, Christian, and Muslim), this discussion of democracy is articulated primarily not in terms of core theological claims, but, rather, in terms of an American "cultural way of being," which for him is exemplified most fully by Ralph Waldo Emerson and Herman Melville, James Baldwin and Toni Morrison.[93] These figures are the central heroes of his argument.

In his desire to find commensurability between Christian and secular moral convictions, West does importantly deny the false and potentially dangerous dichotomizing between the secular and sacred that characterizes the work of some theologians, like Hauerwas, today. And in his resistance to absolutist forms of religious discourse, he rightly highlights the humility that characterizes any proper understanding of public engagement. Furthermore, we do well to recognize, with West, that Christians, in their desire to promote justice and affirm the worth of all, rightly engage in common cause at points with many of their secular counterparts. The problem here is not that West's affirmations of democracy or of a public role for theology are fundamentally misplaced, but that they are inadequately developed. As articulated, West's normative thought fails to give sufficient expression to the way in which theological convictions are rightly determinative of the shape and substance of the normative commitments of a Christian rendering of the prophetic voice, including its democratic meanings and commitments. While we do rightly resist forms of theology that are too starkly differentiated from the surrounding culture, equally problematic are those forms in which it is largely undifferentiated.

Though the heroes of *Democracy Matters* (Emerson, Melville, Baldwin, and Morrison) have much to teach all of us, prophetic Christians included, and though they may be ably utilized in pointing out deficiencies in current political practices, for prophetic Christians such as West the question should not be, "How might I most fully embody this American cultural way of being?," or "How can we forge a new democratic Christian identity in America?," but, "How might I most fully embody the demands of God or live a life of discipleship?" In some cases, the answers to these questions may be the same, but in others, they may not. While there may be distinctive democratic practices and virtues that give expression to the American cultural way of being, for Christians it is ecclesial practices and theological virtues that are primary and decisive in shaping their being in the world. For West, the prophetic voice is a religious voice, but without a more theologically robust articulation of its normative vision, practices, and virtues he lacks the resources to give adequate contemporary expression to it.

Without, that is, a thicker theological framework within which to articulate how we ought to understand and evaluate democratic practices and commitments, West's prophetic Christian pragmatism is in danger of becoming less a religious normative vision than an American or more generally political vision, and in this his ability to speak prophetically is imperiled. In a discussion of Michael Eric Dyson's treatment of the social dimensions of Christianity that resonates with some of the problems I am identifying here with West, Michael Baxter points out that in Dyson's identification of democracy as a fundamental norm of Christianity (clear echoes with West here), "the border between democratic and ecclesiological discourse seems so porous as to be almost nonexistent," and he worries that this leads to the absorption of Christian moral vision into political ideology, thereby foreclosing "the possibility of a fundamental theological critique" of the existing political order.[94]

In West's case, the sorts of worries to which Baxter is pointing are perhaps best illustrated through a more critical interrogation of that value that most fundamentally underwrites his defense of, and commitment to, democracy: human dignity. While I have no desire to deny the significant social and political advances wrought by commitments to dignity, particularly over the last several decades, and while I do want to affirm dignity as a crucial basis for the affirmation of rights in ways that thinkers like Hauerwas might resist, Hauerwasian-like insights and worries are nonetheless instructive here and help to highlight the significance of "thicker," more robust accounts of terms central to West's work.

Specifically, I worry that West's affirmation of dignity is so amorphous, so general that it is vulnerable to being used to underwrite moral positions that stand in considerable tension with a robust rendering of the prophetic. At worst, I worry that it is vulnerable to being conflated or confused with "a political ethic of dignity" that possesses currency not only in academic circles (as in the work of Ronald Dworkin, Peter Singer, and a range of other influential contemporary philosophers[95]), but also in the realms of legal and public opinion. This particular understanding of dignity is highly cognitivist and voluntarist, it emphasizes "self-conscious autonomy" and the "ability to form rational intentions and execute independent decisions over time," and it tends to "exalt reason and volition" as hallmarks of the human.[96] Though West's conceptual treatments of dignity are never very extensive, at points, such as when he characterizes the dignity of persons as "their ability to contradict what is, to change and to be changed," he may seem to assume, however unwittingly, such a view.[97]

Such a position, however, is neglectful of the more fundamental commitment to sanctity that has traditionally served to underwrite a proper recognition of dignity and that can serve to check (what can only appear from a prophetic standpoint as) contemporary rationalist distortions of it. The cognitivism and voluntarism of pure dignity stand in contrast to the recognition of "sanctity," which "refers to the impersonal (i.e., humanly shared) needs and potentials that are antecedent to any calculable merit of achievement" and "encompasses such elements of 'non-cognitive well-being' as the capacity to feel joy, the need to receive care, and the potential to be loved."[98] With its attention to need and its focus on gracious responsiveness to the vulnerabilities of others, it is this latter understanding of human worth and value that is most in keeping with the prophetic. Indeed, it is precisely to some of the most marginal of human lives—the pre-, post-, or non-personal—that regnant notions of dignity are most blind.

While a concern to restore sanctity to its proper place in our moral valuations and judgments need not issue in highly absolutist, unwaveringly restrictive positions regarding abortion, euthanasia, and other associated issues—where it does lead on such issues is well beyond the scope of the current discussion—it is certainly the case that such matters cannot be regarded to be morally neutral or private, as an ethic of pure dignity would have them be. Any discussion about such matters will properly be complex and contentious, as competing values contend with, and are weighed against, one another. This is a conversation, however, to which West can contribute little, as his affirmations about dignity and democracy are so thin as to provide little, if any, concrete guidance. In the worst case, particularly in light of passages that seem to cohere with an ethic of pure dignity and his rather blanket assertion of abortion rights (he states that he aligns himself "firmly with progressive folk who have fought recent attempts to diminish or destroy . . . the legal right to an abortion"[99]), his position is vulnerable to being taken simply to reflect the emerging policy consensus on matters at the margins of life.

The problems presented by the theological thinness of West's project are repeated in his treatments of violence and nonviolence.

VIOLENCE/NONVIOLENCE: POLITICAL AIMS AND THE MARGINALIZATION OF CHRISTIAN PRACTICE

It should be evident from the foregoing that West is concerned to give voice to, and articulate resources for, resisting the violence that surrounds us. As I discussed earlier, he is particularly concerned with the "walking nihilism" that has torn apart black communities and that increasingly threatens us all. His primary response to the violence that threatens to engulf us is a democratic affirmation of the political salience of social care, especially for the marginalized, and of the upbuilding of democratic institutions, practices, and virtues that aid in giving expression to that care. Though they may be articulated in rather general terms, love and social care are real material forces for West that offer hope that existing social conditions might be transformed in the direction of what Martin Luther King, Jr. called the "beloved community." In its broad outlines, then, West's work appears concerned to respond to violence in a manner that resonates in key respects with the prophetic desire to seek and enact justice as *shalom*, justice as the creation of a reconciled and peaceable community.

The primary difficulty, however, is that, as the foregoing pages have argued, this is finally too broad and too general a *political* vision, and in this it fails to articulate sufficiently the distinctive ways in which *theological* considerations shape not only the prophetic Christian desire for peace, but *why* and *how* that peace is sought. Intimations of the broad problem I am attempting to continue to highlight here are discernible in what is lacking in West's work. Despite the general resonances I have just noted, and which I will discuss at greater length momentarily, it is interesting to note that West does not speak explicitly or at length about peaceableness per se, nor does he devote *sustained* attention to practices of forgiveness, nonviolence, reconciliation, and the like as central to, or in some manner conceptually entailed by, a prophetic position. And nowhere in his work does he go so far as to defend something like in-principle pacifism as a corollary of his prophetic pragmatism. Finally, what I have identified as elements of West's thought that point in a peaceable direction are rooted in and rely upon pragmatic-political judgments about the aims or likely success of particular social practices and institutional configurations. Political considerations—albeit of a generally attractive sort—and not considerations rooted in the demands of discipleship ground those features of West's thought that seem to provide insight into how he understands peace and approaches questions relating to the use of political violence. The problems I (continue to) highlight here are perhaps best seen through a more thorough treatment of some of the elements in West's thought that might reasonably be thought to point in a peaceable direction.

Gestures Toward Peace?

It is at least arguable that an orientation toward peace and nonviolence is discernible where one might least expect to find it in West's corpus, namely, in some of his earliest writings, where he adopts rather forthrightly the language of socialist revolution rather than the language of progressive reform that characterizes his more recent work.[100] Though West relies heavily upon Marxist conceptual categories and rhetoric in *Prophesy Deliverance!*, and though his views regarding the use of violence as a tool of liberation are left somewhat sketchy, there are good reasons to interpret him as holding even here that violence should at the very least be strongly resisted in the quest for liberation. First, within this text, he identifies himself with the left-wing Councilist stream of Marxism, which is "committed first and foremost to the norms of individuality and democracy within the workers (and other progressive) movements—and within the future socialist society," rather than with the Leninist stream of Marxism, which views the avoidance of violence in transforming the social order to be "nearly impossible."[101] Furthermore, as noted earlier, his appropriation of Christianity in this early text serves to temper in important respects his appropriation of Marxism. Chastened by an infusion of Christian realism, West is willing to concede that all liberation is penultimate. This, it might reasonably be thought, makes recourse to violence in pursuing a political agenda less likely.

Elsewhere, a peaceable thrust appears even more clearly discernible. Particularly because of his nonviolent ethic and the political possibilities it enables, Martin Luther King, Jr. frequently appears as a hero of many of West's writings from the mid-1980s to the present. In an essay originally published in 1986, West argues that it was King's adoption of a Gandhian commitment to nonviolence as the application of the love ethic of Jesus Christ that provided him with a response to the agonistic implications of Marx and

Nietzsche. The power of King's nonviolent ethic, rooted in a "*profound trust* in the redemptive power of love and in the salvific plan of God," was that it promised to

> transform and even convert one's opponents. The aim is not simply to rely on the moral sense or conscience of the adversary but, if need be, to force the adversary to develop such a sense and conscience. And if one concludes that no such development is possible, then we simply must admit that we are doomed to an unending cycle of violence and oppression—with the old victims of violence soon to become the new perpetrators of violence. Such a nightmare—an inevitable conclusion for Marx and Nietzsche in King's view—radically calls into question the very power of the love ethic of Jesus Christ. For King, if one accepts such a nightmare, then only self-destruction awaits us.[102]

West's evaluation of King's significance in *The American Evasion of Philosophy* is just as forthright. In that work, he claims that King "represents the best of what the political dimension of prophetic pragmatism is about . . . . His all-embracing moral vision facilitated alliances and coalitions across racial, gender, class, and religious lines. His Gandhian method of nonviolent resistance highlighted forms of love, courage, and discipline worthy of a compassionate prophet." By accenting the anti-racist and anti-imperialist implications of his ideals, King serves as a source of inspiration that links "the struggle for freedom in America to those movements in South Africa, Poland, South Korea, Ethiopia, Chile, and the Soviet Union."[103]

The sort of coalition politics King fostered, and the peaceable possibilities of such a politics, finds repeated emphasis in much of West's more recent work. Particularly since the publication of *Race Matters* (1993), West has advocated coalition politics as the model of ethical and political engagement that is most exemplary of his democratic normative vision. Such a model of politics may seem to provide a means of working across, through, and sometimes around differences in creating diverse centers of power that, in seeking to foster liberation and social amelioration, are able to oppose or stand against countervailing forms of unjust power. Such strategies draw upon diverse existing resources and traditions as a means of forging bonds of solidarity and discursive interaction across identities and differences in seeking to alleviate a variety of forms of social suffering. At their best, West would surely contend, coalition strategies can be effective means of peaceably resisting injustice because they capitalize on opportunities to exploit inter-traditional commonalities in addressing collective problems.

In *Democracy Matters*, for example, he suggests coalition strategies are necessary to resist the rise in America of the Constantinian Christianity he claims has corrupted Christianity's traditional emphasis on values such as tolerance and compassion, values central to the workings of a healthy democracy.

Instead, as noted previously, this form of Christianity has functioned to justify the free-market fundamentalism, aggressive militarism, and escalating authoritarianism that characterize the imperial captivity of politics in the contemporary United States. If West is right about the nature of Constantinian Christianity and its connections to these social forces, this is a very bad thing, indeed. Among other things, it threatens to encourage, and it makes many Christians complicit in, the proliferation of violence in our world. West seeks to respond to this situation by suggesting the necessity of a coalition between prophetic Christians, members of other religious groups, and secularists. "It is only with a coalition of the prophetic Christians of all colors, the prophetic Jews and Muslims and Buddhists, and the democratic secularists that we can preserve the American democratic experiment."[104] While there might be good reason to question whether his account of prophetic Christianity is sufficiently robust, his peaceable vision merits respect.

Lingering Ambiguity

A closer look at these elements of West's work reveals that none of them, alone or collectively, give unambiguous or sufficient expression to a peaceable vision. In the end, it remains unclear at best how well West's thought coheres with a prophetic understanding of peaceableness. Consider, first, his upholding of coalition politics as exemplary of his democratic normative vision. Though such a politics may importantly point to possibilities for engagement across a diverse range of traditions, this does not necessarily entail that violence will be eschewed, as on an in-principle pacifist position, or even reduced or subjected to principled limitation, as in just war theory. Indeed, though coalition forms of politics do serve to minimize division and enhance cooperation on one side of a political or moral conflict, it is hardly clear that they alone can minimize violence as a tool for responding to those who stand on the other side of the conflict. For example, West tells us, as I noted earlier, that a coalition politics solicits solidarity with those deeply committed to resisting racism. This is certainly a good thing, something to which we should all be party. But *how* ought we to do so? Can violence ever be a legitimate tool in resisting racism? Certainly, there are those who would claim that it can. But if one contends that violence is not a legitimate tool, can one enter and participate in a coalition with those who would advocate violence? If so, under what terms? West's defense of coalition politics, which is focused primarily on the good ends such a politics may seek to achieve, provides little guidance regarding the permissible means through which these ends may be pursued.

West is unable to give much guidance regarding how the prophetic voice would or ought to address such questions because we find here again the subordination, or reduction, of thick religious commitments to highly general political ends and ideals. Religious commitments—West doesn't specify which ones or how, though apparently these are commitments that are generally shared across a wide range of religious traditions—are significant for coalition politics above all because of their ability to foster desirable political results. Prophetic religious voices, including Christian ones, are significant because they help to "preserve the American democratic experiment." This is underscored elsewhere in *Democracy Matters* in West's characterization of King's enduring significance: "King provided Americans with our last great call to conscience about the intertwined evils of race and empire, calling on us to choose between democracy and white supremacy, between democracy and corporate plutocracy."[105] And in an earlier essay, he asserts that King's principal challenge to us lies in his accenting "the anticolonial, anti-imperialist and antiracist consequences of taking seriously the American ideals of democracy, freedom and equality."[106]

Indeed, in contrast to what would be allowed on King's resolutely nonviolent moral vision,[107] taking democracy seriously is something that West admits, albeit indirectly, might entail the use of violence. In *Democracy Matters*, for example, though harboring reservations about the character of American and British imperialism, he quite clearly approves of the use of military force to defeat German and Italian fascism during World War II. He applauds the "sheer will" of Winston Churchill as he stood "between Nazi domination and any democratic possibility in Europe," and notes favorably the "historical alliance of the American and Soviet empires" that "defeated the fascist forces on the globe." He continues, "The indescribable courage of the U.S. Jim Crow armed forces (365,000 dead) and the incredible gallantry of the Soviet army (twenty million Russian dead) gave the world another chance for democracy matters."[108] However important theological convictions might have been for *King*, it is ultimately considerations about democracy that guide West's thoughts about how political violence might be avoided (through democratic institutions and practices) and about why it might be necessary (to sustain and defend democratic institutions and practices).

The primary difficulty here is not that West endorses the political use of violence, for I have already argued that the prophetic voice does not necessarily reject the political use of violence. Instead, the difficulty is that West's flirtations with the issue simply do not tell us enough about when, why, and how it may legitimately be utilized. It is insufficient to tie the defense of political violence to the defense of democratic institutions and practices. Though he affirms the Allied use of force in World War II, he is critical of the "aggressive militarism" of the George W. Bush administration, with its policy of preemptive military action against potential enemies. It was the embodiment of a "cowboy mythology," a "lone-ranger strategy," in which "one's own interests and aims define what is moral and one's own anxieties and insecurities dictate what is masculine."[109] But what if such an interpretation did not so clearly suggest itself? If matters were slightly different, if imperial political pretensions did not appear so readily discernible, how would this affect West's judgments? What if Iraq *did* pose the imminent threat that the Bush Administration claimed it did? How, in such a case, would West evaluate a decision to intervene militarily? And if West were to judge military intervention to be justifiable in such a case, what means would be legitimately at the United States' disposal? If the political stakes were high enough, if democracy appeared to be under decisive threat in the Middle East, how would he evaluate a president who, in Churchillian fashion, asserted his or her "sheer will" against such an imminent threat? What if this assertion of will included, in Churchillian fashion, directly targeting innocent civilians? Is democracy so great a value that its defense can constitute a Walzerian supreme emergency?

What King recognized, but what West fails to attend to is that, for prophetic Christians, discourse about violence, nonviolence, and peaceableness, as much as discourse about justice, is most fundamentally not about the nature and attractiveness of competing political perspectives or ends, but about the nature and shape of Christian discipleship. Thus, as Daniel Bell has noted, just war thinking in the Christian tradition is not an abstract theory "to be bantered about but a rigorous ecclesial practice which arose out of the church's day-to-day life and shaped that life." It is "a form of Christian discipleship" concerned first of all "about forming the church and only derivatively about speaking to policy makers."[110] The point is not that the Christian will have nothing to say about policy or political matters, nor is it that what she has to say will be wholly distinct from claims that will be forwarded from other camps, religious or not. The point, rather, is that whatever it is that the Christian has to say about such things as political violence and peaceableness will first of all properly be rooted in and reflective of discourse about who God is, what God has made possible, and about what and who God is calling us to be.

CONCLUSION

In his explicit appropriation of the biblical prophets as moral exemplars and inspiration, and in his resolute commitment to foster community that is responsive to voices of suffering and attentive to forces of marginalization and oppression, Cornel West's work resonates deeply with the witness of the prophets, as he intends. Standing alongside the influence of the prophets in West's work, however, is the influence of the American pragmatist tradition, particularly as it finds expression in some of its more recent neo-pragmatist expressions, and this influence leads to some ambivalence in West's thought regarding his understanding of truth and, by extension, to the primary difficulties that finally attend the normative content of his thought and its communal expression. Though there are important influences, themes, and trajectories in his thought that point in a realist direction, he also, especially when evincing the influence of Richard Rorty, seems to veer toward a fairly clear anti-realist conventionalism. West skirts these deep tensions through his adoption of democratic convictions and practices as the primary means through which communities express concern for and respond to suffering, but this only serves to displace the problems that exist with his conception of truth onto his normative commitments. Community for Walzer, in short, *is* democratic community. In contrast to Walzer and Hauerwas, the problem with West's understanding of community and, hence, with his understanding of the prophetic, is not that it is too narrow or closed, but that, because it is tied to an overly general affirmation of democratic commitments and practices, it is not "thick" enough.

Although the prophetic voice is not necessarily incompatible with democratic commitments—indeed, I find relatively uncontroversial the claim that the prophetic voice gives expression to what we would now call irreducibly democratic characteristics and that it thus serves as a crucial source for understanding the historical background and conceptual basis of democratic theory and practice[111]—West's effective reduction of the prophetic voice to democracy is finally unable to give expression to how that voice, whatever else it might also be, is for the prophetic Christian first of all and most basically an expression of divine will, in particular God's justice and God's peace. Without a more substantive construal of that voice, even the most seemingly uncontroversial aspects of his thought, like his affirmation of human dignity, are liable to be distorted by, or absorbed into, regnant forms of political ideology, a result that clearly runs afoul of the prophetic voice's independence. Similarly, though West's work does possess a clearly discernible peaceable thrust, it is guided in this more by political considerations about the nature and shape of democratic convictions and practices than it is by robust convictions about the nature of peace. As such, he is unable to provide any substantive guidance regarding when, why, and how, if at all, the prophetic voice would endorse the use of political violence.

Despite his failures, in some respects West arguably comes the closest of the three figures examined here to serving as a contemporary exemplar of the prophetic voice. With both Walzer and Hauerwas he importantly affirms the significance of community as the primary locus for the apprehension and expression of ethical knowledge, though unlike them, he does not conceive it in highly bounded or closed terms. Furthermore, his thought evinces a critical edge not found in Hauerwas and that arguably provides resources that enable him to resist domination more successfully than Walzer. However, perhaps the most significant contribution he offers is with regard to the character of realism from a non-foundationalist perspective. In those passages in which he appears to uphold a form of realism with regard to meaning and value (though, as I have already noted, because West evinces a good deal of ambivalence on such matters this is not a dominant theme in his work), he offers correctives to difficulties manifest in both Walzer and Hauerwas. What might at these points be called West's critical or faithful realism resists both the conventionalism of Walzer, while still affirming the mediated nature of knowledge, and, because it adopts a critical, revisionist perspective regarding all knowledge claims, the tendency of Hauerwas' thought to conflate the medium and the message.

NOTES

1. Cornel West, "A World of Ideas," in *The Cornel West Reader* (New York: Basic *Civitas* Books, 1999), 294.

2. For discussions of the significance of West's work for the public and potentially transformative role of religious and theological claims, see, for example, Gary Dorrien, "Imagining Social Justice: Cornel West's Prophetic Public Intellectualism," *CrossCurrents* 58, no. 1 (Spring 2008): 6–42 and Mary Doak, "Cornel West's Challenge to the Catholic Evasion of Black Theology," *Theological Studies* 63, no. 1 (February 2002): 87–106.

3. Cornel West, *The American Evasion of Philosophy: A Genealogy of Pragmatism* (Madison: University of Wisconsin Press, 1989), 233. This theme continues to endure for West, as evidenced by its prominence in his most recent book. See Cornel West, *Democracy Matters: Winning the Fight Against Imperialism* (New York: Penguin Press, 2004).

4. Cornel West, "Introduction: To Be Human, Modern and American," in *The Cornel West Reader*, xv.

5. Ibid.

6. West, *The American Evasion of Philosophy*, 228. For a cautionary note regarding West's use of "the tragic," see Elizabeth V. Spelman, "Theodicy, Tragedy and Prophecy: Comments on Cornel West's *The American Evasion of Philosophy*," *APA Newsletter on the Black Experience* 90, no. 3 (Fall 1991): 19–23. Spelman's fundamental worry is that "the structure of feeling" that attends the West's use of the tragic seems to undermine the subversiveness of critiques of white supremacy and other forms of social evil. I do not want to dismiss Spelman's concerns here as unimportant, but I suspect that the differences here between her and West relate to divergent estimations of social hope, and differing understandings of the nature of human evil, or sin.

7. Cornel West, "On My Intellectual Vocation," in *The Cornel West Reader*, 20. See also Cornel West, "Prophetic Religion and the Future of Capitalist Civilization," in Judith Butler, et al., *The Power of Religion in the Public Sphere*, ed. Eduardo

Mendieta and Jonathan VanAntwerpen (New York: Columbia University Press, 2011), 94–95.

8. West, "Introduction: To Be Human, Modern and American," xvi.

9. Ibid., xvii. Even from this very brief treatment of West's diagnosis of the human condition, it is clear that his thought incorporates at least two senses of the tragic: one, a human and finite sense, in which evils are human-made and can be transformed by human effort, and a second, more clearly metaphysical sense, in which "our foes are infinite and transcendental." The first sense testifies to the need for political struggle and resistance. The second, insofar as it is inscribed in "the order of things," is largely resistant to such struggle and testifies to the need for a spirituality of some sort, a "sense of the whole," whether Christian or not. See Lorenzo Simpson, "Evading Theory and Tragedy? Reading Cornel West," *Praxis International* 13, no. 1 (April 1993): 40.

10. West, "Introduction: To Be Human, Modern and American," xvii–xviii.

11. See Ibid. See also Cornel West, "The New Cultural Politics of Difference," in *The Cornel West Reader*, 121.

12. Cornel West, "The Ignoble Paradox of Modernity," in *The Cornel West Reader*, 52.

13. West, "Introduction: To Be Human, Modern and American," xviii–xix.

14. Ibid., xix. In a similar vein, West has elsewhere written that "a deep sense of evil and the tragic must infuse any meaning and value of democracy. The culture of democratic societies requires not only the civic virtues of participation, tolerance, openness, mutual respect and mobility, but also dramatic struggles with the two major culprits—disease and death—that defeat and cut off the joys of democratic citizenship. Such citizenship must not be so preoccupied—or obsessed—with possibility that it conceals or represses the ultimate facts of the human predicament." Cornel West, "Pragmatism and the Sense of the Tragic," in *The Cornel West Reader*, 179.

15. Cornel West, "Nihilism in Black America," in his *Race Matters* (Boston: Beacon Press, 1993), 12. West's discussion of black nihilism has been taken by a number of critics to amount to a "blaming the victim" diagnosis of the plight of contemporary black America that fails to consider adequately the economic and political roots of the current crisis. See, for example, Clevis Headley, "Cornel West on Prophesy [*sic*], Pragmatism, and Philosophy: A Critical Evaluation of Prophetic Pragmatism," in *Cornel West: A Critical Reader*, ed. George Yancy (Oxford: Blackwell, 2001), 72–76; Floyd W. Hayes III, "Cornel West and Afro-Nihilism: A Reconsideration," in *Cornel West*, ed. Yancy, esp. 246–248; and Mark David Wood, *Cornel West and the Politics of Prophetic Pragmatism* (Urbana: University of Illinois Press, 2000), 106–109. West is clearly trying to offer a complex, nuanced analysis that eschews forms of reductionism, and while he does emphasize cultural factors to a degree to which these critics find problematic, he is quite clear that these have political and economic roots. For responses to these critics, see Rosemary Cowan, *Cornel West: The Politics of Redemption* (Oxford: Polity, 2003), 136–138; and Cornel West, "Afterword: Philosophy and the Funk of Life," in *Cornel West*, ed. Yancy, 357–358.

16. West, "Nihilism in Black America," 14. See also Cornel West, "The Political Intellectual," in *The Cornel West Reader*, 293.

17. See West, "The Political Intellectual," 293, and Cornel West, "The Moral Obligations of Living in a Democratic Society," in *The Good Citizen*, ed. David Batstone and Eduardo Mendieta (New York: Routledge, 1999), 10–11.

18. Cornel West, "The Indispensability Yet Insufficiency of Marxist Theory," in *The Cornel West Reader*, 227.

19. West, "A World of Ideas," 298–299. Theologically, it may be useful to think of West as echoing here the best insights of the Social Gospel vision of Walter Rauschenbush, on one hand, and the Christian realism of Reinhold Niebuhr, on the other. In ways that later will become clearer, "West blends the idealism of Rauschenbusch," which holds on to the relevance of the moral values of Christianity (particularly love) in the public sphere, "with Niebuhr's realism about fallen human nature and the limitations this places on human progress . . . . Niebuhr's pessimism tempers Rauschenbusch's optimism and points to the dialectic of hope and despair, idealism and pessimism, which flows throughout West's work." Cowan, *Cornel West*, 72, 78.

20. West, "On My Intellectual Vocation," 22.

21. West, *The American Evasion of Philosophy*, 5.

22. Ibid., 5, 6.

23. Cornel West, "The Political Intellectual," in *The Cornel West Reader*, 278. See also West's "Afterword: The Politics of American Neo-Pragmatism," in *Post-Analytic Philosophy*, ed. John Rajchman and Cornel West (New York: Columbia University Press, 1985), 263–265; and his "Nietzsche's Prefiguration of Postmodern American Philosophy," in *The Cornel West Reader*, 188–207.

24. West, "Afterword: The Politics of American Neo-Pragmatism," 262.

25. Ibid., 263.

26. Richard Rorty, *Philosophy and the Mirror of Nature* (Princeton: Princeton University Press, 1979), 317–318. For a characterization of the foundationalist as fundamentalist, see John E. Thiel, *Nonfoundationalism* (Minneapolis: Fortress Press, 1994), 24.

27. Cornel West, "The Making of an American Radical Democrat of African Descent," in his *The Cornel West Reader*, 14.

28. Cornel West, "Dispensing with Metaphysics in Religious Thought," in his *Prophetic Fragments: Illuminations of the Crisis in American Religion and Culture* (Grand Rapids, MI/Trenton, NJ: William B. Eerdmans Publishing Co./Africa World Press, 1988), 267–268.

29. Ibid., 268, 269. Emphasis in original.

30. Cornel West, "Conclusion: The Author Responds," *Monthly Review* 45, no. 2 (June 1993): 59.

31. West, "Nietzsche's Prefiguration of Postmodern Philosophy," 189–198.

32. West, "The Political Intellectual," 278.

33. Ibid., 279. Emphasis added.

34. Cornel West, *The Ethical Dimensions of Marxist Thought* (New York: Monthly Review Press, 1991), 1.

35. Ibid.

36. Ibid., 3.

37. West, "Afterword: The Politics of American Neo-Pragmatism," 268, 269. See, generally, 268ff. See also West, "Dispensing with Metaphysics in Religious Thought," 269.

38. West, "Nietzsche's Prefiguration of Postmodern American Philosophy," 209–210. Emphasis added.

39. See the nice summary discussion in Cowan, *Cornel West*, 63–65.

40. Wood, *Cornel West and the Politics of Prophetic Pragmatism*, 91.

41. Quoted in Cowan, *Cornel West*, 54.

42. West, *The American Evasion of Philosophy*, 233.

43. C. Stephen Evans, "Realism and Antirealism in Kierkegaard's *Concluding Unscientific Postscript*," in *The Cambridge Companion to Kierkegaard*, ed. Alastair Hannay and Gordon D. Marino (Cambridge: Cambridge University Press, 1998), 170.

44. Ibid., 166.

45. Ibid., 169.

46. Ibid., 172.

47. Cornel West, "A Philosophical View of Easter," in *The Cornel West Reader*, 416.

48. Ibid., 418.

49. George Yancy, "Religion and the Mirror of God: Historicism, Truth, and Religious Pluralism," in *Cornel West*, ed. Yancy, 122.

50. Ibid., 135.

51. West, "A Philosophical View of Easter," in *The Cornel West Reader*, 418–419. West may be somewhat confusing in the way he deploys terminology relating to truth/Truth, reality/Reality, and the like. When he uses these terms in their capitalized forms, I take it that he means to refer to them as understood in their ultimate, unmediated, inaccessible fullness. In most instances, uses of these terms are, as we have seen, occasions for intellectual vice. The only instances in which such terms are properly used in this manner, it seems, is to refer to Jesus Christ. Truth and Reality, West seems to say, are like proper names when used in reference to Jesus Christ.

52. Joerg Rieger, *God and the Excluded: Visions and Blindspots in Contemporary Theology* (Minneapolis: Fortress Press, 2001), 115.

53. West, "A Philosophical View of Easter," in his *The Cornel West Reader*, 419.

54. Ibid.

55. Cornel West, *Prophesy Deliverance! An Afro-American Revolutionary Christianity* (Philadelphia: The Westminster Press, 1982), 98.

56. Ibid.

57. Yancy, "Religion and the Mirror of God," in *Cornel West*, ed. Yancy, 127–128.

58. West, "Conclusion: The Author Responds," 59.

59. Cornel West, "The Historicist Turn in the Philosophy of Religion," in his *The Cornel West Reader*, 370.

60. West, *Prophesy Deliverance!*, 16. For a reading along these lines that instructively puts West in conversation with Ludwig Feuerbach and Emmanuel Levinas, see, Josiah Ulysses Young III, "Existential Aptness and Epistemological Correctness: West and the Identity of the 'Lord,'" in *Cornel West*, ed. Yancy, 167–175.

61. West, *Democracy Matters*, 17.

62. Ibid., 114–115.

63. West, *Prophesy Deliverance!*, 16.

64. Ibid., 17.

65. Ibid.

66. Ibid., 99–100.

67. Ibid., 17–18.

68. Ibid., 18–19.

69. Reinhold Niebuhr, "The Children of Light and the Children of Darkness," in *The Essential Reinhold Niebuhr: Selected Essays and Addresses*, ed. Robert McAfee Brown (New Haven: Yale University Press, 1986), 160. See also the helpful discussion in Cowan, *Cornel West*, 71–78.

70. West, "Nihilism in Black America," 18.

71. Of course, arguments and analyses, as West's own work illustrates, are not marginal in responding to social ills, as they are necessary in diagnosing and determining a proper response to them. West's point, however, is that the materiality and source of social remediation is found most in the networks of care and love of which we are a part. Without such networks of care and love, no amount of argumentation or analysis will succeed in responding adequately to social evil and injustice.

72. West, "Nihilism in Black America," 19. See also, West, "Prophetic Religion and the Future of Capitalist Civilization," 96–97.

73. See West, "Prophetic Religion and the Future of Capitalist Civilization," 98.

74. Cornel West, "Christian Love and Heterosexism," in *The Cornel West Reader*, 407.

75. Cornel West, "The Pitfalls of Racial Reasoning," in *Race Matters*, 28.

76. Cowan, *Cornel West*, 143. For criticism, which I do not share, of West's affirmation of coalition politics, see Clarence Sholé Johnson, *Cornel West and Philosophy: The Quest for Social Justice* (New York: Routledge, 2003), 34–36. The lynchpin of Johnson's critique is that because nihilism is a problem peculiar to blacks, West ought to focus more centrally on the unique significance of race, something he finds marginalized or relativized in a race-transcending coalition politics approach. The primary problem with Johnson's argument is that it incorrectly asserts that nihilism is a problem unique to black communities. West does, of course, write about nihilism in black America, but he does not claim that this is a problem found only in black America. Indeed, in *Democracy Matters*, he writes of it as a multidimensional phenomenon that pervades American social and political culture. See West, *Democracy Matters*, Chapter 2 ("Nihilism in America").

77. James H. Cone, "'Let Suffering Speak:' The Vocation of the Black Intellectual," in *Cornel West*, ed. Yancy, 109.

78. Young, "Existential Aptness and Epistemological Correctness," 168–169.

79. West, *Democracy Matters*, 192.

80. Ibid., 171.

81. West, *The American Evasion of Philosophy*, 232.

82. Cornel West, "Religion, Politics, Language," in *Prophetic Fragments*, 23–24. See also Cornel West, "On Michael Harrington's *The Politics at God's Funeral*," also in *Prophetic Fragments*, 26–27.

83. West, *Democracy Matters*, 146–151.

84. Judith Butler and Cornel West, "Dialogue," in Butler, et al., *The Power of Religion in the Public Sphere*, 105.

85. West, *Democracy Matters*, 160.

86. Ibid., 161.

87. Ibid., 162.

88. West, "Religion, Politics, Language," 23–24. See also West, "On Michael Harrington's *The Politics at God's Funeral*," 26–27.

89. West, *Democracy Matters*, 152.

90. Ibid., 160.

91. West, "The Indispensability Yet Insufficiency of Marxist Theory," 227.

92. West, *Democracy Matters*, 163.

93. See West, *Democracy Matters*, Chapter 3, "The Deep Democratic Tradition in America." The phrase "cultural way of being" is found on p. 68.

94. Michael J. Baxter, C.S.C., "'Overall, the First Amendment Has Been Very Good for Christianity'—*Not!*: A Response to Dyson's Rebuke," *DePaul Law Review* 43, no. 2 (Winter 1994): 433–434. Emphasis added. The article by Dyson to which Baxter is responding, "'God Almighty Has Spoken From Washington, D.C.': American Society and Christian Faith," originally published in the *DePaul Law Review* (vol. 42), is reprinted in Michael Eric Dyson, *Reflecting Black: African-American Cultural Criticism* (Minneapolis: University of Minnesota Press, 1993), 286–319.

95. See, for example, Ronald Dworkin, *Life's Dominion: An Argument about Abortion, Euthanasia, and Individual Freedom* (New York: Alfred A. Knopf, 1993) and Peter Singer, *Rethinking Life and Death: The Collapse of Our Traditional Ethics* (New York: St. Martin's Griffin, 1994).

96. Jackson, *Political* Agape, 188.

97. West, *Prophesy Deliverance!*, 17. It is likely unwise to make too much of this passage and, on its basis, attribute too firm a view about the moral worth of human beings to West. My sense here is that he is simply reflecting a rather common view about the nature of dignity, perhaps informed by Niebuhrian considerations. The more fundamental point, however, is that this is just its greatest weakness, that is, its lack of conceptual thickness and development.

98. Jackson, *Political* Agape, 188.

99. Sylvia Ann Hewlett and Cornel West, *The War Against Parents: What We Can Do for America's Beleaguered Moms and Dads* (Boston: Houghton Mifflin, 1998), 197.

100. In *Cornel West and the Politics of Prophetic Pragmatism*, Mark David Wood argues that there is a clearly discernible shift in West's thought from an early, revolutionary socialist standpoint to a later, progressive reformist standpoint.

101. West, *Prophesy Deliverance!*, 137, 135.

102. Cornel West, "Prophetic Christian as Organic Intellectual: Martin Luther King, Jr.," in his *The Cornel West Reader*, 432.

103. West, *The American Evasion of Philosophy*, 234–235.

104. West, *Democracy Matters*, 169.

105. Ibid., 58.

106. West, "Prophetic Christian as Organic Intellectual," 433.

107. See the discussion in John J. Ansbro, *Martin Luther King, Jr.: The Making of a Mind* (Maryknoll, NY: Orbis Books, 1982), esp. 250–251.

108. West, *Democracy Matters*, 55–56.

109. Ibid., 5–6.

110. Daniel M. Bell Jr., "In War and in Peace: Implications of Just War Theory," *The Christian Century* (September 6, 2005): 26. See also Daniel M. Bell Jr., *Just War as Christian Discipleship: Recentering the Tradition in the Church rather than the State* (Grand Rapids, MI: Brazos Press, 2009).

111. On this, see, for example, John W. De Gruchy, *Christianity and Democracy* (Cambridge: Cambridge University Press, 1995), 40–53.

Chapter 5

The Prophetic Voice as Realist and Non-Foundationalist

The Contours of a Constructive Christian Theological Account

TAKING STOCK

The initial impetus to treat together the figures who form the heart of this project—Michael Walzer, Stanley Hauerwas, and Cornel West—was rooted in the recognition that each of these figures, from resolutely and self-consciously non-foundationalist perspectives, has been understood, and wants to be understood, as an exponent of the prophetic voice in some form. To reiterate, the prophetic voice is properly understood as giving expression to a distinctive, divinely grounded moral vision that seeks forms of justice prioritizing those on society's margins and the fundamental transformation of the social order in the direction of peace and reconciliation. My hope was that these figures could aid in articulating what that voice looks like—particularly from a Christian theological perspective—once one has conceded, as non-foundationalists do, that human perception and knowledge of reality is never had "raw," but is always mediated and shaped by a variety of historical and communal influences, contexts, and traditions.

To be sure, each of these figures does offer insights regarding how we might understand the present possibilities of speaking and acting in a prophetic mode. Drawing heavily on the prophets as exemplars, Michael Walzer articulates an approach to political philosophy that places resistance to domination at its center, while also affirming the centrality of community to moral knowledge and action. From a resolutely theological perspective, Stanley Hauerwas upholds a vision of the church as a peaceable community standing as a distinctive critical, countercultural presence to the pathologies of liberal modernity, particularly its violence. And Cornel West creatively fuses Christian-inspired moral vision with pragmatism and other forms of critical thought in articulating a solidaristic ethic that he hopes can respond to the forms of suffering characteristic of the late twentieth and early twenty-first centuries. These insights are all resonant in varying, but important, degrees with central emphases of the biblical prophetic voice.

Despite these insights, these figures also illustrate how difficult it is to articulate an adequate non-foundationalist account of the prophetic voice. In the three preceding chapters, I have argued that Walzer, Hauerwas, and West all share a fundamental problem, relating to their respective understandings of how the prophetic voice finds communal expression and embodiment. As each turns to some understanding of community as the context within which moral claims are apprehended and expressed, a corollary of their shared non-foundationalist assumptions, truth/reality is reduced to or conflated with some aspect of its communal expression. That is, though rightly recognizing that all knowledge is socially and linguistically mediated, each figure succumbs to the pitfall, intentionally or not, of conflating the medium with the message, thereby losing sight of the crucial realist underpinnings of the prophetic voice. Walzer's conventionalist account of political philosophy reduces the prophetic voice to the contingent shared understandings of particular political communities. Hauerwas' resolute desire to avoid what he diagnoses as the pathologies of liberal modernity leads him to articulate a highly bounded vision of the church in which, however unintentionally, the reality of God is reduced to a particular ecclesial expression. By contrast, West's pragmatic orientation and concern to avoid the potentially absolutist implications of an affirmation of realism lead him to uphold an overly generalized conception of community organized around democratic convictions and practices. There is nothing inherent in the turn to community that makes such an outcome necessary or inevitable, though it is, I concede, an all too real danger, as Walzer, Hauerwas, and West make clear.

In succumbing to this pitfall, each one, in turn, fails to give adequate expression to the normative commitments of the prophetic voice. Walzer's prioritizing of the shared understandings of political community leads him to be blind to the sorts of marginal voices the prophetic will prioritize and it undergirds a defense of political violence that prioritizes the nation-state and fails to attend to the reconciliatory thrust of the biblical witness. Hauerwas' bounded conception of Christian community similarly makes difficult the sort of attention to marginalized voices the prophetic will be concerned with, and it cannot express adequately the just peace the prophetic envisions. Boundaries are precisely what West resists, but this leads him to adopt an overly general democratic ethic that underexpresses the normative commitments of the prophetic voice.

If these three very prominent, highly influential thinkers fail, can the prospects for success be very good? Yes. By learning from the missteps of each of these figures and building upon positive features of their thought, adding to these features themes in minor keys and trajectories not fully developed that do point in genuinely prophetic directions, it is possible to articulate an adequate realist, yet non-foundationalist Christian theological account of the prophetic voice. It is to sketching out the contours of such an account that the remainder of this chapter will be devoted.

Perhaps the most fundamental lesson to be learned from the failures of Walzer, Hauerwas, and West is that, for the prophetic, *truth has primacy*, and this leads to a certain reordering of priorities. In beginning to articulate what an adequate contemporary Christian theological expression of the prophetic might look like, I will thus be concerned, first of all, to suggest what a theological account of truth in a non-foundational context looks like, and then I will draw out the implications of this for its communal expression, especially in and through the church, and its normative content. There is, I will suggest, a natural fit between a certain non-foundationalist construal of truth and its expression in community, on the one hand, and the normative commitments of the prophetic voice, on the other. Indeed, there is a deep sense in which the contemporary expression of the prophetic voice is enabled to come into its own, to retrieve and express some of the deepest insights of its biblical expression, when it is cast in a non-foundationalist frame.

TOWARD A NON-FOUNDATIONALIST CHRISTIAN THEOLOGICAL REALISM

At least as traditionally conceived, religious commitments, by definition, have a realist character.[1] Such commitments are believed to refer to something beyond them, something that transcends or undergirds them, something that gives them meaning and value, something that can stand as a criterion of their adequacy. It is such a conception that Christians characteristically assume when they speak of, think about, pray to, and act in response to God. Thus, the truth of a claim, as I have noted repeatedly, is measured by whether it corresponds to or reflects the reality to which it is meant to refer. Thus, Christians claim that God, as the source of reality and truth—indeed, as reality itself—is the basic fact of the world, the singularity in which the world's plurality achieves a unity. It is God upon which all of our moral claims are dependent, and, insofar as they are true, it is to God that they refer. Insofar as it is concerned to speak about God and so make claims about the way the world *is*, about its creation, fallen state, and ultimate redemption, theology will necessarily be realist in character and universal in its scope and aspirations.

It is just this universalist scope of religious commitments, in particular, and of realist commitments, more generally, that concerns many philosophers and theologians. The chief concern with talk about "truth," "reality," and other associated concepts, a concern that is buttressed by a good bit of historical evidence, is that they too easily take on a fundamentalist or absolutist cast that may lead to coercion, manipulation, and, in some cases, violence. Earlier in the book, such concerns were seen to motivate Walzer's conventionalism and West's tendency, particularly when evincing the influence of Richard Rorty, to veer toward a rejection of realism. In place of the manipulation and compulsion of the philosopher possessed of pure knowledge, Walzer urges a more grounded approach to the elaboration and evaluation of claims via democratic conversation. Similarly, while the connections between concerns about realism and democracy are not explicitly in drawn out West's work, I have suggested that such a connection does exist in his thought, as well.

Of course, as Hauerwas shows, an affirmation of realism need not go hand in glove with an affirmation of abstraction and the rejection of particularity. Hauerwas is just as concerned as Walzer and West are about the potentially deleterious effects of highly abstract claims. As discussed earlier, he claims that the abstraction characteristic of liberal modern ways of knowing serves to underwrite the very sort of violence liberalism wants so badly to avoid. In part (this is not the only impetus; considerations about the nature and structure of biblical narrative are at least as paramount), it is precisely this that leads him to turn to Christian narrative as an expression of truth or, as he more commonly puts it, truthfulness.

Nevertheless, though realist assumptions clearly guide and motivate Hauerwas' work, his realism lies more or less in the background of his thought, and is not fully developed. Most crucially, how his realist commitments sit with or relate to his non-foundationalist commitments is not developed, and it is inattention to such matters that leads to the problems that attend his thought. This inattention may be in large part due to his resistance to ways of understanding knowledge claims apart from their rootedness in a particular tradition. While I will later affirm, with Hauerwas, the centrality of community as a primary mediator of knowledge, an insufficiently critical reliance on tradition runs the risk of conflating the truths mediated in and through tradition with truth itself. However, even if Hauerwas does not develop it sufficiently, it is possible to uphold the integrity of both realist commitments and non-foundationalist assumptions. Showing how this is the case will be largely a matter of developing further and tying together strings of argument from the preceding chapters.

Perhaps the most fundamental element in showing this is the distinction, first noted in the second chapter, between the *meaning or nature of truth*, on the one hand, and the *justification of truth claims*, on the other. The alethiological realism I am concerned to affirm has to do with the nature or meaning of truth claims, not their justification. Realism with regard to truth, then, is non-epistemic in character. What alethiological realism claims is that truth obtains when there is a correspondence between one's words or ideas and the world they describe or objects to which they refer; it is not dependent on an account of how we might determine whether truth, so understood, obtains. Indeed, such a position is entirely compatible with a fallibilist, non-foundational epistemology that highlights the mediated nature of all of our knowledge claims. A fallibilist epistemology does not claim or entail that our claims cannot be true in a correspondence sense, but only that we have no tests that can guarantee that our words properly describe or that our ideas adequately refer. Such an epistemology recognizes that, even (especially?) on a realist conception of truth, we can never be sure that our claims have actually "gotten" reality. We are not God; our claims are always bounded and shaped by a panoply of factors, and so are always subject to revision as we encounter challenges.[2] But it is precisely because realism is compatible with such a fallibilist and revisionist epistemology that it need not entail the sort of absolutism or certitude about which Walzer and West worry. All inquiry into truth is tentative and never final.

This affirmation of the tentative, never fixed character of truth claims is frequently missed by both foundationalist defenders of realism and their postmodern anti-realist critics in their shared assumption that knowledge of objective reality is dependent upon some method of verifying that knowledge with certainty.[3] This assumption has manifested itself more than once in the foregoing. It lurks in George Yancy's earlier-noted contention that West fails to capture the traditionally realist character of religious beliefs because his historicist approach lacks a way of ascertaining whether a particular religion is true. Similarly, it is prominent in the work of Richard Rorty, whose resonance with Walzer and influence on West has been noted. By failing to note the crucial conceptual distinction between alethiology and epistemology, critics of realism frequently, though mistakenly, assume that the inability to show with certainty how claims may be true entails that there are no truths to which our claims might correspond. What these sorts of assumptions neglect is the non-epistemic character of a realist account of the meaning of truth.

Because knowledge is mediated and fallible, our claims about truth will have an approximative and aspirational character. Returning to the discussion in the previous chapter of realist trajectories in West's work, what West sometimes seems to uphold is a realist construal of the meaning of theological claims that also contends, like Kierkegaard before him, that our particular descriptions of or beliefs about the world are never adequate in describing that to which they refer; they are never exhaustive of reality. To believe otherwise is to cling to forms of surety that are likely to have dire consequences for others. This does not mean, however, that there is no reality to which our descriptions or beliefs properly aspire to refer. Rather, it means that no particular claim we make can ever fully and finally capture that reality. We continue to uphold correspondence to extralinguistic reality as the ideal by which our claims are measured, but recognize that particular expressions of that ideal will all, finally, be inadequate and partial. Though our claims may point to or provide intimations of the fullness of that reality, offering approximations of it, they will never fully capture it, at least not this side of the eschaton. Thus, for example, Christians affirm that the Kingdom to which they witness has a present, though incomplete, reality. We have clues to its character, partial foretastes of its existence, but its fullness is something held in anticipation. So understood, futurity is the basic form of theological truth.[4]

Such a conception of theological truth and its apprehension is in keeping with fundamental considerations about the nature and tasks of Christian discipleship. It is in Jesus Christ that God meets human beings in their particularity. Among other things, for Christians this means that it is in Jesus that the relational character of God is most fully and profoundly revealed and known. Knowledge of and responsiveness to God in Christ takes the form of discipleship—following after—and so is not primarily propositional, but relational in form. The Kingdom proclaimed by Jesus elicits a response as one seeks proper relationship to God, self, and the other in light of the reality he proclaims. This is a crucial feature of Jesus' teachings noted in the first chapter. His often indirect and excessive parabolic and hyperbolic teachings could not be ignored and were subject to varied understanding and even misunderstanding. But in inviting plural reception and appealing to people where they were, they also often served to open new horizons of understanding and action in response to the in-breaking reality of the Kingdom. Similarly, if they are truly taken seriously, the transformative initiatives of the Sermon on the Mount demand to find embodied practice. Of course, though such practices, when successful, will be analogically reflective of Jesus' own practice, such embodiment will always be in contexts distinct from Jesus' own. Thus, discipleship most essentially consists not of the possession of a discrete set of truths to be instantiated in the same manner in various particular situations, but is, instead, a following after in the quest to give fuller and richer expression to what we might call God's unfolding truth. It is better understood in terms of "the recognition, seeking and following of a person into new situations." Our apprehension and embodiment of the truth Jesus discloses thus "might be seen as something always on the move, and the follower of Jesus becomes a wayfarer."[5]

THE CHURCH AS A COMMUNITY OF BECOMING

Not only is our apprehension of truth marked by fallibility, it is also mediated in and through the communities of which we are a part. For Christians, the church is the primary community through which reality is apprehended. What are the implications of the foregoing claims, then, for how we ought to understand Christian community, for ecclesiology? If the follower of Jesus, in foregoing surety, is a wayfarer, this has profound implications for how we might understand the nature of the church that such disciples comprise. In keeping with this vision of discipleship, the church will be a community that understands itself not in terms of security and stability, but in terms of becoming. It is a people grasping for ever fuller and adequate expressions of a dynamic, but underdetermined identity.[6] What emerges from an understanding of the church along these lines is an affirmation of the centrality of ecclesiology, such as one finds in Hauerwas, but recast in conceptual terms resistant to the erection of boundaries and use of oppositional spatial metaphors. It will be a vision of the church that, though sharing some emphases with postliberal categories and assumptions, will have little regard for the sort of dichotomizing that often characterizes Hauerwas' work, precisely because the vision of truth that animates it will welcome the sorts of reconfigurations that are generated through contact with "others."

Within theology, the non-foundationalist recognition that our apprehension of reality is inescapably shaped by and mediated through a variety of social and historical factors, as well as by a variety of forms of shared behavior and linguistic practice, has led some, particularly those labeled postliberal, to emphasize that it is only by locating ourselves in relation to and following other authoritative practitioners of a tradition that we acquire and grow in theological knowledge. To posit some other basis for critical theological reflection would be to assume the possibility of occupying the sort of neutral standpoint that such a position grants does not exist. It is assumptions of these sorts, already discussed at length, that motivate much of Hauerwas' work and lead him to highlight the church as the primary locus for the expression of theological truth. In this fundamental move, his thought moves in just the right direction.

The difficulty with Hauerwas' project, as I have noted, is not that it has a community-oriented, ecclesiological focus, but that his ecclesiology, in an effort to demarcate clearly the church from that which might imperil its identity, tends to emphasize the coherence, continuity, and reception of an already established identity. At more than one point, I noted Hauerwas tends to articulate the relationship between the church and world in ways that evince a self-assuredness regarding his interpretation of the Christian story and an accompanying general unwillingness to adjust or examine that story in light of challenges to his reading of it. I noted, for example, that he is generally unreceptive to feminist challenges to aspects of his thought, accusing them instead of harboring some of the most pathological assumptions about modernity. Similarly, Hauerwas' general tendency is to depict the relationship between the church and world unidirectionally; the world is reshaped by the church, but not the other way around. He largely follows Lindbeck in affirming that no world is more real than the scriptural world and that it is Scripture that therefore rightly provides the interpretive framework through which believers come to understand reality. The proper relation of church to world is one in which the church, as bearer of that interpretive framework, absorbs the world, rather than being absorbed by it. As I argued earlier, these and other similar features of his thought lead to problems both with articulating how it is to *God's truth*, rather than a particular expression of it, that the church witnesses and with attending to the claims of those on the margins prioritized by the prophetic voice.

However, recognition of the centrality of the church for theological knowledge and practice need not entail that received tradition is static or incapable of growth. Admitting the mediated nature of all knowledge, recognizing that there is no noncircular way to make theological claims or to evaluate nontheological claims theologically, and affirming the generative character of received tradition need not entail the sort of communal closure one finds in Hauerwas. This is because granting authority to received tradition need not be uncritical. Though the commitments of communally borne tradition do rightly—indeed, inescapably—constitute something like a precondition or starting point for any sort of critical inquiry into the truth of claims, it is precisely these commitments that subsequently get tested, evaluated, and possibly revised as we subject our partial, fallible claims to critical inquiry.[7] Although we necessarily begin *here*, openness to the dynamism of God's truth will almost certainly lead us to journey elsewhere.

Because the truth that one finds expressed in and through the church is incomplete and fragmentary, the identity of the church is itself incomplete and subject to revision and rearticulation as it encounters new or different voices that may enable it to become a fuller and more faithful expression of Christ's body. If we affirm that all of our theological claims are partial and fallible and therefore describe the church, as the embodiment of those claims, as underdetermined and always becoming, the understanding of the relationship between church and world one finds in Hauerwas cannot hold. There can be no surety that any expression of the church—even (especially?) the idealized version one finds in Hauerwas—has "gotten it right" and the world "gets it wrong." There can be no assurance that the church provides *the* interpretive framework for the world because the church itself is incomplete and, indeed, bears the world's darkness. This darkness is well-attested to by a well-documented and, in some instances, still ongoing history of exclusions based on race, gender, and other factors.[8]

A church that learns from and is responsive to its "others," precisely in giving up forms of theological surety, finds itself faced with new opportunities to discern the transfiguring presence of the Spirit. Such openness to the challenges posed by others means that the boundaries between church and world will often not be capable of clear demarcation and their relationship will properly have a reciprocal, dialogical character. Though in redeeming the world the church does reconfigure the world (Hauerwas is surely right this far), the absorption of the world into Christian reality also rightly refigures and even transfigures Christianity and the church. The church reinvents itself by incorporating into its identity and self-narration "other" voices that offer "'perturbations' in tradition." Such voices "disrupt the consistency of belief and practice while rippling outward to establish a new pattern," but "within and in obedience to its redeeming incarnational grammar."[9] This does not indicate a lessening of desire on the part of the church to witness to the truth. On the contrary, the only way the church can hope to continue to approximate the truth it finds in Christ is by relinquishing surety, embracing the risk of encountering others, and, in light of such encounters, correcting its most distorted and enhancing its most salutary features.

Yet how is the relationship between generative community and transformative engagement with the other negotiated? Both tradition and innovation have their rightful place in the theological task, and it is not clear at this point whether, or how, in any particular instance of theological reflection, one or the other ought to have priority. There is an abiding tension between a critical, innovative mode that challenges current expressions of ecclesial reality, on the one hand, and a more traditional, conservative mode that subjects challenges to critical scrutiny, on the other. The real theological significance of the critical, innovative mode, however, is the manner in which it enables Christian theology more fully to become itself, to give ever more adequate expression to its incarnational grammar.[10] With regard to the prophetic voice, this manner of negotiating these moments of theological reflection is clarified as we turn from considerations about the *form* that voice takes in light of non-foundationalist assumptions, to considerations about its *content*.

THE COMMUNITY OF TRUTH IS A COMMUNITY OF JUSTICE

Though the foregoing provides some sense of the form prophetic truth and community take from a non-foundationalist perspective, this is not all that can be said about the nature of theological truth or its communal expression in the church. To stop here would not clarify how this position is to be distinguished from a postmodern "play of difference" and it would fail to give sufficient expression to the content of the incarnational grammar that guides the church's critical vocation. In this section, I want to suggest that, for those concerned to uphold a realist construal of truth, the acceptance of non-foundationalist assumptions (along with the attendant rejection of surety and recognition of the significance of "others") creates a space that is hospitable to—indeed, that actively solicits—a prophetic construal of justice. In short, a realist, but non-foundationalist understanding of theological truth goes hand in hand with a prophetic understanding of justice. This distinguishes this position from other forms of difference affirmation and clarifies, by making explicit its theological authorization, how attention to the other is central to ecclesial identity.

The connection between a non-foundationalist construal of truth and prophetic justice has already been gestured toward a few times in the preceding chapters. In chapter 3, in seeking a way beyond Hauerwas' tendency to reduce apprehension of truth to its expression in the church, I noted, following Tyler Roberts, the renunciative character of theology. This aspect of theology, which finds partial, though insufficient, expression in Hauerwas' work, highlights the limitations and inadequacies of human imagination regarding the divine. Bearing in mind the limitations and partiality of our apprehension of God, a task the renunciative character of theology shares with a non-foundationalist realism, Roberts argues that our apprehension of God must attend to the margins. Similarly, from a self-consciously liberationist perspective, West has contended that the power of particular Christian claims finds important measure in their power to effect social transformation and amelioration, in their power, in short, to "let suffering speak." Indeed, this connection between knowledge of God and attention to the margins is characteristic of liberation theology generally, which has continually placed an emphasis on both the limited and perspectival nature of our apprehension of God, on the one hand, and the ways in which this apprehension can be enriched through attention to the margins, on the other. For liberation theologies, "the notion of truth is not watered down" through a self-consciousness of limits and a concomitant appeal to the margins, "but expanded."[11]

This connection between the apprehension of truth and the doing of justice is hardly accidental for many liberation theologians, for they characteristically find authorization for their claims in the biblical, especially prophetic, witness. As chapter 1 makes clear, a prophetic understanding of truth and community is inseparable from substantive claims about the nature of justice and peaceableness. The essential character of God *is* justice.[12] Biblically, God is known as justice is done by attending especially to those who are most vulnerable and at society's margins. Such justice is not characterized a by a neutral, appraisive fairness that disregards outcomes, but rather is focused specifically on upsetting and alleviating the deep-rooted causes and effects of injustice, particularly in their political, economic, and religious dimensions. It is expressed as the steadfast love of God is imitated and embodied in individual lives and communal structures and practices. To know God, therefore, is to know and do justice at the margins, or, more accurately, to know God ever more adequately is to do God's justice ever more adequately.

Ecclesiologically, then, the church is a particular community of truth that is also a particular community of justice. Because there is an organic connection between God's character and actions and the character and actions of the community that seeks to know God, the church's identity and vocation is constituted and defined essentially by its willingness to follow God and Jesus in caring for the vulnerable at society's margins. Just as God's character finds expression through a steadfast love that self-givingly moves toward and on behalf of humanity, so the church is characterized by similar movements to the margins. In contemporary parlance, then, the church's primary religious and ethical responsibility is to foster solidaristic forms of relationship with those at the margins and, on the basis of such relationships, to challenge and to seek to redeem existing ecclesial and societal structures and practices. There is a necessary connection between orthodoxy and orthopraxy, as the being of the church, which is always also (at least this side of the eschaton) a becoming, finds ever truer expression only as it is constructed from the outside, in.[13] As with the prophets and Jesus Christ, the church gives proper expression to its belief in God only as it enacts God's way of being in the world, only as it advocates for and enacts practices of justice understood in terms of attention to and solidarity with society's most marginal and vulnerable.

We can get a better, more concrete sense of what this might look like by examining some examples. In both examples, the normative position the prophetic voice stakes out—while remaining compatible with a range of nontheological voices—is irreducibly theological. Within the distinctive context of contemporary politics and social challenges, the demands of prophetic justice sketched here reflect, and serve as creative responses to, God's character and demands.

Consider, first, the nature and limitations of Hauerwas' treatments of race and racism. At least one thing a justice-oriented ecclesiology will entail is a greater willingness of the church to alter its practices to recognize and respond more fully to those voices that have been excluded from it and from society at large. In order to be credible, a truly prophetic ecclesiology "requires a community of reference composed of weak and strong, oppressor and oppressed alike–a reconciled people whose radical ecclesiology is a politics of peace."[14] Hauerwas' recent difference-affirming gestures (discussed in chapter 3) notwithstanding, it is not clear that this is a lesson he has learned fully. This is especially evident with his engagement with race. In a recent essay in which he engages the work of Will Campbell to address race, Hauerwas writes that the "'lot more' to this 'race thing' is sin and redemption," particularly the denial of God's absolute sovereignty. "The categories of race, or the classification of people by color, do not exist in the new creation enacted by Jesus Christ. The Christian message on race is quite simply the Gospel: that is, 'while we were yet sinners, Christ died for us' (Rom 5:8)."[15] In response to racism, we are not to "do" anything; rather we are to *be* reconciled to God and man.[16]

But what does *this* mean? Without more specificity about what being reconciled means in this context, it is hard not to be suspicious that, intentionally or not, Hauerwas is letting himself and others too easily off the hook here. In an earlier essay on King, he writes that the story of the black struggle in America "is not my story, though I pray that God will make that story my story, for I hope to enjoy the fellowship of the communion of saints."[17] Of course, the first part of this claim is simply not true. Insofar as Hauerwas' own life (and the lives of his fellow white citizens) has been inscribed, as he recognizes, by white racism, King's story, and the story of black struggle in America more generally, *is* his story, "*albeit experienced and interpreted from very different perspectives*."[18] If he is truly to embrace the insights radical democracy has to offer the church, as he claims he desires in some of his most recent works, if he is to offer more than a deferred eschatological hope for racial reconciliation that implicitly colludes with the deafening silence prevalent among other Anglo-American ethicists and theologians,[19] he must demonstrate how embodied Christian practices can provide a constructive response to racism.

As Derek Woodard-Lehman suggests, "The conversion required to effect a full disavowal of both" state violence and states of violence associated with white supremacy "cannot merely be a discourse of resurrection; it must generate communities of resurrection."[20] Generating such communities may, of course, entail education about the nature and legacy of racism. It may involve active forms of resistance against racial injustice. It may find expression through pulpit and congregational exchanges between predominantly white and predominantly black churches. But the prophetic voice requires more than these sorts of measures. It requires the "performance of penitent memory." Concretely, this could mean something like the following: For Hauerwas, this could take the form of challenging his own United Methodist Church community penitently to seek reunification with those denominations (e.g., the African Methodist Episcopal and Christian Methodist Episcopal Churches) whose creation is rooted in racial division. "This reunion might best be effected by the resignation of UMC bishops and transfer of UMC property to a truly *uniting* Methodist Church, a costly repentance transferring *actual* power and assets. These officers would serve, or not serve, at the behest of those formerly excluded from full communion"[21] There would be, of course, similar opportunities for other denominations with similar histories.

As a second example, consider how a distinctly prophetic understanding of poverty alleviation might shape Christian engagement with welfare policy. One common way to view poverty is to see it primarily as a kind of cultural pathology: excepting innocent victims of misfortune like young children or elderly who lack families to care for them, the poor are largely victims of their own deficiencies. Robust government social safety net programs are likened to hammocks that lull "able-bodied people into lives of dependency and complacency."[22] Public policy should focus primarily on providing incentives for the poor to change their ways and lift themselves out of their self-imposed suffering. Such a position makes it easier to justify cuts to public programs, such as the Supplemental Nutrition Assistance Program (SNAP) or even the Patient Protection and Affordable Care Act ("Obamacare"), rendering responsiveness to immediate needs a function not of public policy but of individual and private charity. For example, Mike Conaway, a Republican member of the U.S. House of Representatives from Texas, defended a 2013 proposal to cut billions from SNAP assistance by arguing that Jesus' claim in Matthew 25:40—"Truly I tell you, just as you did it to one of the least of these . . . , you did it to me"—referred to the personal obligations of individuals, but not the government.[23] In essence, poverty alleviation is properly a function of personal responsibility and private charity.

The prophetic voice, however, will view poverty alleviation not as a function of charity, but as an obligation of public justice. At least two theological claims are central here. First, as Duncan Forrester has noted, "poverty is an issue of justice . . . because poor people bear a disproportionate burden of pain" and because the poor possess a "privileged place in the heart of God"[24] (recall their place in what Nicholas Wolterstorff calls God's "quartet of the vulnerable"). The poor experience shorter lives, poorer health, have fewer opportunities, and experience greater strain in their relationships with family members and others. "Good relationships are expressed and strengthened by a just distribution of material things; poverty and deprivation put pressure on family and other relationships; and poor people tend to be marginalized by the broader community."[25] Second, the importance of such claims is deepened and buttressed by the long-standing theological insight that wealth is not simply the possession of individuals to dispose of as they please. As Matthew Tuininga has noted, from the early church fathers to Aquinas, Calvin, and beyond, Christian tradition has long held that "excess wealth belongs to the poor." The earth and its resources are a gift from God to human beings in common. Property rights are secondary, "qualified by the obligations of stewardship and justice and subject to the regulation of the government. It is inherently unjust when the poor do not have what they need."[26]

It is possible to go further here and argue that ensuring such normative obligations is a matter not simply of effective government regulation of property, but also of active government intervention and provision of social goods. While it would be naive and shortsighted to ignore the good that private charity, including especially that of churches, can effect in responding to social problems like poverty, such efforts are, by themselves, insufficient. A more adequate response to our normative obligations is an "all hands on deck" approach, where private and public entities work together, with the latter picking up the slack when necessary, especially in lean times, when responsiveness to social need is most necessary but least likely to be forthcoming from private sources.[27] Such times can lead to what Lester Salamon, Director of the Center for Civil Society Studies at Johns Hopkins University, has called philanthropic insufficiency, which "occurs when the voluntary sector can't generate enough resources to provide social insurance at a sufficient scale," as in the wake of the Great Recession of 2008. Private charity can also fail to deliver sufficient resources because of philanthropic particularism, in which charity focuses on particular groups, especially those considered most "deserving," and philanthropic paternalism, which is a result of the narrow control of charitable power by those with the most resources, who then channel that power "toward the interests and needs of those who already hold large amounts of power."[28] In light of such challenges, prophetic justice will often affirm an important role for the state in meeting the needs of society's most vulnerable.

In enabling the pursuit of justice in these and other ways, the vision of the prophetic voice outlined here constitutes a meaningful expression of political theology. In its biblical and theological grounding and concern to give faithful expression to discipleship, this understanding of the prophetic voice is as concerned with theological integrity as are those Jeffrey Stout has labeled "enclave" theologians. It avoids, however, lapsing into the forms of utopianism and identity politics to which they are liable. Though John Milbank, especially, is among the theologians Stout identifies as most guilty of conceiving of the church ideologically as an "enclave society,"[29] if my earlier analysis is correct, it is fitting to include Hauerwas in this group, as well. Like other enclave theologians, he commonly "makes a negative example of believers, especially theologians, who have identified with movements of democratic reform in the broader society," and frequently holds up secular thinkers, especially philosophical liberals, "as symbolic representatives of the secularism that supposedly defines the broader society."[30]

Furthermore, though the understanding articulated here is as concerned to be as politically engaged and focused on healing the world as those often described as theological liberals seek to be, it does not lapse into the tendency (which I have argued is seen—however unintentionally or unwittingly—in West), to abandon concern with expounding and elaborating the integrity of a distinctly theological vision. Theology ought to be done critically and in conversation with voices outside of the church, but this does not entail that those who undertake it become "alienated theologians" who, though remaining preoccupied with God-talk, "abandon some or all of the basic commitments of their faith communities."[31] Indeed, a key element of the theological task on this understanding of the prophetic voice is to give more adequate expression to what the church most fully is and to speak robustly in defense of the normative values that define it.[32]

The character of this position as a form of political theology is shown further in how it can aid in correcting and refiguring how we might understand democracy and rights, concepts that have proven to be controversial elements of the treatments of justice previously canvassed. In chapter 3, I noted Hauerwas' worries about the prevalence of talk, especially among Christians, about liberal democracy and rights. He worries that such talk compromises the distinct witness of the Christian church because its abstract and ahistorical character reduces politics to a procedural system of rules for interest-driven individuals. I argued that his wholesale rejection of such concepts is problematic because, as engagement with some of his feminist critics helped to illustrate, it is overdrawn and undermines concerns about justice proper to the prophetic voice. Nevertheless, though problematic, Hauerwas' position is not without merit. Broadly understood, the sorts concerns to which he gives voice arguably find expression in West, who, in locating democracy at the heart of Christianity, seems at points to reduce Christian religious vision to a form of political expression. In this, however, he is unable to give adequate expression to the sometimes distinctive shape and content of Christian public engagement. As I have noted, this is evident in his characterization of rights talk as the form of discourse that is to guide Christian public engagement in a pluralistic society because it gives expression to society's common moral language and in his identification of human dignity as a central normative concept.

An adequate prophetic Christian affirmation of rights and democracy will be most fundamentally rooted not in considerations about individual autonomy or about how such concepts enhance the ability of a religious vision to gain leverage in public, pluralistic conversations (though such things, properly framed, are certainly worthy of affirmation), but simply in the logic of the social and political shape of an animating religious vision. For his part, Hauerwas mistakenly discusses rights and democracy as if they are wholly creations of the Enlightenment. And West, though seemingly attuned at points to the biblical basis for such talk, finally and problematically treats democracy and rights as political terms in their own right, with their own conceptual autonomy. These sorts of distortions can be gotten beyond, however, by attending self-consciously to the *pre-Enlightenment, theological* roots of rights and democracy. We can and should affirm, with Walzer and West, and against Hauerwas, the normative importance of democracy and rights from the perspective of the prophetic voice, but such affirmations have a *derivative* status. On a Christian theological account of the prophetic, they properly find authorization in biblical and theological concepts. This is provided, above all, by the basic affirmations that God's care extends to all bearers of the *Imago Dei*—particularly the weak and vulnerable—and that institutional structures and practices ought to embody and reflect that care. These roots have been extended and enhanced in a variety of subsequent, though still pre-Enlightenment, theological movements, particularly in figures within the Eastern Church who synthesized elements of Stoicism and the biblical heritage, and early free-church understandings of religious liberty and covenant responsibility.[33]

Some readers will surely note that, in some key respects, this discussion of prophetic justice is not terribly different from what one finds in West. Like the normative content of the ecclesial vision outlined here, his normative thought, as I noted in the last chapter, is marked above all by a concern to attend to the margins, to stand in solidarity with those who suffer and to seek to alleviate that suffering. However, as also noted in the previous chapter, if we understand a theological construal of the prophetic voice primarily or only in terms of political concepts such as democracy or rights, and ignore or subsume the theological grounding for such concepts, as West tends to do, it is liable to lose the critical edge that gives it its independence. At worst, it is susceptible to supporting normative commitments with which it should have no truck, barter, or trade. While, as I noted in the Introduction, West is frequently an exemplary performer of the prophetic, his conceptual rendering of it is problematically underdeveloped.

The difference between West's position and the one outlined here, then, is not vast, but it is significant, and it has to do with what concepts and language are most fundamental and prioritized in shaping how the prophetic is understood. When the normative commitments of the prophetic are allowed to float free from their theological moors, they are susceptible to being co-opted by forms and expressions of political discourse to which they may bear some terminological and even conceptual similarity, but from which they are substantively distinct. It is through the prioritization of the theological convictions that underlie prophetic justice—such as communal responsiveness to, and imitation of, the steadfast love of God through concern above all with the vulnerable, the weak, the needy—that a Christian theological account of the prophetic maintains a distinct and critical standpoint vis-à-vis other contending political visions. Such convictions are particularly important for how an adequate contemporary expression of the prophetic mode regards questions of violence and nonviolence, for it ultimately seeks to foster, in Christ-like manner, transformative practices and outcomes of just peacemaking.

GLIMPSING PROPHETIC PEACE: FROM JUST WAR TO JUST PEACE

In the preceding chapters, I have argued that a theologically adequate understanding of justice, coupled with an understanding of the incompleteness of the Kingdom, leads to the affirmation of just war as a regrettable, though permissible, response to injustice. It should now be clear that there are two senses in which the Kingdom is incomplete. First, it is incomplete in the sense, already discussed in the previous chapters, that the fullness of its peace will be realized only eschatologically. In the interim, coercion may sometimes be needed to restrain sin, precisely as an expression of neighbor love. But the Kingdom is also incomplete in a second, related, sense, gestured toward in earlier chapters, but developed most fully here. Knowledge and embodiment of the Kingdom in and through the church is partial and halting and always in a state of becoming. One implication of this is that one of the primary vocational tasks of the church is to become ever more what it is called to be, to give ever more adequate expression to its incarnational grammar. With regard to the matter of political violence, this means that the church will seek ever more adequate ways to embody the full peaceableness realized in Christ. Though *in extremis* violence will sometimes be a justifiable response to injustice, such a response, as the just war tradition makes clear, is *exceptional*. As I will suggest here, the primary vocation of the church is to foster practices and outcomes of just peace*making*.

As discussed, Hauerwas' all-or-nothing defense of pacifism is theologically rooted in an all-or-nothing, realized eschatology, in which the Kingdom is understood as fully present in Christ and embodied especially, if it takes its vocation seriously, in an understanding of the church that defines itself over and against the world. Though the peaceable Kingdom inaugurated by Christ is not yet fully present in the world, Christians embody a different history than the world and are the first fruits of the new Kingdom made present in Christ. These stark contrasts, in turn, derive much of their force from Hauerwas' bounded conception of the church and his understanding of its highly dichotomous relationship to the liberal nation-state, which he claims embodies a false history of godlessness. Despite some ambiguity, Hauerwas contends that his Christological nonviolence does not entail nonresistance or withdrawal from social and political responsibility.[34] Indeed, his project is inspired in good measure by his recognition that Jesus confronted and fought the powers, though not on their terms. In its peaceable vocation, the church exercises a distinctive form of social and political power that does not seek control, but looks to Jesus' suffering servanthood for its inspiration and substance.

I have argued in the foregoing, however, that some expressions of just war theory are justifiable and for theological reasons relating to the love of one's neighbor in a fallen world. Hauerwas' strict division between church and world and its accompanying eschatology are normatively and theologically problematic. One problematic implication of his wholesale rejection of (even a limited and constrained) violence for the sake of a theologically pure, thoroughgoing pacifism is that it would allow unjust violence to be visited upon others (albeit regretfully and tragically) for the sake of a theological vision. From the perspective of the prophetic, however, this cannot be squared with a determination to attend to vulnerable and marginalized others. Emphasizing, against Hauerwas, the futurity of the fullness of the Kingdom and attending to the recalcitrance of sin, Christian just war theorists contend that violent coercion may in some cases be a justifiable, love-impelled response to protect vulnerable others from imminent, unjust threats. Despite this tragic concession to violence, this position remains animated by a concern for peaceableness, as one of its chief goals is to create conditions where a true peace—*just* peace—can gain a foothold and grow.

Though Hauerwas' position ultimately fails to compel, his peaceable witness needs to be respected, not only because of its theological seriousness, but also because violence, though sometimes tragically justifiable, can never be a sufficient response to injustice. He is surely right that, even in cases of humanitarian intervention, violence is never the quick fix its advocates often portray it to be.[35] At least as it is most commonly articulated, just war theory constitutes a largely *reactive* standpoint that seeks to provide guidance regarding how to respond to imminent or already existing conditions of violence. It provides guidance, for example, regarding when, how, and why a country might intervene in another country to protect and endangered group from unjust assault. But it generally does not provide concrete guidance regarding how such conditions might be avoided or how their severity might be defused, even if it may hope for such a result. In short, it is not *proactive*.

A truly prophetic vision will actively seek to foster the fuller realization of both justice and peace. It will, I suggest, seek to embody a standpoint that in recent years has been termed the just peacemaking paradigm. The just peacemaking paradigm is not intended to supplant just war theory or, for that matter, pacifism; instead, its goal is to *supplement* these dominant understandings of how Christians, in the context of contemporary social and political institutions and practices, ought to respond to injustice. In this, it seeks to offer a fuller theological expression of the concern for peaceableness that underwrites both just war theory and pacifism. One of its primary goals is to affirm, strengthen, and extend both pacifism's commitment to nonviolent action and just war theory's commitment to justice. As David Gushee and Glen Stassen, one of the chief architects of the theory, explain, it "fills out the original intention of the other two paradigms. It encourages pacifists to be what their name means: peace*makers*. And it calls just war theorists to thicken the content of their underdeveloped principles of last resort and just intention."[36]

Theologically understood, the just peacemaking paradigm is an attempt to highlight how basic theological convictions and practices may be brought to bear in proactive efforts to enhance and extend present opportunities for the expression of God's justice and peace. By seeking to create opportunities for, and expressions of, true justice, this paradigm hopes to create opportunities for the expression of true peace. It seeks to highlight and exploit the synergy perceived to exist between theological convictions and the opportunities of the historical moment, in which the need for peacemaking has been widely recognized and its implementation is enabled by the presence of a variety of institutional structures and practices. The paradigm recognizes that it is only through active enactment of transformative practices of justice, particularly at the margins, that conditions will be created such that the peace of God's Kingdom may be glimpsed.

Grounding the paradigm are three theological convictions that cohere with central characteristics of the prophetic voice outlined here. It is provided with its distinctive shape, above all, by an understanding of discipleship grounded in an embodied Christology that emphasizes Jesus' transforming initiatives, discussed in chapter 1, and the modes of action they offer to resist forces of bondage. Second, in keeping with central elements of the prophetic voice, the paradigm is concerned to advance justice. Embodied in affirmations of democracy, human rights, and other related normative commitments and practices, this grounding element gives expression to the liberating and transformative power of God in the world. Third, these affirmations of democracy and rights, in turn, are supported by a vision of broadly inclusive community. Through practices that range from fostering grassroots modes of engagement to enhancing international forms of cooperation, this vision seeks to build broader, new forms of community through material expressions of love that overflow the boundaries that divide people.[37] It is finally something like this paradigm that will most fully characterize a robust contemporary articulation of the prophetic commitment to peace. The sort of creative and constructive engagement with diverse others that is central to the paradigm gives concrete expression to the church's vocation to ever more adequately embody the just and peaceable witness of Jesus Christ.

In these last few pages, I want to flesh out the position I am seeking to articulate here through an interpretation of a painting by American folk artist Edward Hicks (1780–1849). Hicks' well-known series of *Peaceable Kingdom* paintings provide Hauerwas with the title of one of his books and represent for him a concrete vision of what the Kingdom of God rightly looks like.[38] There is an undeniable resonance between the vision Hicks depicts and Hauerwas' understanding of the nature and tasks of Christian ethics. This should hardly be surprising, as Hicks was a Quaker who, like Hauerwas, had pacifist commitments. Nevertheless, on the basis of one of his later *Peaceable Kingdom* paintings from 1847, held in the Denver Art Museum, I want to read Hicks as presenting a somewhat more complicated vision than Hauerwas recognizes and even than Hicks himself perhaps intended.

Much of the painting can be interpreted as presenting a rather straightforward depiction of the vision of peaceableness of Isaiah 11; indeed, some early versions (from the mid-1820s) were bordered by an inscription of Isaiah 11:6. In the 1847 version of the painting (Figure 5.1), the better portion of the foreground of the canvas depicts many of the animals from the scriptural passage, many in a state best described as placid. In the bottom center of the painting, a leopard in a state of repose looks directly at the viewer, with what appears to be a goat lying just behind it, underneath the legs of another, standing leopard. Behind and to the right of the lounging leopard stand a wolf and lamb, both seemingly unfazed by the other's presence. Rounding out the biblical menagerie, Hicks has also placed in the painting an ox, a bear,

Figure 5.1 Edward Hicks, The Peaceable Kingdom, c. 1847. Denver Art Museum Collection: Gift of Charles Bayly, Jr., 1954.236 © Denver Art Museum.

and a lion (no snake is depicted), among others. Completing the depiction of the passage from Isaiah, in the bottom right quadrant of the painting, a child, hand out-raised and bearing an olive branch—a clear Christological reference—emerges from the animals. At the left center of the painting, in the background, a depiction of William Penn's treaty with Native Americans gives expression to an earthly manifestation of the natural vision depicted in Isaiah. Penn and his men, one of whom has his arms out stretched at his side in a clearly peaceable posture, greet a group of Native Americans, one of whom is holding what appears to be a ceremonial pipe.

Despite Hicks' clear and powerful depiction here both of the eschatological vision of Isaiah and of the in-breaking reality of the Kingdom, there are important elements of the painting that appear to point to his recognition of the incompleteness of the presence of that reality, a recognition that would have been underscored for Hicks by eighteenth-century divisions within his own Society of Friends. Though most of the animals are in a posture of repose and/or have rather placid expressions of their faces, there are some notable exceptions to this. Though no threat is apparent, the standing leopard, under which the goat lies, has its ears pinned back, back arched, tail tucked, and teeth exposed, as if it feels threatened. Similarly, the bear, which dominates the bottom right corner of the painting, appears to have backed into or been bumped by the leopard in the foreground, and is looking back over its right shoulder, teeth exposed. Furthermore, the child with the olive branch, though present, seemingly struggles to emerge from the animals and proclaim peace in the midst of the conflict around him. His body is not fully visible, and in the painting his path seems blocked by the snarling bear.

I suggest that the juxtaposition of the depiction of the Penn and the Native Americans with the conflict among the animals might reasonably be understood to convey that, though this-worldly intimations of the peace of God's Kingdom may be had, the fullness of the peace of that Kingdom is not yet realized. It might be suggested that the embodiment of that peace in Quaker dealings (Penn was a Quaker) with Native Americans points to its fullness within a particular religious expression, while the disorder among the animals points to lingering disorder in the "world," but such an interpretation hardly seems compelling, as the disorder among the animals likely represents divisions within Hick's own Quaker faith.[39] It is just this sort of realization of the incompleteness of the Kingdom—of the eschatological futurity of its fullness—that leads me to affirm the possibility of violence as an always temporary and exceptional, but sometimes theologically justified, response to injustice in extreme cases.

Nevertheless, in his depiction of Penn and the Native Americans, especially, Hicks gives powerful expression to the claim made here, that the peaceable vision of scripture is not merely an eschatological vision, but is an in-breaking, if incomplete, reality that can and does find earthly expression. He recognizes that we anticipate and offer glimpses of the Kingdom that is yet to come fully as we engage justly and seek peaceable relation with the other, as Penn did in remarkable ways in his own context. One aspect of the power of Hicks' painting lies precisely in his recognition that God's peace is a just peace—this recognition should hardly be surprising, given that the connection is made explicitly in the Isaiah passage itself (see vv. 4–5)—that properly shapes and guides how we encounter the other. The vision of biblical justice and peace glimpsed in Isaiah rightly has a claim on us, now.

Indeed, the consistent gesture of the child bearing the olive branch, across the canvas and toward the Penn party, in this and a number of other versions of the painting, points us to the deeper thrust of Christian peaceableness, indeed, of Christian *prophetic* peaceableness. Even if the peaceable kingdom is not fully present, Hicks seems to want to say, expressions of it, however rare and fragile, are present possibilities, and it is to such expressions that our attention finally is properly devoted. Though the prophetic vision outlined here contends that responding to injustice and establishing the conditions for true peace will sometimes allow the use of political violence, with Hicks, it is most concerned with the entwined practices of establishing justice, fostering community-building, and fomenting practices of peacemaking. Indeed, violence is permissible only insofar as it is judged necessary to foster the conditions of a truly just peace. It is finally only through such practices of just peace*making* that the contemporary prophetic church will be able to give ever more adequate communal expression to the vision of reality that served as the impetus for the hope of Israel's prophets and that finds full embodiment in Jesus Christ.

NOTES

1. I say "as traditionally conceived" to account for contemporary religious or theological non-realists, such as Don Cupitt, Grace Jantzen, Gordon Kaufman, and Sallie McFague. For instructive discussion, see Christopher J. Insole, "Why Anti-Realism Breaks Up Relationships," *Heythrop Journal* 63, no. 1 (January 2002): 20–28.

2. See, for example, Timothy P. Jackson, "Naturalism, Formalism and Supernaturalism: Moral Epistemology and Comparative Ethics," *Journal of Religious Ethics* 27, no. 3 (Fall 1999): 481.

3. C. Stephen Evans, "Realism and Antirealism in Kierkegaard's *Concluding Unscientific Postscript*," in *The Cambridge Companion to Kierkegaard*, ed. Alastair Hannay and Gordon D. Marino (Cambridge: Cambridge University Press, 1998), 170.

4. See the helpful discussion in Alistair McFadyen, "Truth as Mission: The Christian Claim to Universal Truth in a Pluralistic Public World," *Scottish Journal of Theology* 46, no. 4 (1993): 447–451.

5. Ibid., 446–447.

6. Paul Murray's recent work on theological rationality makes similar suggestions about the character of ecclesiology, to which I am indebted. He advocates a radicalizing of the Vatican II image of the church as the "pilgrim people of God." See Paul D. Murray, *Reason, Truth and Theology in Pragmatist Perspective* (Leuven: Peeters, 2004), 157; and his "On Valuing Truth in Practice: Rome's Postmodern Challenge," *International Journal of Systematic Theology* 8, no. 2 (April 2006): 163–183.

7. See Murray, *Reason, Truth and Theology in Pragmatist Perspective*, 109.

8. See, for example, James Logan, "Liberalism, Race, and Stanley Hauerwas," *CrossCurrents* 55, no. 4 (Winter 2006): 522–533 and Derek Alan Woodard-Lehman, "Body Politics and the Politics of Bodies: Racism and Hauerwasian Theopolitics," *Journal of Religious Ethics* 36, no. 2 (June 2008): 295–320.

9. Sue Patterson, *Realist Christian Theology in a Postmodern Age* (Cambridge: Cambridge University Press, 1999), 148. See also the insightful discussion by Romand Coles, "Storied Others and Possibilities of *Caritas*: Milbank and Neo-Nietzschean Ethics," *Modern Theology* 8, no. 4 (October 1992): 331–351.

10. See Murray, *Reason, Truth and Theology in Pragmatist Perspective*, 156–157.

11. Joerg Rieger, *God and the Excluded: Visions and Blindspots in Contemporary Theology* (Minneapolis: Fortress Press, 2001), 116.

12. Though there does not seem to be the same strict textual equation with God and justice as there is with God and love, such a claim should be relatively uncontroversial, given the close connections between God's *hesed* (steadfast love) and justice, as well as the characteristic use of *sedaqah* (righteousness) to denote a quality of an actor known through his or her actions.

13. See Ian A. McFarland, *Listening to the Least: Doing Theology from the Outside In* (Cleveland: The Pilgrim Press, 1998), especially 94–95.

14. Woodard-Lehman, "Body Politics and the Politics of Bodies," 308.

15. Stanley Hauerwas, "Race: The 'More' It Is About: Will D. Campbell Lecture: University of Mississippi, 2006," in Stanley Hauerwas and Roman Coles, *Christianity, Democracy, and the Radical Ordinary: Conversations between a Radical Democrat and a Christian* (Eugene, Oregon: Cascade Books, 2008), 98, 99.

16. Ibid., 100–101.

17. Stanley M. Hauerwas, "Remembering Martin Luther King Jr. Remembering," in his *Wilderness Wanderings: Probing Twentieth-Century Theology and Philosophy* (Boulder, Colo.: Westview Press, 1997), 225.

18. James Logan, "Liberalism, Race, and Stanley Hauerwas," 526.

19. See Ibid., 527.

20. Woodard-Lehman, "Body Politics and the Politics of Bodies," 315.

21. Ibid., 316.

22. Arthur Delaney and Michael McAuliff, "Paul Ryan Wants 'Welfare Reform Round 2,'" *Huffington Post*, March 20, 2012, accessed May 24, 2017, http://www.huffingtonpost.com/2012/03/20/paul-ryan-welfare-reform_n_1368277.html.

23. Editors, "Faith and Food Stamps: WWJD?," *Political Theology Today*, June 4, 2013, accessed May 24, 2017, http://www.politicaltheology.com/blog/faith-and-food-stamps-wwjd/.

24. Duncan B. Forrester, *Christian Justice and Public Policy* (Cambridge: Cambridge University Press, 1997), 104.

25. Ibid.

26. Matthew J. Tuininga, "Justice for the Poor in the Heidelberg Catechism: The Eighth Commandment," *Do Justice*, October 9, 2017, accessed October 24, 2017, http://dojustice.crcna.org/article/justice-poor-heidelberg-catechism-eighth-commandment.

27. See, for example, Rob Reich and Christopher Wimer, *Charitable Giving and the Great Recession* (Stanford, CA: Stanford Center on Poverty and Inequality, 2012).

28. Mike Konczal, "The Voluntarism Fantasy," *Democracy Journal*, 32, Spring 2014, accessed January 9, 2018, https://democracyjournal.org/magazine/32/the-voluntarism-fantasy.

29. See, especially, John Milbank, *Theology and Social Theory: Beyond Secular Reason* (Oxford: Blackwell, 1990).

30. Jeffrey Stout, *Democracy and Tradition* (Princeton: Princeton University Press, 2004), 115.

31. Ibid.

32. Discussion of how the prophetic voice as I have articulated it here might serve as a constructive contributor to civil discussion in a pluralistic society is an important topic, but one that is beyond the purview of the current discussion. For instructive thoughts on such matters, with which I am highly sympathetic, see Christopher J. Eberle, "Religious Reasons in Public: Let A Thousand Flowers Bloom, But Be Prepared to Prune," *St. John's Journal of Legal Commentary* 22, no. 2 (2007): 431–443.

33. For instructive discussion, see Nicholas Wolterstorff, *Justice: Rights and Wrongs* (Princeton: Princeton University Press, 2008); Michael L. Westmoreland-White, "Setting the Record Straight: Christian Faith, Human Rights, and the Enlightenment," *Annual of the Society of Christian Ethics* (1995): esp. 76–85; and Max L. Stackhouse, *Creeds, Society, and Human Rights: A Study in Three Cultures* (Grand Rapids, MI: William B. Eerdmans Publishing Co., 1984), Chapter 2.

34. See the discussion in chapter 3, note 120.

35. See Stanley Hauerwas, Linda Hogan, and Enda McDonagh, "The Case for Abolition of War in the Twenty-First Century," *Journal of the Society of Christian Ethics* 25, no. 2 (Fall/Winter 2005): 29–31.

36. David P. Gushee and Glen H. Stassen, *Kingdom Ethics: Following Jesus in Contemporary Context*, second edition (Grand Rapids, MI: William B. Eerdmans Publishing Co., 2016), 332. See also Mark J. Allman and Tobias L. Winright, "Growing Edges of Just War Theory: *Jus ante bellum, just post bellum*, and Imperfect Justice," *Journal of the Society of Christian Ethics* 32, no. 2 (Fall/Winter 2012): 173–191. Allman and Winright argue that just peacemaking theory is not an alternative to just war theory or pacifism, but a corrective to them, especially the "myopia" (174) of the former: "From a just war angle, just peacemaking serves as a *jus ante bellum* category, which hopefully minimizes the likelihood that wars erupt in the first place. This hope is implied in the *jus ad bellum* criterion of last resort, and we think it stems from the *jus ad bellum* criterion of right intent" (176).

37. For a good summary statement of these animating convictions and their expression through a variety of concrete practices, see Duane K. Friesen, John Langan, S.J., and Glen Stassen, "Introduction: Just Peacemaking as a New Ethic," in *Just Peacemaking: Ten Practices for Abolishing War*, ed. Glen H. Stassen (Cleveland: The Pilgrim Press, 1998), 1–28.

38. See Stanley Hauerwas, *The Peaceable Kingdom: A Primer in Christian Ethics* (Notre Dame: University of Notre Dame Press, 1983), xiii.

39. For discussion of these divisions, see Eleanore Price Mather, *Edward Hicks: His* Peaceable Kingdoms *and Other Paintings* (Newark: University of Delaware Press and New York: Cornwall Books, 1983), 26–29, 36–41. See also the brief, but informative, discussion in Holland Cotter, "Finding Endless Conflict Hidden in a Peaceable Kingdom," *New York Times*, June 16, 2000.

Bibliography

Ackerly, Brooke A. *Political Theory and Feminist Social Criticism*. Cambridge: Cambridge University Press, 2000.

Albrecht, Gloria. *The Character of Our Communities: Toward an Ethic of Liberation for the Church*. Nashville: Abingdon Press, 1995.

Allman, Mark J. and Tobias L. Winright. "Growing Edges of Just War Theory: *Jus ante bellum, jus post bellum*, and Imperfect Justice." *Journal of the Society of Christian Ethics* 32, no. 2 (Fall/Winter 2012): 173–191.

Anderson, Bernhard W. "Introduction: Mythopoeic and Theological Dimensions of Biblical Creation Faith." In *Creation in the Old Testament*, edited with an introduction by Bernhard W. Anderson, 1–24. Philadelphia: Fortress Press, 1984.

Ansbro, John J. *Martin Luther King, Jr.: The Making of a Mind*. Maryknoll, NY: Orbis Books, 1982.

Aristotle. *Nicomachean Ethics*, translated by Terence Irwin. Indianapolis: Hackett, 1985.

Augustine, Saint. *The City of God*, translated by Henry Bettenson. Harmondsworth, England: Penguin Books, 1972.

Balfour, Lawrie. "The Appeal of Innocence: Baldwin, Walzer, and the Bounds of Social Criticism." *The Review of Politics* 61, no. 3 (Summer 1999): 373–401.

Baxter, Michael J., C.S.C. "'Overall, the First Amendment Has Been Very Good for Christianity' – *Not!*: A Response to Dyson's Rebuke." *DePaul Law Review* 43, no. 2 (Winter 1994): 423–446.

Beach-Verhey, Timothy A. "Exemplifying Public Discourse: Christian Faith, American Democracy, and Martin Luther King Jr." *Journal of the Society of Christian Ethics* 24, no. 2 (Fall/Winter 2004): 115–136.

Beem, Christopher. "American Liberalism and the Christian Church: Stanley Hauerwas vs. Martin Luther King Jr." *Journal of Religious Ethics* 23, no. 1 (Spring 1995): 119–133.

Bell, Daniel M., Jr. *Just War as Christian Discipleship: Recentering the Tradition in the Church rather than the State*. Grand Rapids, MI: Brazos Press, 2009.

———. "In War and in Peace: Implications of Just War Theory." *The Christian Century*, September 6, 2005, 26–33.

Benhabib, Seyla. "Feminism and Postmodernism: An Uneasy Alliance." In Seyla Benhabib, Judith Butler, Drucilla Cornell, and Nancy Fraser, *Feminist Contentions: A Philosophical Exchange*, 17–34. New York: Routledge, 1995.

———. *Situating the Self: Gender, Community and Postmodernism in Contemporary Ethics*. New York: Routledge, 1992.

Biggar, Nigel. *In Defence of War*. Oxford: Oxford University Press, 2013.

———. "Is Stanley Hauerwas Sectarian?" In *Faithfulness and Fortitude: In Conversation with the Theological Ethics of Stanley Hauerwas*, edited by Mark Thiessen Nation and Samuel Wells, 141–160. Edinburgh: T & T Clark, 2000.

Birch, Bruce C. *Let Justice Roll Down: The Old Testament, Ethics, and Christian Life*. Louisville: Westminster John Knox Press, 1991.

Bounds, Elizabeth M. "Conflicting Harmonies: Michael Walzer's Vision of Community." *Journal of Religious Ethics* 22, no. 2 (Fall 1994): 355–374.

Brueggemann, Walter. *The Prophetic Imagination*, second edition. Philadelphia: Fortress Press, 2001.

———. "Covenant as a Subversive Paradigm." In Walter Brueggemann, *A Social Reading of the Old Testament: Prophetic Approaches to Israel's Communal Life*, edited by Patrick D. Miller, 43–53. Minneapolis: Fortress Press, 1994.

———. *Texts Under Negotiation: The Bible and the Postmodern Imagination*. Minneapolis: Fortress Press, 1993.

Butler, Judith and Cornel West. "Dialogue." In Judith Butler, et al., *The Power of Religion in the Public Sphere*, edited by Eduardo Mendieta and Jonathan VanAntwerpen, 101–108. New York: Columbia University Press, 2011.

Cahill, Lisa Sowle. "Just Peacemaking: Theory, Practice, and Prospects." *Journal of the Society of Christian Ethics* 23, no. 1 (Spring/Summer 2003): 195–212.

———. "The Bible and Christian Moral Practices." In *Christian Ethics: Problems and Prospects*, edited by Lisa Sowle Cahill and James F. Childress, 3–17. Cleveland: The Pilgrim Press, 1996.

———. *Love Your Enemies: Discipleship, Pacifism, and Just War Theory*. Minneapolis: Fortress Press, 1994.

Childress, James F. "Righteousness." In *The Westminster Dictionary of Christian Ethics*, edited by James F. Childress and John Macquarrie, 556. Philadelphia: The Westminster Press, 1986.

Clapp, Rodney. "Practicing the Politics of Jesus." In *The Church as Counterculture*, edited by Michael L. Budde and Robert W. Brimlow, 15–37. Albany: State University of New York Press, 2000.

Coakley, Sarah. *Powers and Submissions: Spirituality, Philosophy, and Gender*. Oxford: Blackwell, 2002.

Cohen, Joshua. "Book Review of *Spheres of Justice*." *Journal of Philosophy* 83, no. 8 (August 1986): 457–468.

Coles, Romand. "The Wild Patience of John Howard Yoder: 'Outsiders' and the 'Otherness of the Church.'" *Modern Theology* 18, no. 3 (July 2002): 305–331.

———. "Stored Others and Possibilities of *Caritas*: Milbank and Neo-Nietzschean Ethics." *Modern Theology* 8, no. 4 (October 1992): 331–351.

Cone, James H. "'Let Suffering Speak:' The Vocation of the Black Intellectual." In *Cornel West: A Critical Reader*, edited by George Yancy, 105–114. Oxford: Blackwell, 2001.

Cotter, Holland. "Finding Endless Conflict Hidden in a Peaceable Kingdom." *New York Times*, June 16, 2000.

Cowan, Rosemary. *Cornel West: The Politics of Redemption*. Oxford: Polity, 2003.

Cross, Frank Moore. *Canannite Myth and Hebrew Epic: Essays in the History of the Religion of Israel*. Cambridge: Harvard University Press, 1973.

Dahl, Robert A. *Democracy and Its Critics*. New Haven: Yale University Press, 1989.

De Gruchy, John M. *Christianity and Democracy: A Theology for a Just World Order*. Cambridge: Cambridge University Press, 1995.

Dean, William. "The Challenge of the New Historicism." *Journal of Religion* 66, no. 3 (July 1986): 261–281.

Delaney, Arthur and Michael McAuliff. "Paul Ryan Wants 'Welfare Reform Round 2.'" *Huffington Post*, March 20, 2012. Accessed May 24, 2017. http://www.huffingtonpost.com/2012/03/20/paul-ryan-welfare-reform_n_1368277.html

Dempsey, Carol. *Hope Amid the Ruins: The Ethics of Israel's Prophets*. St. Louis: Chalice Press, 2000.

Doak, Mary. "Cornel West's Challenge to the Catholic Evasion of Black Theology." *Theological Studies* 63, no. 1 (February 2002): 87–106.

Domeris, William R. "Leadership, Status and Position in the Early Jesus Community." In *A Democratic Vision for South Africa: Political Realism and Christian Responsibility*, edited by Klaus Nürnberger, 97–108. Pietermaritzburg, South Africa: Encounter Publications, 1991.

Donahue, John, S. J. "Biblical Perspectives on Justice." In *The Faith That Does Justice: Examining the Christian Sources for Social Change*, edited by John C. Haughey, S.J., 68–112. New York: Paulist Press, 1977.

Dorrien, Gary. "Imagining Social Justice: Cornel West's Prophetic Public Intellectualism." *CrossCurrents* 58, no. 1 (Spring 2008): 6–42.

Dula, Peter and Alex Sider, "Radical Democracy, Radical Ecclesiology." *CrossCurrents* 55, no. 4 (Winter 2006): 482–504.

Dworkin, Ronald. *Life's Dominion: An Argument about Abortion, Euthanasia, and Individual Freedom*. New York: Alfred A. Knopf, 1993.

Dyson, Michael Eric. "'God Almighty Has Spoken From Washington, D.C.': American Society and Christian Faith." In *Reflecting Black: African-American Cultural Criticism*, edited by Michael Eric Dyson, 286–319. Minneapolis: University of Minnesota Press, 1993.

Eberle, Christopher J. "Religious Reasons in Public: Let a Thousand Flowers Bloom, But Be Prepared to Prune." *St. John's Journal of Legal Commentary* 22, no. 2 (2007): 431–443.

Editors. "Faith and Food Stamps: WWJD?" *Political Theology Today*, June 4, 2013. Accessed May 24, 2017. http://www.politicaltheology.com/blog/faith-and-food-stamps-wwjd/

Ellacuría, Ignacio. "The Political Nature of Jesus' Mission." In *Faces of Jesus: Latin American Christologies*, edited by José Míguez Bonino, 79–92. Maryknoll, NY: Orbis Books, 1984.

Elshtain, Jean Bethke. “How to Fight a Just War.” In *Strike Terror No More: Theology, Ethics, and the New War*, edited by Jon L. Berquist, 231–235. St. Louis: Chalice Press, 2002.

———. “Review Essay: Theology and Political Life.” *Modern Theology* 12, no. 3 (July 1996): 367–376.

Evans, C. Stephen. “Realism and Antirealism in Kierkegaard’s *Concluding Unscientific Postscript*.” In *The Cambridge Companion to Kierkegaard*, edited by Alastair Hannay and Gordon D. Marino, 154–176. Cambridge: Cambridge University Press, 1998.

Fergusson, David. *Community, Liberalism and Christian Ethics*. Cambridge: Cambridge University Press, 1998.

Fiddes, Paul S. *The Creative Suffering of God*. Oxford: Clarendon Press of Oxford University Press, 1989.

Flanders, Henry Jackson, Jr., Robert Wilson Crapps, and David Anthony Smith. *People of the Covenant: An Introduction to the Hebrew Bible*, fourth edition. New York: Oxford University Press, 1996.

Forrester, Duncan B. *Christian Justice and Public Policy*. Cambridge: Cambridge University Press, 1997.

Fretheim, Terrence E. *The Suffering of God: An Old Testament Perspective*. Philadelphia: Fortress Press, 1984.

Freyne, Seán. “The Ethic of Jesus: The Sermon on the Mount Then and Now.” In *Ethics and the Christian Life*, edited by Seán Freyne, 41–57. Dublin: The Columba Press, 1991.

Friesen, Duane K., John Langan, S. J., and Glen Stassen. “Introduction: Just Peacemaking as a New Ethic.” In *Just Peacemaking: Ten Practices for Abolishing War*, edited by Glen H. Stassen, 1–28. Cleveland: The Pilgrim Press, 1998.

Galston, William A. “Community, Democracy, Philosophy: The Political Thought of Michael Walzer.” *Political Theory* 17, no. 1 (February 1989): 119–130.

Gardner, E. Clinton. *Justice and Christian Ethics*. Cambridge: Cambridge University Press, 1995.

Gushee, David P. and Glen H. Stassen. *Kingdom Ethics: Following Jesus in Contemporary Context*, second edition. Grand Rapids, MI: William B. Eerdmans Publishing Co., 2016.

Gustafson, James M. “The Sectarian Temptation: Reflections on Theology, the Church and the University.” *Proceedings of the Catholic Theological Society of America* 40 (1985): 83–94.

Gutiérrez, Gustavo. *A Theology of Liberation*. Maryknoll, NY: Orbis Books, 1972.

Hanson, Paul D. *The People Called: The Growth of Community in the Bible*, with a New Introduction. San Francisco: Harper and Row, 2001.

———. “The Origin and Nature of Prophetic Political Engagement in Ancient Israel.” In *Let Justice Roll: Prophetic Challenges in Religion, Politics, and Society*, edited by Neal Riemer, 1–21. Lanham, MD: Rowman and Littlefield Publishers, 1996.

Harink, Douglas. “For or Against the Nations: Yoder and Hauerwas, What’s the Difference?” *Toronto Journal of Theology* 17, no. 1 (Summer 2001): 167–185.

Hartt, Julian. “Theological Investments in Story: Some Comments on Recent Developments and Some Proposals.” In *Why Narrative? Readings in Narrative*

Theology, edited by Stanley Hauerwas and L. Gregory Jones, 279–292. Grand Rapids, Mich.: William B. Eerdmans Publishing Co., 1989.

Hauerwas, Stanley. "Democratic Time: Lessons Learned From Yoder and Wolin." *CrossCurrents* 55, no. 4 (Winter 2006): 534–552.

———. *Performing the Faith: Bonhoeffer and the Practice of Nonviolence.* Grand Rapids, MI: Brazos Press, 2004.

———. "Where Would I Be Without Friends?" In *Faithfulness and Fortitude: In Conversation with the Theological Ethics of Stanley Hauerwas*, edited by Mark Thiessen Nation and Samuel Wells, 313–332. Edinburgh: T & T Clark, 2000.

———. *Sanctify Them in Truth: Holiness Exemplified.* Nashville: Abingdon Press, 1998.

———. *Wilderness Wanderings: Probing Twentieth-Century Theology and Philosophy.* Boulder, CO: Westview Press, 1997.

———. "Failure of Communication *or* A Case of Uncomprehending Feminism." *Scottish Journal of Theology* 50, no. 2 (1997): 228–239.

———. *In Good Company: The Church as Polis.* Notre Dame: University of Notre Dame Press, 1995.

———. *Against the Nations: War and Survival in a Liberal Society.* Notre Dame: University of Notre Dame Press, 1992.

———. *The Peaceable Kingdom: A Primer in Christian Ethics.* Notre Dame: University of Notre Dame Press, 1992.

———. *After Christendom? How the Church is to Behave if Freedom, Justice, and a Christian Nation Are Bad Ideas.* Nashville: Abingdon Press, 1991.

———. "Why the Truth Demands Truthfulness: An Imperious Engagement with Hart." In *Why Narrative? Readings in Narrative Theology*, edited by Stanley Hauerwas and L. Gregory Jones, 303–310. Grand Rapids, MI: William B. Eerdmans Publishing Co., 1989.

———. *Christian Existence Today: Essays on Church, World, and Living In Between.* Durham, NC: The Labyrinth Press, 1988.

———. "Epilogue: A Pacifist Response to the Bishops." In *Speak Up for Just War or Pacifism: A Critique of the United Methodist Bishop's Pastoral Letter "In Defense of Creation,"* edited by Paul Ramsey, 149–182. University Park: The Pennsylvania State University Press, 1988.

———. "Will the Real Sectarian Please Stand Up?" *Theology Today* 44, no. 1 (April 1987): 87–94.

———. "On the 'Right' to be Tribal." *Christian Scholar's Review* 16, no. 3 (March 1987): 238–241.

———. "Should Christians Talk So Much About Justice?" *Books and Religion* 14, nos. 5–6 (1986): 5, 14–16.

———. "Pacifism: Some Philosophical Considerations." *Faith and Philosophy* 2, no. 2 (April 1985): 99–104.

———. *A Community of Character: Toward a Constructive Christian Social Ethic.* Notre Dame: University of Notre Dame Press, 1981.

———. *Truthfulness and Tragedy: Further Investigations into Christian Ethics.* Notre Dame: University of Notre Dame Press, 1977.

Haucrwas, Stanley and Romand Coles. *Christianity, Democracy, and the Radical Ordinary: Conversations between a Radical Democrat and a Christian*. Eugene, OR: Cascade Books, 2008.

Hauerwas, Stanley, Linda Hogan, and Enda McDonagh. "The Case for Abolition of War in the Twenty-First Century." *Journal of the Society of Christian Ethics* 25, no. 2 (Fall/Winter 2005): 17–35.

Hauerwas, Stanley and Will Willimon. "Why *Resident Aliens* Struck a Chord." *Missiology: An International Review* 19, no. 4 (October 1991): 419–429.

Hauerwas, Stanley and William H. Willimon. *Resident Aliens: Life in the Christian Colony*. Nashville: Abingdon Press, 1989.

Haughey, John C., S.J. "Jesus and the Justice of God." In *The Faith That Does Justice: Examining the Christian Sources for Social Change*, edited by John C. Haughey, S.J., 264–290. New York: Paulist Press, 1977.

Hayes, Floyd W., III. "Cornel West and Afro-Nihilism: A Reconsideration." In *Cornel West: A Critical Reader*, edited by George Yancy, 245–260. Oxford: Blackwell, 2001.

Hays, Richard B. *The Moral Vision of the New Testament: A Contemporary Introduction to New Testament Ethics*. San Francisco: HarperSanFrancisco, 1996.

Healey, Joseph P. "Peace, Old Testament." In *The Anchor Bible Dictionary. Vol. 5*, edited by David Noel Freedman, 206–207. New York: Doubleday, 1992.

Healy, Nicholas M. *Hauerwas: A (Very) Critical Introduction*. Grand Rapids, MI: William B. Eerdmans Pub. Co., 2014.

Headley, Clevis. "Cornel West on Prophesy, Pragmatism, and Philosophy: A Critical Evaluation of Prophetic Pragmatism." In *Cornel West: A Critical Reader*, edited by George Yancy, 59–82. Oxford: Blackwell, 2001.

Heschel, Abraham J. *The Prophets*. New York: Perenniel Classics, 2001.

Hewlett, Sylvia Ann and Cornel West. *The War Against Parents: What We Can Do for America's Beleaguered Moms and Dads*. Boston: Houghton Mifflin, 1998.

Hill, Thomas E., Jr. "Servility and Self-Respect." *The Monist* 57, no. 1 (1973): 87–104.

Hultgren, Arland J. "Jesus of Nazareth: Prophet, Visionary, Sage, or What?" *Dialog* 33, no. 4 (Fall 1994): 263–273.

Insole, Christopher J. "Why Anti-Realism Breaks Up Relationships." *Heythrop Journal* 43, no. 1 (January 2002): 20–33.

Jackson, Timothy P. *Political* Agape*: Christian Love and Liberal Democracy*. Grand Rapids, MI: William B. Eerdmans Pub. Co., 2015.

———. *The Priority of Love: Christian Charity and Social Justice*. Princeton: Princeton University Press, 2002.

———. *Love Disconsoled: Meditations on Christian Charity*. Cambridge: Cambridge University Press, 1999.

———. "Naturalism, Formalism, and Supernaturalism: Moral Epistemology and Comparative Ethics." *Journal of Religious Ethics* 27, no. 3 (Fall 1999): 477–506.

———. "Ambivalences About Nature and Naturalism: A Supernaturalist Response to Theodore W. Nunez." *Journal of Religious Ethics* 27, no. 1 (Spring 1999): 137–144.

———. "Liberalism and *Agape*: The Priority of Charity to Democracy and Philosophy." *The Annual of the Society of Christian Ethics* (1993): 47–72.

Johnson, Clarence Sholé. *Cornel West and Philosophy*. New York: Routledge, 2003.

Kallenberg, Brad J. *Ethics as Grammar: Changing the Postmodern Subject*. Notre Dame: University of Notre Dame Press, 2001.

Katongole, Emmanuel. *Beyond Universal Reason: The Relation Between Religion and Ethics in the Work of Stanley Hauerwas*. Notre Dame: University of Notre Dame Press, 2000.

Kenneson, Philip D. *Beyond Sectarianism: Re-Imagining Church and World*. Harrisburg, Penn.: Trinity Press International, 1999.

Klassen, William. *Love of Enemies: The Way to Peace*. Philadelphia: Fortress Press, 1984.

Kloppenborg, John S. "Alms, Debt, and Divorce: Jesus' Ethics in their Mediterranean Context." *Toronto Journal of Theology* 6, no. 2 (Fall 1990): 182–200.

Konczal, Mike. "The Voluntarism Fantasy." *Democracy Journal*, 32, Spring 2014. Accessed January 9, 2018. https://democracyjournal.org/magazine/32/the-voluntarism-fantasy

Kraybill, Donald B. *The Upside-Down Kingdom*, second edition. Scottdale, PA: Herald Press, 1990.

Kymlicka, Will. *Liberalism, Community and Culture*. Oxford: Clarendon Press of Oxford University Press, 1989.

Lafer, Gordon. "Universalism and Particularism in Jewish Law: Making Sense of Political Loyalities." In *Jewish Identity*, edited by David Theo Goldberg and Michael Krausz, 177–211. Philadelphia: Temple University Press, 1993.

Leith, Mary Joan Winn. "Know." In *The Oxford Companion to the Bible*, edited by Bruce M. Metzger and Michael D. Coogan, 416–417. New York: Oxford University Press, 1993.

Lindbeck, George. *The Nature of Doctrine: Religion and Theology in a Postliberal Age*. Philadelphia: The Westminster Press, 1984.

Lischer, Richard. *The Preacher King: Martin Luther King, Jr. and the Word That Moved America*. New York: Oxford University Press, 1995.

Logan, James. "Liberalism, Race, and Stanley Hauerwas." *CrossCurrents* 55, no. 4 (Winter 2006): 522–533.

Lovin, Robin W. *Reinhold Niebuhr and Christian Realism*. Cambridge: Cambridge University Press, 1995.

Macedo, Stephen, "Hauerwas, Liberalism, and Public Reason: Terms of Engagement?" *Law and Contemporary Problems* 75, no. 4 (2012): 161–180.

Malina, Bruce J. *The Social Gospel of Jesus: The Kingdom of God in Mediterranean Perspective*. Minneapolis: Fortress Press, 2001.

Martin, Dale. *The Corinthian Body*. New Haven: Yale University Press, 1995.

Mather, Eleanore Price. *Edward Hicks: His* Peaceable Kingdoms *and Other Paintings*. Newark/New York: University of Delaware Press/Cornwall Books, 1983.

Mathewes, Charles T. "Appreciating Hauerwas: One Hand Clapping." *Anglican Theological Review* 82, no. 2 (Spring 2000): 343–360.

Mays, James Luther. "Justice: Perspectives from the Prophetic Tradition." *Interpretation* 37, no. 1 (January 1983): 5–17.

McCarthy, Thomas. "Private Irony and Public Decency: Richard Rorty's New Pragmatism." *Critical Inquiry* 16, no. 2 (Winter 1990): 355–370.

McFadyen, Alistair. "Truth as Mission: The Christian Claim to Universal Truth in a Pluralistic Public World." *Scottish Journal of Theology* 46, no. 4 (1993): 437–456.

McFarland, Ian A. *Listening to the Least: Doing Theology from the Outside In*. Cleveland: The Pilgrim Press, 1998.

McWilliams, Warren. "Divine Suffering in Contemporary Theology." *Scottish Journal of Theology* 33, no. 1 (1980): 35–53.

Meeks, Wayne A. *The Origins of Christian Morality: The First Two Centuries*. New Haven: Yale University Press, 1993.

———. "A Hermeneutics of Social Embodiment." *Harvard Theological Review* 19, nos. 1–3 (January–July 1986): 176–186.

Mendenhall, George E. "The Monarchy." *Interpretation* 29, no. 2 (April 1975): 155–170.

———. *The Tenth Generation: The Origins of the Biblical Tradition*. Baltimore: The Johns Hopkins University Press, 1973.

Milbank, John. *Theology and Social Theory: Beyond Secular Reason*. Oxford: Blackwell, 1990.

Miscamble, Wilson D. "Sectarian Passivism?" *Theology Today* 44, no. 1 (April 1987): 69–77.

Moore, Andrew. *Realism and Christian Faith: God, Grammar, and Meaning*. Cambridge: Cambridge University Press, 2003.

Mott, Stephen. *Biblical Ethics and Social Change*, second edition. New York: Oxford University Press, 2011.

Murphy, Debra Dean. "Community, Character, and Gender: Women in the Work of Stanley Hauerwas." *Scottish Journal of Theology* 55, no. 3 (2002): 338–355.

Murray, Paul D. "On Valuing Truth in Practice: Rome's Postmodern Challenge." *International Journal of Systematic Theology* 8, no. 2 (April 2006): 163–183.

———. *Reason, Truth and Theology in Pragmatist Perspective*. Leuven: Peeters, 2004.

Myers, Ched. "'I Will Ask *You* a Question': Interrogatory Theology." In *Theology Without Foundations: Religious Practice and the Future of Theological Truth*, edited by Stanley Hauerwas, Nancey Murphy, and Mark Nation, 91–116. Nashville: Abingdon Press, 1994.

Newman, Louis E. "The Quality of Mercy: On the Duty to Forgive in the Judaic Tradition." *Journal of Religious Ethics* 15, no. 2 (Fall 1987): 155–172.

Niebuhr, Reinhold. "The Children of Light and the Children of Darkness." In *The Essential Reinhold Niebuhr: Selected Essays and Addresses*, edited by Robert McAfee Brown, 160–81. New Haven: Yale University Press, 1986.

———. *The Nature and Destiny of Man, Volume II: Human Destiny*. Louisville: Westminster John Knox Press, 1964.

———. *An Interpretation of Christian Ethics*. San Francisco: Harper and Row, 1963.

Nolan, Albert. *Jesus Before Christianity*. Maryknoll, NY: Orbis Books, 1978.

O'Day, Gail. "The Gospel of John." In *The New Interpreter's Bible*, volume 9, edited by Leander Keck, 491–865. Nashville: Abingdon Press, 1995.

O'Donovan, Oliver. *The Desire of the Nations: Rediscovering the Roots of Political Theology*. Cambridge: Cambridge University Press, 1996.

Okin, Susan Moller. *Justice, Gender, and the Family*. New York: Basic Books, 1989.

Orend, Brian. *Michael Walzer on War and Justice*. Montreal: McGill-Queen's University Press, 2000.

Patterson, Sue. *Realist Christian Theology in a Postmodern Age*. Cambridge: Cambridge University Press, 1999.

Pincoffs, Edmund. *Quandaries and Virtues: Against Reductivism in Ethics*. Lawrence: University Press of Kansas, 1986.

Placher, William C. "Postliberal Theology." In *The Modern Theologians: An Introduction to Christian Theology in the Twentieth Century*, second edition, edited by David F. Ford, 343–356. Oxford: Blackwell, 1997.

———. *Unapologetic Theology: A Christian Voice in a Pluralistic Conversation*. Louisville: Westminster/John Knox Press, 1989.

Quirk, Michael J. "Beyond Sectarianism?" *Theology Today* 44, no. 1 (April 1987): 78–86.

Rasmusson, Arne. *The Church as* Polis. *From Political Theology to Theological Politics as Exemplified by Jürgen Moltmann and Stanley Hauerwas*. Notre Dame: University of Notre Dame Press, 1995.

Rawls, John. *A Theory of Justice*. Cambridge: The Belknap Press of Harvard University Press, 1971.

Reynolds, Terrence P. "A Conversation Worth Having: Hauerwas and Gustafson on Substance in Theological Ethics." *Journal of Religious Ethics* 28, no. 3 (Fall 2000): 395–421.

Reich, Rob and Christopher Wimer. *Charitable Giving and the Great Recession*. Stanford, CA: Stanford Center on Poverty and Inequality, 2012.

Rieger, Joerg. *God and the Excluded: Visions and Blindspots in Contemporary Theology*. Minneapolis: Fortress Press, 2001.

Roberts, Tyler T. "Michael Walzer and the Critical Connections." *Journal of Religious Ethics* 22, no. 2 (Fall 1994): 333–353.

———. "Theology and the Ascetic Imperative: Narrative and Renunciation in Taylor and Hauerwas." *Modern Theology* 9, no. 2 (April 1993): 181–200.

Rorty, Richard. *Contingency, Irony, and Solidarity*. Cambridge: Cambridge University Press, 1989.

———. *Philosophy and the Mirror of Nature*. Princeton: Princeton University Press, 1979.

Siesler, John. "Righteousness." In *The Oxford Companion to the Bible*, edited by Bruce M. Metzger and Michael D. Coogan, 655–656. New York: Oxford University Press, 1993.

Simpson, Lorenzo. "Evading Theory and Tragedy? Reading Cornel West." *Praxis International* 13, no. 1 (April 1993): 32–45.

Singer, Peter. *Rethinking Life and Death: The Collapse of Our Traditional Ethics*. New York: St. Martin's Griffin, 1994.

Smith, Scott. "Hauerwas and Kallenberg and the Issue of Epistemic Access to an Extra-Linguistic Realm." *Heythrop Journal* 45, no. 3 (July 2004): 305–326.

Sobrino, Jon. *No Salvation Outside the Poor: Prophetic-Utopian Essays*. Maryknoll, NY: Orbis Books, 2008.

———. *Jesus the Liberator: A Historical-Theological Reading of Jesus of Nazareth*, trans. Paul Burns and Francis McDonagh. Maryknoll, NY: Orbis Books, 1993.

Spelman, Elizabeth V. "Theodicy, Tragedy and Prophecy: Comments on Cornel West's *The American Evasion of Philosophy*." *APA Newsletter on the Black Experience* 90, no. 3 (Fall 1991): 19–23.

Spohn, William C. *Go and Do Likewise: Jesus and Ethics*. New York: Continuum, 2000.

Stackhouse, Max L. "Liberalism Dispatched vs. Liberalism Engaged." *The Christian Century*, October 18, 1995, 962–967.

———. *Creeds, Society, and Human Rights: A Study in Three Cultures*. Grand Rapids, MI: William B. Eerdmans Publishing Co., 1984.

Stout, Jeffrey. *Democracy and Tradition*. Princeton: Princeton University Press, 2004.

———. *Ethics After Babel: The Languages of Morals and Their Discontents*. Boston: Beacon Press, 1988.

Surin, Kenneth. "The Impassibility of God and the Problem of Evil." *Scottish Journal of Theology* 35, no. 1 (1982): 97–115.

Tanner, Kathryn. *Theories of Culture: A New Agenda for Theology*. Minneapolis: Fortress Press, 1997.

Taylor, Charles. "What is Human Agency?" In Charles Taylor, *Human Agency and Language: Philosophical Papers I*, 15–44. Cambridge: Cambridge University Press, 1985.

Thiel, John E. *Nonfoundationalism*. Minneapolis: Fortress Press, 1994.

Tucker, Gene M. "The Role of the Prophets and the Role of the Church." In *Prophecy in Israel: Search for an Identity*, edited by David L. Petersen, 159–174. Philadelphia: Fortress Press, 1987.

Tuininga, Matthew J. "Justice for the Poor in the Heidelberg Catechism: The Eighth Commandment." *Do Justice*, October 9, 2017. Accessed October 24, 2017. http://dojustice.crcna.org/article/justice-poor-heidelberg-catechism-eighth-commandment

Walzer, Michael. *In God's Shadow: Politics in the Hebrew Bible*. New Haven: Yale University Press, 2012.

———. *Arguing About War*. New Haven: Yale University Press, 2004.

———. *Thick and Thin: Moral Argument at Home and Abroad*. Notre Dame: University of Notre Dame Press, 1994.

———. "Shared Meanings in a Poly-Ethnic Democratic Setting: A Response." *Journal of Religious Ethics* 22, no. 2 (Fall 1994): 401–405.

———. "Two Kinds of Universalism." In *The Tanner Lectures on Human Values, XI*, edited by Grethe B. Peterson, 509–556. Salt Lake City: University of Utah Press, 1990.

———. "A Particularism of My Own." *Religious Studies Review* 16, no. 3 (July 1990): 193–197.

———. "The Communitarian Critique of Liberalism." *Political Theory* 18, no. 1 (February 1990): 6–23.

———. *The Company of Critics: Social Criticism and Political Commitment in the Twentieth Century*. New York: Basic Books, 1988.

———. *Interpretation and Social Criticism*. Cambridge: Harvard University Press, 1985.

———. *Spheres of Justice: A Defense of Pluralism and Equality*. New York: Basic Books, 1983.

———. "Philosophy and Democracy." *Political Theory* 9, no. 3 (August 1981): 379–399.

———. *Just and Unjust Wars: A Moral Argument with Historical Illustrations*. New York: Basic Books, 1977.

Walzer, Michael and Ronald Dworkin. "'Spheres of Justice': An Exchange." *New York Review of Books* (July 21, 1983): 43–46.

Warnke, Georgia. *Justice and Interpretation*. Cambridge: MIT Press, 1993.

Webb, Elizabeth A. "Power in Weakness: Feminist Reclamations of the Suffering of Christ." *Religious Studies Review* 38, no. 4 (December 2012): 199–205.

Webb, Stephen H. "A Hyperbolic Imagination: Theology and the Rhetoric of Excess." *Theology Today* 50, no. 1 (April 1993): 56–67.

Weber, Max. *The Sociology of Religion*, Introduction by Talcott Parsons with a New Forward by Ann Swidler. Boston: Beacon Press, 1993.

Welch, Sharon. *A Feminist Ethic of Risk*, revised edition. Minneapolis: Fortress Press, 2000.

———. "Communitarian Ethics After Hauerwas." *Studies in Christian Ethics* 10, no. 1 (1997): 82–95.

Wells, Samuel. *Transforming Fate into Destiny: The Theological Ethics of Stanley Hauerwas*. Carlisle, UK: Paternoster Press, 1998.

West, Cornel. "Prophetic Religion and the Future of Capitalist Civilization." In Judith Butler, et al., *The Power of Religion in the Public Sphere*, edited by Eduardo Mendieta and Jonathan VanAntwerpen, 92–100. New York: Columbia University Press, 2011.

———. *Democracy Matters: Winning the Fight Against Imperialism*. New York: Penguin Press, 2004.

———. "Afterword: Philosophy and the Funk of Life." In *Cornel West: A Critical Reader*, edited by George Yancy, 346–362. Oxford: Blackwell, 2001.

———. *The Cornel West Reader*. New York: Basic *Civitas* Books, 1999.

———. "The Moral Obligations of Living in a Democratic Society." In *The Good Citizen*, edited by David Batstone and Eduardo Mendieta, 5–12. New York: Routledge, 1999.

———. *Race Matters*. Boston: Beacon Press, 1993.

———. "Conclusion: The Author Responds." *Monthly Review* 45, no. 2 (June 1993): 57–60.

———. *The Ethical Dimensions of Marxist Thought*. New York: Monthly Review Press, 1991.

———. *The American Evasion of Philosophy: A Genealogy of Pragmatism*. Madison: University of Wisconsin Press, 1989.

———. *Prophetic Fragments: Illuminations of the Crisis in American Religion and Culture*. Grand Rapids, MI/Trenton, NJ: William B. Eerdmans Publishing Co./Africa World Press, 1988.

———. "Afterword: The Politics of American Neo-Pragmatism." In *Post-Analytic Philosophy*, edited by John Rajchman and Cornel West, 259–272. New York: Columbia University Press, 1985.

———. *Prophesy Deliverance! An Afro-American Revolutionary Christianity*. Philadelphia: Westminster Press, 1982.

Westmoreland-White, Michael L. "Setting the Record Straight: Christian Faith, Human Rights, and the Enlightenment." *Annual of the Society of Christian Ethics* (1995): 75–96.

Whitmore, Todd. "Beyond Liberalism and Communitarianism in Christian Ethics: A Critique of Stanley Hauerwas." *Annual of the Society of Christian Ethics* (1989): 207–225.

Williams, Rowan. *On Christian Theology*. Oxford: Blackwell, 2000.

Wilson, Robert R. *Prophecy and Society in Ancient Israel*. Philadelphia: Fortress Press, 1980.

Winch, Peter. "Authority." In *Political Philosophy*, edited by Anthony Quinton, 97–111. Oxford: Oxford University Press, 1967.

Wink, Walter. *Collected Readings*, edited by Henry French. Minneapolis: Fortress Press, 2013.

———. "Beyond Just War and Pacifism: Jesus' Nonviolent Way." *Review and Expositor* 89, no. 2 (Spring 1992): 197–214.

———. "Jesus and the Domination System." In *Society of Biblical Literature 1991 Seminar Papers*, edited by Eugene H. Lovering, 265–286. Atlanta: Scholar's Press, 1991.

Wittenberg, Gunther. "Authoritarian and Participatory Decision-Making in the Old Testament." In *A Democratic Vision for South Africa: Political Realism and Christian Responsibility*, edited by Klaus Nürnberger, 85–96. Pietermaritzburg, South Africa: Encounter Publications, 1991.

Wood, Mark David. *Cornel West and the Politics of Prophetic Pragmatism*. Urbana: University of Illinois Press, 2000.

Woodard-Lehman, Derek Alan. "Body Politics and the Politics of Bodies: Racism and Hauerwasian Theopolitics." *Journal of Religious Ethics* 36, no. 2 (June 2008): 295–320.

Woodhead, Linda. "Can Women Love Stanley Hauerwas? Pursuing an Embodied Theology." In *Faithfulness and Fortitude: In Conversation with the Theological Ethics of Stanley Hauerwas*, edited by Mark Thiessen Nation and Samuel Wells, 161–188. Edinburgh: T & T Clark, 2000.

Wolf, Susan. "Moral Saints." *Journal of Philosophy* 79, no. 8 (August 1982): 419–439.

Wolterstorff, Nicholas. *Justice: Rights and Wrongs*. Princeton: Princeton University Press, 2008.

———. "Suffering Love." In *Philosophy and the Christian Faith*, edited by Thomas V. Morris, 196–237. Notre Dame: University of Notre Dame Press, 1988.

———. "Christianity and Social Justice." *Christian Scholar's Review* 16, no. 3 (March 1987): 211–228.

———. "Why Care About Justice?" *The Reformed Journal* 36, no. 8 (August 1986): 9–14.

Yancy, George. "Religion and the Mirror of God: Historicism, Truth, and Religious Pluralism." In *Cornel West: A Critical Reader*, edited by George Yancy, 115–138. Oxford: Blackwell, 2001.

Yoder, John Howard. "The Constantinian Sources of Western Social Ethics." In John Howard Yoder, *The Priestly Kingdom: Social Ethics as Gospel*, 135–147. Notre Dame, Ind.: University of Notre Dame Press, 1984.

Young, Iris Marion. *Justice and the Politics of Difference*. Princeton: Princeton University Press, 1990.

Young, Josiah Ulysses, III. "Existential Aptness and Epistemological Correctness: West and the Identity of the 'Lord.'" In *Cornel West: A Critical Reader*, edited by George Yancy, 167–175. Oxford: Blackwell, 2001.

Index

About the Author

Christopher J. Libby is Associate Professor of Religion and Philosophy at Missouri Valley College, Marshall, Missouri. He earned his Ph.D. in Religion—Ethics and Society from Emory University.